Fencing
in the Dark

Fencing in the Dark

Japan, China, and the Senkakus

SUNOHARA Tsuyoshi

Japan Publishing Industry Foundation for Culture

PUBLISHER'S NOTE
This book follows the Hepburn system of romanization of Japanese words. Japanese personal names are written in the conventional Japanese order: family name followed by given name. All personal titles of the public figures mentioned in this book are as of the publication date of the Japanese hardcover edition in 2013.

Fencing in the Dark: Japan, China, and the Senkakus
Sunohara Tsuyoshi. Translated by the Japan Institute of International Affairs (JIIA).

Published by
Japan Publishing Industry Foundation for Culture (JPIC)
2-2-30 Kanda-Jinbocho, Chiyoda-ku, Tokyo 101-0051, Japan

First English edition: February 2020

© 2013 Sunohara Tsuyoshi
English translation © 2020 The Japan Institute of International Affairs (JIIA)
All rights reserved

Originally published in hardcover in 2013 under the Japanese title *Anto Senkaku kokuyuka* and then released in paperback in 2015, supplemented with a dialogue between the author and Nagashima Akihisa, special advisor to Prime Minister Noda at the time. Both editions were published by SHINCHOSHA Publishing Co., Ltd.

English publishing rights arranged with SHINCHOSHA Publishing Co., Ltd.

This publication is the result of a collaborative effort between the Japan Institute of International Affairs (JIIA) and Japan Publishing Industry Foundation for Culture (JPIC).

Book design: Miki Kazuhiko, Ampersand Works
Jacket and cover photograph: aflo

Printed in Japan
ISBN 978-4-86658-115-6
https://www.jpic.or.jp/

CONTENTS

CHAPTER
4 The Summit Meeting

CHAPTER
5 The Final Decision

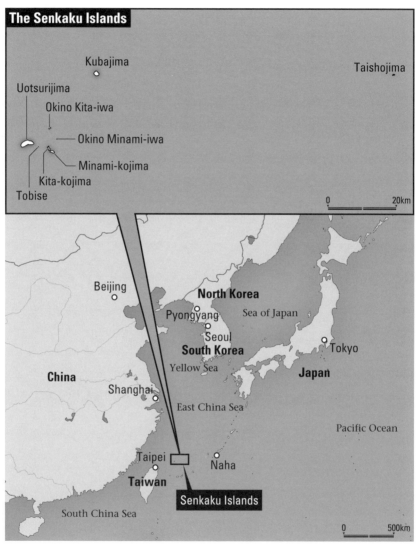

The Senkaku Islands

Kubajima

Taishojima

Uotsurijima

Okino Kita-iwa

Okino Minami-iwa

Minami-kojima

Kita-kojima

Tobise

0   20km

Beijing

North Korea

Pyongyang

Sea of Japan

Seoul

South Korea

Tokyo

China

Yellow Sea

Japan

Shanghai

East China Sea

Pacific Ocean

Taipei

Naha

Taiwan

Senkaku Islands

South China Sea

0   500km

Map design: Amitani Takahiro (atelier PLAN)

Fencing in the Dark

Introduction to the English Edition

Did Noda and Ishihara conspire to nationalize the Senkaku Islands? This is the question I heard from many of my friends and associates who visited Japan in late 2012. While I told them all that I did not believe it for a minute, I could not, in my heart of hearts, entirely dismiss the possibility.

A number of sources have been cited for the rumor that Democratic Party of Japan (DPJ) Prime Minister Noda Yoshihiko and Tokyo Governor Ishihara Shintaro were secretly conspiring behind everyone's backs to create a justification for the government to purchase the three Senkaku Islands, but Japanese and US government officials were agreed from day one in attributing it to China. Japanese China-watchers have noted in this connection that China reacted especially viscerally to the term "nationalization."

No matter how many times Japan tried to explain that this was a simple real estate transaction involving the transfer of title from a private Japanese individual to the Japanese government, this explanation fell on deaf ears in a China where the Chinese Communist Party exercises unchallenged one-party rule. Instead, China steadfastly maintained that the purchase was nationalization orchestrated by "Team Japan" with Noda and Ishihara pulling the strings, that it hid far more than its surface significance, and that it could only have been a strategic conspiracy. At least this is how Japanese observers saw Chinese bottom-line thinking on this.

Looking a bit more closely at the issue, it is worth noting that Chinese government ships had been violating Japan's territorial waters with increasing frequency for several years prior to the purchase. This clearly suggested to many that China, which was already embroiled in maritime territorial disputes with multiple countries facing on the South China Sea, was now moving to extend its game and open a new front in the East China Sea. Almost every day brought new reports of Chinese incursions into Japan's territorial waters, and the Japanese people were beset with nagging anxiety about the future. The feeling rapidly spread that Japan had to do something to counter these Chinese trespasses lest the area become another South China Sea situation. As if in proof of this widespread sense of alarm, governor Ishihara's appeal for crowdfunding to buy the Senkakus quickly drew nearly 1.5 billion yen in donations.

The US responded deftly to this psychological warfare between Japan and China. At first, President Barack Obama staked out a position of neutrality. As one ranking US official asked, "What would be the point of Japan and China—much less the United States and China—clashing over a few barren rocks in the middle of the ocean that nobody even lives on?" Nor was this person alone, as almost nobody understood or sympathized with the Noda administration's bid to buy the Senkakus. Looking back at the US position when Argentina and the UK went to war over the Falklands in the 1980s, it is clear that the US posture was informed by great-power geopolitical realism in not wanting to get involved in what it deemed an insignificant scuffle over insignificant islands.

This may have been a matter of vital importance for Japan, but it did not even register on the US radar. Still the US quickly realized that the perception gap had to be addressed before it ate away at the very foundations of the Japan-US alliance. At the same time, it was also realized that the China-sponsored conspiracy theory could not be allowed to become the conventional wisdom and had to be exorcised, lest it prove a corrosive legacy for the bilateral relationship.

It was the same sense of impending peril that largely motivated me to write this book. More than half a century having passed since the war's end, the Japan-US alliance has become a "common good" underpinning peace, stability, and prosperity in the Asia-Pacific region, yet its structure is still fragile. The sterile back-and-forth over relocating the US Futenma airbase in Okinawa is but one face of this fragility.

In my quest to author a non-fiction documentary that would set out the facts of the Senkaku story as best they can be known and would withstand the scrutiny of future historians, I was blessed with the understanding support not only of Noda Yoshihiko, one of the drama's principal players, but of numerous other people central to the DPJ administration, and I would like to express anew my sincere appreciation to them for their openness. I also owe a special debt of gratitude to Tsuchiya Shinya at Shinchosha for his understanding and support throughout the long process of interviews, research, and everything else that was so essential to producing this work.

Following the publication of this work in Japanese, a number of people familiar with events within the government came forth with new information and insights. This is most gratifying, and I hope to be able to incorporate their contributions in a follow-up piece before long.

Sunohara Tsuyoshi
September 2019

CHAPTER
1

Strained to the Breaking Point

Chinese fishing boat rams Japan Coast Guard patrol ship in Senkaku waters.
Jiji Press

The September 2010 collision involving a Chinese fishing boat and a Japan Coast Guard patrol ship occurred in the waters off the coast of the Senkaku Islands. A behind-the-scenes struggle between Japan and China was already underway when the decision was made to arrest the Chinese captain of the vessel.

The Kantei in Turmoil

In an unprecedented turn of events, a Chinese vessel and a patrol boat from Japan's 11th Regional Coast Guard Headquarters collided off the coast of Okinawa Prefecture's Senkaku Islands a little after 10:00 a.m. on September 7, 2010. About twelve hours later, at 10:30 p.m., the Regional Coast Guard Headquarters petitioned the Naha District Court for an arrest warrant for the Chinese captain of the fishing vessel. Following the issue of the warrant, the captain was arrested on charges of obstruction of performance of official duties. The arrest took place a little after 2:00 a.m. on September 8.

Leading up to the collision, two Coast Guard patrol boats, the *Yonakuni* and the *Mizuki,* were giving chase to a Chinese fishing vessel in Japan's territorial waters off the northwestern coast of Kubajima of the Senkaku Islands and ordering it to stop. Ignoring the Coast Guard orders and steering the vessel himself, the Chinese captain of the vessel rammed one of the patrol boats. Coast Guard officers on site determined this action constituted "obstruction of performance of official duties" and took action to arrest the captain.

The incident was reported to Maehara Seiji, the Democratic Party of Japan (DPJ) Kan Cabinet Minister of Land, Infrastructure, Transport and Tourism (MLIT) with jurisdiction over the Coast Guard. Maehara soon convinced himself that the "arrest was unavoidable." Known as the foremost hardliner within the administration at the time of the incident, Maehara would later justify his decision in these words.

"When I saw the video recording that would later be leaked to the public, I immediately thought, 'This is a criminal act.' There was a gaping hole in the patrol boat's hull. Patrol boats are constructed differently from Maritime Self-Defense Force battleships, and the damage to the hull was sufficient to raise serious concern the ship might sink."

Minister of Foreign Affairs Okada Katsuya was visiting Germany when the news broke and had quickly sent a comment to the Kantei (Prime Minister's Official Residence) saying that Japan should go ahead with the arrest and take a resolute stand to show that Japan was a "nation under the rule of law."

Chief Cabinet Secretary Sengoku Yoshito recalls those tense moments. "To the best of my memory, Okada and Maehara did say that we should go ahead [with the arrest]. But practically, the Coast Guard was already taking action [ahead of any political decision]." In other words, Sengoku's interpretation of events is that, at least in its earliest stages, the drama of the arrest was being played out in the waters off the Senkaku Islands without stopping to seek a government decision on whether or not to make the arrest.

According to newspaper reports, the Coast Guard patrol boats discovered a Chinese trawler illegally operating in Japan's territorial waters approximately 15 kilometers northwest of Kubajima of the Senkaku Islands in the East China Sea. At around 10:55 a.m. on September 7, the trawler was ordered to stop for inspection. The Chinese captain of the fishing vessel suddenly made a sharp left turn and rammed the midsection of the *Mizuki* on its starboard side. Before this collision, the *Yonakuni* had discovered the fishing vessel operating illegally in Japanese waters and had ordered it to stop. Ignoring the order, the fishing vessel had scraped the stern of the patrol boat and fled. The fishing vessel finally stopped before 1:00 p.m., at which time Coast Guard officers boarded the vessel for inspection.

The captain was arrested a few minutes after 2:00 a.m. the following day, September 8, within Japan's territorial waters at a location approximately seven kilometers north of Uotsurijima in the Senkaku Islands. The captain was then transported by patrol boat to Ishigaki Port, arriving there at 7:25 a.m. The Ishigaki Coast Guard Office immediately transferred the captain to its offices in Ishigaki City for questioning. This is the basic outline of the incident as reported by the media.

It should be noted that there was a 13-hour gap between when the Coast Guard took the captain into custody and when he was actually arrested.

Sengoku is recorded to have made the following comment at his regular press conference on the morning of September 8 at the Kantei. "Japan's position on the Senkaku Islands is that no territorial issue exists. We shall take strict action in accordance with Japanese laws and regulations, taking into account the severity of the violation." The statement indicates that a political decision had already been reached on arresting the captain. Asked why more than half a day had passed before an arrest had been made and if this was out of diplomatic concerns, Sengoku replied, "This time was needed for procedural matters because this was the first time making an arrest on suspicion of obstruction of performance of official duties. And no, the delay was not due to diplomatic concerns.

"These judicial procedures [arrest by Coast Guard and turning the suspect over to the public prosecutors office] had never before been undertaken. In the case of the fishing vessel, the petition for an arrest warrant didn't move forward quickly and everything else took time. The fact that the incident took place at sea further delayed the process."

That is how Sengoku later described what was happening behind the scenes on the day of the incident. Sengoku's right-hand man, Deputy Chief Cabinet Secretary Fukuyama Tetsuro, recalls, "The outcome was that the [Chinese fishing] vessel had been stopped, and matters had moved on to where a decision had to be made on whether to make an arrest. So the question was, 'What should we do?'"

According to Fukuyama, it was around 9:00 p.m. on September 7 when he was first shown the video recording of the incident, which was later leaked to the public by an active-duty Coast Guard officer. Having closely examined the video and discussed it at the Kantei, Fukuyama explains that the judgment was made that, "This is an extremely serious and malicious incident and an arrest is unavoidable." Later that evening (10:30 p.m.), a petition was filed with the district court for an arrest warrant, which warrant was then served in the early hours the next day (a little after 2:00 a.m. on September 8).

"We shall take strict action in accordance with Japanese laws and regulations."

Following the arrest of the Chinese captain of the fishing vessel, Prime Minister Kan Naoto met with the media at the Kantei on the evening of September 8. In a statement made at this time, Prime Minister Kan sought to emphasize that the government had not erred in its judgment. Asked whether he would "face China with a firm attitude," the prime minister avoided giving a clear answer and instead twice repeated the phrase, "We will respond in accordance with the laws."

Whatever the intent of these words, there is no question but that the Kan Cabinet had taken a historic first step. In line with the resolute attitude advocated by Maehara and others, the Kan Cabinet had, for the first time in a case pertaining to the Senkaku Islands, arrested a Chinese national on criminal charges (obstruction of performance of official duties) under domestic Japanese laws.

As the deputy to Chief Cabinet Secretary Sengoku, Fukuyama worked to make sure the major players at the Kantei were all on the same page. "I think the decision-makers in the first instance were Minister Maehara as the MLIT minister with direct jurisdiction and Foreign Minister Okada. The crux of the issue was whether or not to make an arrest. But our incoming information was saying that it was an extremely malicious ramming and members of the Coast Guard had been put at extreme risk of life and limb." Fukuyama goes on to explain, "Basically, the judgment that the arrest should be made was made by the Foreign Minister and the MLIT Minister. In our earlier discussions with Sengoku, we had said that if the two ministers called for an arrest, we would just have to do it."

Prior to this incident, Japanese authorities had taken Chinese nationals into custody in the waters around the Senkaku Islands on numerous occasions. However, all of these cases were deemed to be violations of the Immigration Control and Refugee Recognition Act and the individuals involved were immediately deported. As will be discussed below, in an incident that occurred on March 24, 2004, seven individuals aboard what was believed to be a Chinese vessel landed on Uotsurijima. The Liberal Democratic Party (LDP) Koizumi Cabinet that was in power at the time opted not to make arrests. Instead, Prime Minister Koizumi Junichiro made the political decision to waive prosecution and to go straight to deportation.

According to Sengoku, in February 2009, the Coast Guard had compiled an Arrest Manual dedicated to incidents occurring in the Senkaku area. This had been done under the instruction of the LDP Aso Taro Cabinet prior to the transfer of power to the DPJ. Later, under the cabinet of Prime Minister Noda Yoshihiko, the process of preparing legislation to cope with Chinese and Taiwanese fishing vessels violating Japan's territorial waters was launched under the concept of "maritime police authority." But at the time of the collision in September 2010, all that the DPJ's Sengoku had to go on was the Arrest Manual formulated at Coast Guard initiative under LDP administration.

Maehara, who looked to Sengoku as his mentor in political matters, vociferously rebutted criticisms leveled against his party by the LDP. "In the first place, the Manual was prepared under the LDP. All we did was to act in accordance with the provisions of this document," he argued. Maehara would go on to assert that the DPJ was not in error in making the judgments and taking the actions that it did after the collision incident. "The decision of the Koizumi Cabinet [not to go further than deportation based on the Immigration Control and Refugee Recognition Act] addressed the question of landing. That incident was of a completely different character from the ramming."

Coast Guard officers had taken on the moniker *Umizaru* (sea monkeys) after the recent eponymous movie that had proved to be a big commercial success. Driven by a strong sense of mission as defenders of the nation's front lines, Sengoku noted, the Coast Guard in certain respects constituted a "battle group." For Sengoku, who at one point in the course of the Diet debate had referred to Japan's Self-Defense Forces as an "apparatus of violence," the Coast Guard was not sufficiently conscious of its status as a "judicial police force" operating under the "maritime police" name.

"It's all well and good that the Coast Guard said 'We have made an arrest, and we have an Arrest Manual to go by.' So I asked, 'What happens after you make an arrest? Do you have guidelines on what to do after an arrest?'" recalls Sengoku.

According to Sengoku, the Arrest Manual contained nothing on what to do next. "In other words, there was no manual on handing the suspect over to the public prosecutor and no guidelines on what to do with the arrestee or how to go about trying the case in court."

"Maybe they were just itching to make an arrest somewhere. After all, [the Coast Guard] is all about 'offense and defense.' That's the mentality."

With this interpretation of the Coast Guard's organizational psychology, Sengoku sought out staff members in the Chief Cabinet Secretary's Office with expertise in the judicial processes of arrest, prosecution, and trial. Those who were tapped for brainstorming sessions on what to do next were officers seconded from the National Police Agency. At the same time, Sengoku held intermittent meetings with Prime Minister Kan, Foreign Minister Okada, and MLIT Minister Maehara to devise a solution to the situation. Already at this point, Sengoku was telling himself, "This is going to develop into a terrible mess unless a political decision is made [on a final resolution]."

Naturally enough, the greatest concern that dogged Sengoku and Fukuyama at this point was the anticipated Chinese reaction. Based on past experience, there was every reason to expect China to take strident action. Working back from this realization, Sengoku and Fukuyama knew that their biggest headache would be to decide what to do with the Chinese captain who had been arrested on charges of obstruction of performance of official duties.

Beginning immediately after the collision, Sengoku and Fukuyama started receiving messages from the Chinese side delivered through various routes and quarters but all with the same intent: "Please give special consideration to this case." But there was a fundamental difference between this case and the 2004 case when Chinese activists who landed on the Senkaku

Islands were charged with violating the Immigration Control and Refugee Recognition Act. Given that the captain had been arrested for obstruction of performance of official duties, criminal procedures could not be avoided. Both Sengoku and Fukuyama were convinced the "judicial process" of a nation under the rule of law left no room for political intervention.

Fukuyama recalls, "The same message was being delivered to us through various routes. 'Give special consideration to this case.' But there was no way to suspend criminal procedures other than through the exercise of the command authority."

Sengoku describes the situation bluntly. "If you want to dispose of a matter in this particular way, you have to represent it as having been done on the front lines. The political side should not be demanding 'Release the man!' My background as a lawyer told me, 'If political considerations were to determine the outcome, and if that ever became public knowledge, the aftermath would be disastrous.'"

The three principal actors in the drama approached the incident from different positions, but all agreed that "an arrest should be made." First, the Coast Guard, committed to its mission as the border guard on the seas, took a strong and unyielding position. Second, Maehara had already been labeled by China as a "nationalist and hardliner toward China" going back to 2005 when, as the President of the Democratic Party, he had stated that "China poses a military threat." Third, Okada was known within the ranks of his party as a "fundamentalist" who was not given to easy compromise and insisted on a principled approach. This unexpected trio calling for an arrest had already become too loud and too strong for the Kantei to stop.

"Japan and China must endeavor to ensure the development of a mutually beneficial relationship based on common strategic interests."

These words were uttered by Prime Minister Kan to members of the press at the Kantei on the evening of September 13, five days after the arrest. Kan was strongly suggesting that Japan was prepared to act to prevent a negative impact on bilateral relations. The statement was affected by the schedule of diplomatic events that loomed on the near horizon. In particular, Kan was feeling the weight of the upcoming Asia-Pacific Economic Cooperation (APEC) Conference scheduled to be held in Yokohama in November. Kan felt that Japan bore a heavy responsibility as the host country for ensuring the success of the conference.

Given that Chinese leaders were expected to participate in the APEC Yokohama Conference, there was a strong desire to set the stage for improving bilateral ties in time for the conference.

This was the truth about the atmosphere that prevailed in the Kantei. Kan had another worry—the United Nations (UN) General Assembly Meeting set for the end of September, where he was scheduled to engage in his first summit meeting with Chinese Premier Wen Jiabao. Kan calculated that a re-set button on Japan-China relations had to be pushed by the time of this meeting in New York. Otherwise, the clock could run out on ensuring the participation of Premier Wen Jiabao and President Hu Jintao in the November APEC Conference. Another major event was looming, the Asia-Europe Meeting (ASEM) summit conference scheduled for October 4–5 in Brussels. But at this point, Kan had already decided he would not go to Brussels because it created a schedule conflict with the special session of the Diet.

"At this rate, I won't be able to have meaningful talks with China in New York. That is unacceptable."

Sengoku recalls a very irritated Prime Minister Kan just before leaving for New York. Kan came close to yelling when he ordered Sengoku and others to put an end to the matter as soon as possible. Media reports suggest that Sengoku and Fukuyama were mulling the possibility of ending the matter quickly by avoiding a trial through the process of summary indictment. But this path was blocked because the Chinese captain was unyielding in his denial of the charges brought against him. Things quickly spun out of control.

Under the Japanese legal system, the denial of charges unavoidably results in detention pending trial, which in turn implies the prolongation of the case. Consequently, on September 19, more than ten days after the incident, the Ishigaki Branch of the Naha District Public Prosecutors Office applied for an extension of the period of detention. On the same day, the Ishigaki Summary Court authorized a ten-day extension lasting through September 29.

Regarding the discussions taking place in the Kantei at around this time, Sengoku recalls Kan dropping the following words. "If both the Foreign and MLIT ministers are saying so, I suppose an extension of the period of detention is alright. There is no choice but to go along." Led by the combative stances of Maehara and Okada, the prime minister had agreed to "making the arrest." Pushed further by momentum, Kan was now giving his tacit approval to extending the period of detention.

With no way of knowing what was going on in the Kantei, China stepped up its protest when the period of detention was extended. On September 19, the day of the extension, Ma Zhaoxu, chief spokesman for China's Ministry of Foreign Affairs released the following statement. "If the Japanese side compounds its errors by insisting on its own way of thinking, China shall respond with strong retaliatory measures." Ma asserted, "Japan must accept all responsibility for the results," then repeated the demand for immediate and unconditional release of the Chinese captain of the fishing vessel.

Prior to this, China had on several occasions summoned the Japanese ambassador to China, Niwa Uichiro, to strongly protest the arrest. Parallel to this, China had taken a number of counter-measures, including suspending bilateral government negotiations on an agreement for the development of natural gas fields in the East China Sea and the visit to Japan by officers of the National People's Congress. During this same period, the state-owned Xinhua News Agency carried a number of reports underscoring the fact that various means were being used to send a political message to Japan. These included the temporary suspension of all ministerial exchanges with Japan, cancellation of aviation talks for increasing the number of flights between the two countries, and postponement of the Japan-China Comprehensive Conference on Coal.

"China shall take strong counter-measures if Japan fails to immediately and unconditionally release the Chinese captain of the fishing vessel."

According to Xinhua News, Deputy Minister Wang Guangya of the Ministry of Foreign Affairs phoned Ambassador Niwa on September 19 to repeat this statement. Ambassador Niwa is reported by the Ministry of Foreign Affairs of Japan to have answered in the following manner. "We call for a calm and cautious response so as not to further escalate the situation." Touching on the fact that China had transported drill-like materials to the rig it had constructed in the Shirakaba Gas Field (Chinese name: Chunxizo Gas Field) in the East China Sea, Ambassador Niwa hinted at counter-measures by stating, "If the Chinese side violates the agreement, Japan will have no choice but to consider taking appropriate measures."

In the early hours of September 12, five days after the incident, Ambassador Niwa had been again summoned, this time by State Councillor (with vice-premier status) Dai Bingguo, China's top foreign policy official. This became an occasion for an unprecedented protest. It was the fifth time that the Japanese ambassador had been summoned since the incident occurred on September 7, an extreme and disrespectful departure from diplomatic protocol.

However, seen from a different perspective, China's hardline stance can be interpreted as having been an indication of Beijing's strong desire to "settle the matter quickly and peacefully." Fukuyama underscores this by saying that the back-channel messages coming from China were calling for "somehow settling the problem amicably."

These conciliatory messages reflected the moderate stance toward Japan advocated by the Hu Jintao leadership team's policy of pursuing a "mutually beneficial relationship based on common strategic interests." Having said that, the leadership knew any sharp deterioration in relations with Japan would inflame the anti-Japanese sentiments of younger generations, and it feared the criticism and protest could easily shift focus from the Japanese government to the Chinese government and ultimately to the Communist Party's one-party rule.

Fukuyama explains, "We had gotten to the point where there was no way left for political intervention other than the exercise of the command authority. We tried to explain this to the Chinese side, but they couldn't understand what we were trying to convey."

True to Fukuyama's description of the situation, China's mistrust of Japan was soaring to new heights beginning around this time and China was seen to be descending into a type of national hysteria.

Deng Xiaoping had famously left behind the legacy of "shelving the question" of the Senkaku Islands, explains Fukuyama. However, the Chinese leadership was feeling increasingly frustrated by the fact that, notwithstanding this long established understanding, Japan was now insisting on dealing with the captain in accordance with Japanese domestic laws, since making it a domestic legal issue then gives rise to suspicions that the DPJ was changing Japan's position vis-a-vis China.

In the face of the negative chain reaction that was rapidly spreading throughout China, Fukuyama and his team at the Kantei repeatedly messaged China that, "There is no reason for such suspicions. We have no intention of fighting over this." (Fukuyama) But China would not be satisfied by words that were not accompanied by the release of the captain and moved to ratchet up the stand-off. It was as if China had surrendered to its own angry impulses.

Harassment

"If Japan continues to ignore the situation, China will be left with no option but to take the necessary forceful action."

This, the most strongly worded warning to be given since the start of the incident, came from Premier Wen Jiabao, reputed to be the leading Japanophile among China's leaders. Addressing Chinese residents in the United

States in a meeting held in New York on September 21, Wen repeated China's demand for the immediate and unconditional release of the Chinese captain of the fishing vessel. China Central Television led off its noon news broadcast on September 22 Beijing time with a summary of Wen's statement, which was seen and noted throughout China.

A few days earlier, the Japanese and Chinese diplomatic teams had reached something of an unspoken agreement that the meeting between Kan Naoto and Wen Jiabao scheduled to be held in New York would not occur. Due to growing bilateral tension resulting from the extension of the captain's detention, neither country made any formal effort to sound the other side out about the upcoming meeting. Consequently, the meeting was simply allowed to die a natural death.

Both sides seem to have been motivated by the same fear of suggesting a meeting only to be rejected by the other side. The embarrassment of such a rejection would have exposed both Kan and Wen to domestic and international criticism. Furthermore, it would not be surprising if both sides had calculated that if a meeting were in fact to materialize, the ensuing risk the meeting would be seen as a head-on clash of opposing views and would critically damage the bilateral relationship was too great.

Acting in conjunction with the stern warning by Wen, China's Ministry of Foreign Affairs released a statement from Deputy-Director-General Jiang Yu of its Information Division on the evening of September 22 which contained the wording: "Japan's devious excuses do not hold any water." It was clear to all observers that both this and Wen's warning were aimed at securing the release of the Chinese captain whose period of detention was coming to an end on September 29.

Sengoku explains what was going through his mind at the time. "Something had to be done quickly. We felt that a single charge of obstruction could end up overturning our bilateral diplomatic relations if it were mishandled."

With Prime Minister Kan in New York, Sengoku was left in charge of the Kantei as its "control tower" and was running around with Fukuyama to put out the fire. The specific actions they took were to utilize every available channel to send the message to Cheng Yonghua, the Chinese ambassador to Japan, that "Japan is a nation under the rule of law and must proceed in a calm and orderly fashion in accordance with established legal procedures." The idea was to find a path to an early release of the captain and a return to normal.

"I believe the other side understood our intent. It was rumored at the time that we [the DPJ] had no direct channels with China. But those allegations were completely wrong."

While confidently relating his story, Fukuyama candidly admits that they failed to gain the full understanding of the Chinese side. "Of course, the Ministry of Foreign Affairs was using its diplomatic channels to convey our position in detail. Beyond that, we were being contacted through every conceivable link with China. However, from a legal perspective, there was simply no procedural alternative to extending the detention of the captain. The only option that remained was the exercise of command authority."

Two weeks after the incident and on the same date as the China Central Television noon broadcast, the September 22 Internet edition of the *New York Times* carried a shocking story reporting that the Chinese authorities had banned the export of rare metals to Japan. Needless to say, rare metals are essential and indispensable to the parts and components of hybrid cars, energy-efficient home appliances, and other products. Based on reports from Japanese trading companies, the Japanese government had already confirmed that customs clearance of exports of rare metals from China had stopped on September 21.

"We know that orders have been issued suspending new contracts for the sale and the portside loading of rare metals."

This statement was made on September 24 by Minister of Economy, Trade and Industry (METI) Ohata Akihiro. The venue was a post-cabinet meeting press conference where Ohata also announced that a full-fledged investigation had been launched to confirm all the pertinent details. METI already knew at this point that exports to other countries had not been affected. Ohata proceeded to state, "Issuance of Japan-bound export permits has been suspended, and new applications are not being accepted," indicating that this information had been received from trading companies. He strongly suggested that Japan had been "singled out" and that China had intentionally suspended its exports of rare metals to Japan.

The banning of rare metal exports to Japan was very likely a violation of the World Trade Organization (WTO) rules. Ohata leveraged this point to say, "It is important to deal with this matter appropriately and in accordance with WTO rules." The idea was this oblique reference would serve to restrain China, but it was clear to all that this would hardly make any difference.

On September 24, the same day that Ohata had revealed the shocking information on the Chinese rare metals export ban to Japan at METI, Sengoku announced a new shocking fact at the Kantei.

"Last night, September 23, we were informed by the Chinese government that four Japanese nationals have been detained by Chinese authorities for questioning in the city of Shijiazhuang, Hebei Province. The information is that they are under house arrest in Shijiazhuang on charges related to the Military Facilities Protection Law and Criminal Procedures Law." Sengoku added that the four individuals were employees of Fujita Corporation, a middle-echelon Japanese general contractor engaged in the removal of abandoned chemical weapons.

On the previous day, the state-owned Xinhua News Agency had reported that four Japanese were being questioned by the national security authorities in Shijiazhuang for trespassing on military zones located in Hebei Province and illegally filming "military targets." The Xinhua report claimed that legal action was being taken against the four and strongly hinted that the four might be taken into custody for questioning, this action apparently designed to jolt the Japanese side.

It was well known that entry into military controlled zones containing People's Liberation Army (PLA) and the People's Armed Police military, tary bases, facilities, and housing is strictly regulated for security reasons. Taking this into consideration, the view quickly spread throughout Japan that punishment for the four accused individuals could go beyond simple deportation. The feeling was that if they were found guilty of unauthorized entry and filming inside military facilities, they could be subjected to severe penalties, including capital punishment.

Given such speculation, the press peppered Sengoku with the question: "Is this Chinese action a response to the Senkaku Islands incident?" Sengoku responded, "Judging from the laws that have been invoked on the Chinese side, we believe this is unrelated to the claims that China is making in connection with the incident that occurred in the vicinity of the Senkaku Islands." On the subject of the rare metals export ban, Sengoku responded, "We have not confirmed that any official announcement has been made by the Chinese government concerning the export of rare metals to Japan. We want to ascertain the pertinent facts as soon as possible, and will take appropriate action once the facts are confirmed."

Sengoku avoided adding any further comments. However, there was no doubt in Japan and throughout the rest of the world that both cases constituted retaliatory measures manufactured by the Chinese side in response to the actions taken by the Japanese government in the Chinese fishing vessel collision incident.

Application of Article V

While the Kantei was struggling to respond to Chinese harassment, Premier Wen Jiabao, China's "control tower," was in New York addressing the UN. His proclamation was clear for all to understand. "When it comes to sovereignty, national unity, and territorial integrity, China will not yield or compromise."

Wen's speech entitled "Getting to Know the Real China" delivered at the UN General Debate contained the following statements. "China will strive toward democracy and open its doors to the world. China's development will not harm anyone or pose a threat to anyone." The words were meant to put a stop to the theories of "China as a threat" that were gaining traction in the United States. At the same time, Wen emphasized a firm commitment to certain principles. "China values friendship and also sticks to principles. It firmly upholds its national core interests. When it comes to sovereignty, national unity, and territorial integrity, China will not yield or compromise."

The previous evening (September 22), Wen had addressed a group of American business and government leaders. This speech contained a similar statement. "The Chinese people will never compromise on issues related to Taiwan and Tibet." Yet in his UN speech, he only spoke of never yielding or compromising on sovereignty, national unity, and territorial integrity, with no reference to any specific region such as Taiwan or Tibet.

In Japan, Wen's seemingly purposeful omission was interpreted as intending to focus attention on the Senkaku Islands and to state by implication that China would continue to treat the Senkaku Islands as part of its "national core interest" on par with Taiwan and Tibet. As Japan saw it, Wen was directing his statement not only to Japan and the United States but to the entire international community.

On the same day as Wen's UN speech (September 23), Maehara Seiji reached out to Secretary of State Hillary Clinton, who held a special place in the Obama administration, with a fevered pitch.

"The Japan-US alliance is important not only for the security of Japan. It is also extremely important as a public good that buttresses the security of the entire Asia-Pacific region. It is our desire to further strengthen Japan-US cooperative relations through strategic dialogue as we continue to overcome a diverse range of challenges."

It was shortly before this that Kan Naoto had won the election for the presidency of the DPJ, and it was in the ensuing cabinet reshuffle that Kan conducted after his election that Maehara's long cherished wish to become foreign minister had been fulfilled.

In his meeting with Secretary Clinton in a New York hotel, Maehara started off with an emphatic exposition of his views on the "significance of the Japan-US alliance." Arriving at the crux of the problem at hand, which was of course the matter of the Senkaku Islands, Maehara solicited a response by saying, "We find it very reassuring that the United States takes the position that the Senkakus fall under the provisions of the Japan-US Security Treaty."

Unhesitatingly, Clinton responded, "Obviously the Security Treaty applies to the Senkakus." With this statement, Clinton confirmed that the Japan-US Security Treaty was applicable to the Senkaku Islands. This was the first meeting between the Japanese foreign minister and the US secretary of state to take place after the reshuffling of the Kan Cabinet and the appointment of Maehara as foreign minister. Maehara took this occasion to outline the response of the Japanese government to the Chinese fishing boat's collision with a Coast Guard ship off the coast of the Senkaku Islands during his term as MLIT minister. "There are no outstanding territorial issues in the East China Sea. Japan will deal calmly with this matter under the provisions of domestic laws." With these explanations, Maehara succeeded to a degree in gaining Clinton's understanding. According to explanations provided by a Foreign Ministry officer who was present at the meeting, Maehara and Clinton also exchanged views on China's maritime expansion in the East China Sea and agreed to continue carefully monitoring the situation there and to stay in close contact and coordination.

Clinton's statement that the Japan-US Security Treaty applies to the Senkaku Islands was immediately confirmed by the top civilian and military officers at the Pentagon (Department of Defense). Meeting with the press on the same day, September 23, Secretary of Defense Robert Gates stated that the US will uphold its responsibilities to the alliance. Michael Mullen, chairman of the Joint Chiefs of Staff, supplemented Gates' statement by adding that the US naturally has a responsibility in that area. Thus the United States unequivocally confirmed that it would intervene in the defense of the Senkaku Islands.

Prior to this, the Obama administration had strictly avoided making any public statements on the war of nerves between Japan and China over the Senkaku Islands. This silence on the Senkaku problem was calculated to avoid unnecessarily irritating the Chinese side in line with the Obama administration's commitment to deepening its strategic dialogue with China. But the situation had now clearly changed with China's ban on rare metal exports to Japan and its taking Japanese businessmen into custody. China's hardline approach thus encouraged the United States to adjust its moderate line and to send a clear message intended to check Chinese actions.

"Because of the cooling in Japan-US relations, China is testing how far it can go [on territorial issues]."

So said former Deputy Secretary of State Richard Armitage about a week before the Pentagon's heartening statement of support. The occasion was a September 15 talk given at the Japan National Press Club in Tokyo's Uchi-saiwai-cho by this Republican doyen of Japan hands. Bearing in mind China's hardline responses following the Chinese fishing vessel ramming off the coast of the Senkaku Islands, Armitage theorized that China was not only testing Japan with its actions but was also interested in gauging the depth of the US commitment to Asian security.

Armitage sounded a strong alarm on China, saying, "China must realize that all territories come under the Japan-US Security Treaty." Moreover, he also directed his attention to the Kan Cabinet with this advice. "A strategic vision for the future of Japan-US relations should be presented through a joint statement with President Obama." He later went to the Kantei and repeated the same message directly to Sengoku. "China is testing Japan."

"A joint Japan-US military exercise in a location such as Palau would send an effective message to China."

By making this proposal in his speech at the Japan National Press Club, Armitage was suggesting that China's military harassment of Japan could be stopped if Japan were to engage in joint military exercises for the defense of isolated islands. As it turned out, before coming to Japan, Armitage had presented this idea in the form of a personal suggestion to Kurt Campbell, a close Clinton aide.

Clinton's unambiguous statement in Japan-US foreign ministerial talks in New York that the Japan-US Security Treaty applies to the Senkaku Islands had been set in motion by Campbell as a direct result of a suggestion from Armitage. However, this was merely a rearrangement of an earlier logic. In 1990, during the Clinton administration, Walter Mondale, who was then serving as US ambassador to Japan, had made a statement to the effect that the United States will not defend the Senkaku Islands if it comes under attack from a foreign country. Responding to this statement, Campbell, who was then Deputy Assistant Secretary of Defense, formulated a carefully crafted logic to explain the statement. That same logic had simply been recycled and rearranged for use by the Obama administration.

Campbell had put together the following interpretation of what would occur in case Japan and China became embroiled in conflict over the

Senkaku Islands. Under the provisions of Article V of the Japan-US Security Treaty, in the case of an "armed attack against either Party in the territories under the administration of Japan [e.g., Senkaku Islands]," "each Party… declares that it would act to meet the common danger." What Clinton had done in her meeting with Maehara was to restate this interpretation in simple terms, which was to say that the Japan-U.S. Security Treaty applies to the Senkaku Islands.

Quasi-Legal Measures

"Taking into consideration the future of Japan-China relations, it is not appropriate to continue the detention any longer." These were the words Deputy Chief Prosecutor Suzuki Toru of the Naha District Public Prosecutors Office read from a prepared statement. The time was a few minutes after 2:00 p.m. on September 24, and the occasion was a press conference that had been called that same afternoon. Suzuki carefully eyed the document as he announced the decision to release the Chinese captain of the fishing vessel without indictment. There was no precedent whatsoever for a public prosecutor to refer to Japan-China relations as an extenuating circumstance.

Even while referring to Japan-China relations, Suzuki emphasized that this was "merely one of a number of considerations." When the press asked whether a political judgment lay behind the decision to release the captain, Suzuki several times repeated the same explanation to directly deny any political intervention. "The judgment was made by the public prosecution authorities."

On the same day, the Public Prosecutor General was meeting with the deputy chief prosecutor of the Fukuoka High Public Prosecutors Office and the chief public prosecutor of the Naha District Public Prosecutors Office. The venue for this prosecutors' summit meeting was the Supreme Public Prosecutors Office located in Tokyo's Kasumigaseki area. Contemporary media reports indicate that it is highly likely that the decision to release the captain was ultimately made in this meeting. A few hours after Suzuki's press conference, Justice Minister Yanagida Minoru chimed in with a similar explanation: The decision was made by the District Public Prosecutors Office in consultation with the Fukuoka High Public Prosecutor Office and the Supreme Public Prosecutors Office.

Notwithstanding these statements, rumors spread like wild fire throughout Japan that this was the result of "wrongful political intervention by the Kantei [Sengoku]."

As Prime Minister Kan was travelling abroad at this time, Sengoku was in charge at the Kantei. Sengoku recalls those days saying, "I thought we already needed to be considering the option of releasing the captain." Sengoku readily admits that, with an eye to the importance of relations with China, he began looking for an early resolution immediately after the incident. He further explained, "It would have been possible to make a political decision on whether or not to have the prosecutors file for detention within 24 hours after the captain was taken into custody, but . . ." With this explanation, Sengoku directly refuted the prevailing view that the Kantei had intervened politically.

Deputy Chief Cabinet Secretary Fukuyama who was working closely with Sengoku in the Kantei to cope with the crisis concurs. "As we are a nation under the rule of law, there was no way we could short-circuit the criminal procedures that had been set in motion." Hardline Maehara and Okada had from the very start cited being a nation under the rule of law as their rationale for calling for the arrest of the captain. As such, it cannot be denied that the team of Sengoku and Fukuyama found their hands had been tied to a considerable extent.

"Considering the prevailing atmosphere, public opinion would have really exploded if the command authority had been invoked to resolve the situation. Command authority had not been used in decades. If we had taken that course, we probably would have been condemned as cowards."

While evoking the difficult position they faced, Fukuyama prefaced this with, "Apart from whether or not this would have been possible," and made a revealing confession, "but when I think back on whether we could have done anything differently, there is just one regret that weighs heavily on my mind."

It is worth bearing in mind that, before taking the post of deputy chief cabinet secretary, Fukuyama had served a stint as senior vice-minister for foreign affairs. According to Fukuyama, a Chinese diplomat (consul) residing in Japan met with the Chinese captain of the fishing vessel soon after his arrest and throughout the period of his detention. Given that China did not recognize Japan's territorial claims to the Senkaku Islands, the Chinese government was fearful that the captain might sign formal documents admitting to the charges that had been leveled against him (obstruction of performance of official duties). As the Chinese government saw the situation, signing could imply that the Chinese people recognized Japan's sovereignty over the islands. With this in mind, Fukuyama says it is impossible to state that the Chinese consul was not telling the captain not to sign any kind of document placed before him.

As previously noted, the team of Sengoku and Fukuyama was mulling a very different resolution scenario at the outset. The captain would be encouraged to come clean and admit his guilt. The case would then go through the process of summary indictment, followed by immediate deportation. But even without retaining legal counsel, the captain refused to sign anything during arraignment proceedings. Faced with this refusal, the prosecutors moved to extend the period of detention. This seriously impacted the early-resolution scenario that the Kantei was hoping for at the outset. Instead, China embarked upon a series of radical harassments against Japan.

Fukuyama took the position that the situation would not have been prolonged and the rapid deterioration in Sino-Japanese relations could have been avoided if the captain had shown greater flexibility instead of adamantly refusing to sign the prosecutor's record of oral statements during the period of detention. In other words, what Fukuyama continues to regret to this day is that the Chinese consul was granted permission to meet with the captain.

What would have been the implication of the captain signing the record of oral statements and admitting to obstruction of performance of official duties? To repeat, his signature could be automatically interpreted to be an admission that Japan's domestic laws did in fact apply to the Senkaku Islands and the surrounding waters. With this possible interpretation in mind, "That is why," Fukuyama says, "the Chinese side went to great lengths to avoid this outcome."

China had begun to make open claims on the sovereignty of the Senkaku Islands well before the incident. Thus from the Chinese perspective, it was absolutely unacceptable that the incident should end with criminal procedures under Japanese domestic law, since such an outcome would signal China's acceptance of the exercise of Japanese sovereignty in the Senkaku Islands. The Chinese position becomes easier to understand if we look at the situation as paralleling Japan's position on the Northern Territories.

As Japan sees it, the Soviet Union, and now Russia, wrongfully wields effective control over Japan's Northern Territories. As a result, for a Japanese national to obtain a visa from the Russian government to visit the Northern Territories would constitute an admission by that individual that the Northern Territories are Russian territory. The acquisition of a visa under Russian domestic law followed by a landing on any of the Northern Territories four islands would immediately weaken the Japanese position that the Russian occupation of the Northern Territories is illegal. This is why, except in special cases (called "visa-waiver travel" by Japanese nationals who previously resided on the islands), the Ministry of Foreign Affairs does not permit Japanese citizens to travel to the Northern Territories.

While prefacing this with the qualification that he does not know what the Chinese consul told the captain, Fukuyama explains that the captain was absolutely adamant in his refusal. Fukuyama would repeatedly return to this "response error" and the possibility that this contributed to worsening the situation.

"There is no truth to the allegation that command authority was exercised." Justice Minister Yanagida Minoru read this prepared statement following the decision to release the captain. Considering that the Kantei had itself ruled out the extra-legal option of exercising command authority, it is clear that moving forward calmly with criminal procedures, as Fukuyama put it, was the only real option. The legal process unfolded with this as the starting point. The captain was detained. But because the captain refused to sign the oral statements, no definite conclusion could be reached and the period of detention was extended. This course of events served to engage the Chinese side even more, explained Fukuyama.

The moment the decision was made to extend the period of detention, the Chinese side must have thought, "We have repeatedly asked Japan to do something about this. But instead Japan has gone forward with criminal procedures and is preparing to indict." Hence the very strongly worded statement by Wen Jiabao at the United Nations.

At the time of the incident, public prosecutors were reeling from a case of evidence tampering and falsification of investigative materials that had taken place at the Special Investigation Department of the Osaka District Public Prosecutors Office. Now that the Senkaku Islands incident had developed into a major diplomatic tussle, if the Chinese captain of the fishing vessel were to be indicted and put on trial, the case would be in court for several months, during which time the captain would have to be detained in Japan. This would certainly lead to an escalation on the Chinese side, and could even lead to a contingency situation.

From various reports carried by the media at the time, it can be surmised that the senior public prosecutors were deeply concerned about the risk of falling into this type of negative spiral of events. Sengoku has stuck to his story that the captain was released on the judgment of the public prosecutors, and explains that immediately before the final policy direction was settled, the Ishigaki Branch of the Naha District Public Prosecutors Office contacted the Kantei with the request that they wanted to sound out the

STRAINED TO THE BREAKING POINT

Ministry of Foreign Affairs. Sengoku admits that a senior Foreign Ministry official was rushed to Okinawa following this request.

This and related events are recorded in the October 21, 2010, proceedings of the House of Councillors Judicial Affairs Committee. The developments are given in chronological order based on statements made by Nishikawa Katsuyuki, director-general of the Ministry of Justice Criminal Affairs Bureau, in response to questions from Sakurauchi Fumiki, a Your Party member of the House of Representatives.

- ➢ September 22: Public prosecutors decide to ask the Ministry of Foreign Affairs for a briefing on the state of Japan-China relations following the collision. This request is relayed from the prosecutors' office to the Ministry of Foreign Affairs via the Justice Ministry.
- ➢ September 23: The Foreign Ministry responds to the Justice Ministry saying a Foreign Ministry official will go to Naha District Prosecutors Office to provide the briefing. This information is relayed by the Justice Ministry to public prosecutors.
- ➢ September 23, afternoon: District prosecutors meet with the Foreign Ministry officer at the Naha District Prosecutors Office and receive the briefing on the state of Japan-China relations following the incident.
- ➢ September 24, morning: A meeting is held at the Supreme Prosecutors Office for consultations between the Supreme Prosecutors Office, Fukuoka High Public Prosecutors Office, and Naha District Public Prosecutors Office and it is decided to release the suspect without indictment. Following this, public prosecutors relay the policy decision on releasing the suspect to the Justice Ministry official handling this case.
- ➢ September 24, 11:55 a.m.: The director-general of the Ministry of Justice Criminal Affairs Bureau (Nishikawa) reports to Justice Minister Yanagida on the public prosecutors' policy decision to release the suspect and the reasons for the decision.
- ➢ September 24, 12:30 p.m.: The vice-minister of justice contacts Deputy Chief Cabinet Secretary Takino Kinya to inform him of the policy decision to release the captain.
- ➢ September 24, 2:30 p.m.: The Naha District Public Prosecutors Office holds a press conference to announce the policy decision to release the captain and the reasons for the decision.

STRAINED TO THE BREAKING POINT

According to Parliamentary Vice-Minister for Foreign Affairs Kikuta Makiko who was present on this occasion, the principal exchange took place between the director of the Justice Ministry's Public Security Division and the director of the Foreign Ministry's China and Mongolia Division, while the vice-minister of justice, vice-minister for foreign affairs, and Deputy Chief Cabinet Secretary Takino basically affirmed what was said by the two divisional directors. Regarding the decision-making process that followed, Kikuta explained that Deputy Chief Cabinet Secretary Takino consulted Chief Cabinet Secretary Sengoku, who then approved the dispatch. At the same time, the vice-minister for foreign affairs reported to Foreign Minister Maehara, who was then in New York, and Maehara gave his consent.

According to Kikuta, even after the public prosecutors had reached a final policy decision on releasing the captain, the director of the Justice Ministry's Public Security Division contacted the director of the Foreign Ministry's China and Mongolia Division, and this information was then conveyed to Maehara in New York. Finally, Maehara responded, "We will respect this as the public prosecutors' decision."

It is not known what the Ministry of Foreign Affairs and the public prosecutors said to each other, but it would be no surprise if the two sides had developed a mutual understanding to the effect that, "From the perspective of Japan-China diplomatic relations, the release of the captain is indispensable to an early settlement of the incident." It is extremely likely that this understanding was condensed and encapsulated in the statement made by Deputy Chief Prosecutor Suzuki Toru of the Naha District Public Prosecutors Office: Taking into consideration the future of Japan-China relations, it is not appropriate to continue the detention any longer.

Deputy Chief Cabinet Secretary Fukuyama, a first-hand witness to this outcome and the developments that preceded it, shares this observation. "Honestly, I think it was totally unnecessary to note Diplomatic Issue on the document of *nolle prosequi*." According to Fukuyama, the public prosecutors were suspending indictment in consideration of the fact that this was the captain's first offense, that there was no premeditation, that his actions had been impulsive, and that the probability of a repeat offense was low. Thus, Fukuyama emphasizes, "Diplomatic considerations were not the reason for suspending indictment."

Fukuyama goes on to add this criticism. "First, the prosecutors had no business referring to diplomatic considerations. Second, this gave the impression that Japan yielded to strong pressure from China in an incident where a Chinese national had obstructed the performance of official duties. As far as impressions go, that was extremely unfortunate."

Katayama Yoshihiro, the Kan Cabinet's minister of internal affairs and communications, made the following comment to members of the press after the announcement of the public prosecutors' decision. Starting out with the caveat, "I was not directly involved in this case," Katayama, continued, "Looking at the big picture, I assume a high-level political decision was behind it all. In a broad sense, you can say the public prosecutors are part of the government."

Katayama continued. "The entire government was constantly engaged in discussing this problem, and I believe an overall political decision existed in the background, which I think is fine. It would be childish to allow an escalation to endanger our relations with China. The Japanese side was a little more mature in its response."

"This outcome is the result of a cool-headed decision reached by the public prosecutors under domestic laws based on a comprehensive evaluation of the nature of the incident and other factors."

Speaking at a press conference in New York on the afternoon of September 24 (the morning of September 25, Japan time) after the Naha District Public Prosecutors Office's decision to release the captain, Prime Minister Kan was emphatic that there had been no political intervention in reaching the decision to release the captain. On the other hand, the Ministry of Foreign Affairs released the following statement through its press secretary on September 25.

There is no doubt that the Senkaku Islands are clearly an inherent territory of Japan, in light of historical facts and based upon international law. Indeed, the Senkaku Islands are now under the valid control of Japan. There exists no issue of territorial sovereignty to be resolved concerning the Senkaku Islands.

The Government of Japan handled the most recent incident duly and strictly in accordance with domestic law as a case involving obstruction of the performance of official duty by a Chinese fishing trawler. Thus, the demand by the Chinese side for apology and compensation is completely groundless and is utterly unacceptable.

Steady development of Japan-China relations is extremely important not only for both countries but also for the region as well as the international community. It is important for both Japan and China to continue making efforts to realize Mutually Beneficial Relationship based on Common Strategic Interests from a broader perspective.

On the same day, the Chinese captain of the fishing vessel returned to Fujian Province in southern China on an airplane chartered by the Chinese government. Following the captain's return, the Chinese Ministry of Foreign Affairs released a statement labeling the legal measures taken by Japan illegal and void and demanding that "Japan must apologize and pay compensation to the Chinese side for this incident." The statement contains a strong protest against the detention of the captain and claims the detention "severely infringed upon Chinese territorial sovereignty." Prior to this, all statements made by the Chinese Foreign Ministry regarding the Senkaku Islands were labeled "statements of the spokesperson." However, this particular statement was assigned a higher standing and was understood to represent a more general expression of the position taken by the Chinese government on the incident.

Maehara was still in New York when this statement was released. Asked to comment, Maehara evaded the question, saying, "I haven't had a chance to see it." But he checked China by stressing, "There is no territorial issue in the East China Sea. If the same kind of incident occurs in the future, we will once again take a resolute stance."

Meeting with the press at the Kantei on the afternoon of September 24, Sengoku said, "This is simply the outcome of the calm pursuit of legal processes and procedures based on Japanese law." Here again, Sengoku repeated his claim that the decision to release the captain was made independently by the public prosecutors. But the method used to close the case continued to attract broad-based criticism and expressions of dissatisfaction from many parties concerned, such as the justice and diplomatic communities, as well as Coast Guard front lines personnel at all levels. Critics were saying that the Kan Cabinet was using the public prosecutors as a convenient cover for its own political decision, and that the outcome was simply the result of weak-kneed diplomacy.

As previously mentioned, Maehara remained wedded to the position that "Japan will deal calmly with this matter under the provisions of domestic laws." Given this position, Sengoku and Fukuyama had concluded from the very start that the appearance could not be given that any laws had been bent to make way for a political decision. Again as previously noted, in light of the actions taken by the Chinese side to ban the export of rare metals to Japan and to take Japanese businessmen into custody, it was clear that it was not in Japan's national interest to continue with time consuming legal procedures.

These two conflicting problems had to be resolved simultaneously. To achieve this end, some way had to be devised for the Chinese captain of the fishing vessel to be released as soon as possible. There is no doubt that the path to such a solution was indirect inducement as practiced by Sengoku, who was regarded as a master manipulator of the bureaucracy.

The process of arresting and detaining the captain had been rushed through the Kan Cabinet by the combined forces of Maehara's nationalism and Okada's fundamentalism. Sengoku, who had responded to these attitudes with his own brand of pragmatism says, "Once the arrest had been made and the suspect detained, there was no other way to settle the matter."

Sengoku explains the basic principle that he abided by. "Once you step over the threshold of judicial process, the decision has to remain within the judiciary until the bitter end. Maybe I make too much of this because of my own legal background. But what can you do? This is the Japanese system."

Asked about persistent rumors concerning the possibility of extra-legal measures, Sengoku laughs it off and says. "As was done by the Fukuda Cabinet, 'extra-legal measures' could perhaps have been an option at the time of sentencing, but it would not be right to interfere in the work of a court on the judicial process prior to final verdict or the work of public prosecutors. Obstruction of performance of official duties is far too minor a charge for considering that route."

In his reference to the Fukuda Cabinet, Sengoku was recalling the 1977 Japan Airlines hijacking perpetrated by members of the Japanese Red Army. In resolving the standoff through extra-legal measures, Prime Minister Fukuda Takeo spoke the now famous words, "Human life is weightier than the whole Earth." Fukuda not only accepted the demands of the hijackers and agreed to release other Red Army members serving prison sentences but also agreed to top it off with a ransom payment.

However, no one's life was at stake in the collision off the Senkaku Islands. For Sengoku, who liked to refer to himself as a "dyed-in-the-wool lawyer," the situation did not call for extra-legal measures. At best, there was room for quasi-legal measures, but nothing more than that.

At the ASEM Meeting

"Well, hello. Why don't we sit down?"

Prime Minister Kan was in Brussels, Belgium, on October 4, 2010, to attend the Asia-Europe Meeting (ASEM). After the banquet that evening, he came face-to-face with China's Premier Wen Jiabao in the corridor of the royal palace where the banquet was held and called out to Wen inviting him to sit down a bit. The two, each accompanied only by his interpreter, sat on a couch and began to talk.

Initially, Kan had decided not to attend ASEM due to a scheduling conflict with the special session of the Diet. But the anticipated first meeting with Wen in New York at the end of September had failed to materialize due to the collision incident. Even now that the captain had been released, China had not softened its position on demanding an "apology and compensation." Back in Japan, the House of Representatives Budget Committee had become the scene of a heated tug-of-war between the ruling and opposition parties over the submission to the Diet of the video tape that showed the Chinese boat ramming the Japan Coast Guard patrol ship and proved the captain's guilt.

It was against this backdrop that Kan suddenly announced on September 27 that he had changed his schedule and was going to Belgium after all. This was because Kan had learned through his own channels that Wen Jiabao would be attending ASEM.

One of the reasons Kan decided to go was that he feared ASEM would turn into a kangaroo court if he did not go. With all the leaders of Asia and Europe gathered together, Wen Jiabao could very easily get away with one-sided claims on the Senkaku Islands. Kan felt he had to be in Belgium to make the appeal that the "Senkaku Islands are an inherent part of the territory of Japan."

Kan was scheduled to host the APEC Summit Meeting in Yokohama in the middle of the following month, November. It was anticipated that President Hu Jintao would be present at this conference as usual. As the host country, Japan would have to welcome the leaders of the participating countries and ensure the success of the conference. With this in mind, Kan concluded that the most important and most urgent diplomatic issue before him was that of restoring relations with China as soon as possible. Given that, Kan calculated that he needed to meet Wen Jiabao at the earliest opportunity to find a path to improved relations.

"It went rather well and we were able to talk naturally and normally" is how Kan described his exchange with Wen Jiabao. However, contrary to Kan's description, the 25-minute private conversation had been carried out in an extremely tense atmosphere. "The islands are integral to the territory of China." Wen was repeating the standard Chinese position, to which Kan responded head-on, "They are an inherent part of Japan, and there is no territorial issue."

"We agreed that the current state of Japan-China relations is not desirable, and we confirmed that we will pursue a mutually beneficial relationship based on common strategic interests." As agreed with Wen, Kan met the press with these words after the brief meeting and strongly implied that some progress had been achieved.

On October 3, immediately before leaving for Belgium, Kan had met with the press at the Kantei and had been asked about the response to the collision incident. Leading off as usual with a series of "well, yes" as was his habit, Kan answered, "Several bilateral talks are scheduled. I believe it is necessary to explain Japan's position in the course of these talks." But when he was asked directly whether a meeting with Chinese leaders had been scheduled, Kan dismissed the question and answered more brusquely than usual. "Nothing has been planned."

Insofar as nothing had been arranged through official diplomatic channels at that point in time, Kan was correct in saying that no meeting had been scheduled with Wen Jiabao. But the possibility of holding some kind of meeting with Wen was never zero. Kan's response to the query about a meeting with Wen had been voiced in what may have been a mechanical and unemotional tone. Contrary to his tone, it is possible that Kan had already received signals behind the scenes that an unofficial meeting to explore ways to improve bilateral relations could be arranged with the Chinese side after arriving in Belgium.

"I am here to meet some people on my own, not as an envoy. There is nothing more I can say."

This was the explanation Hosono Goshi gave the press when they surrounded him at a Beijing hotel on the evening of September 29, 2010, a week before the Japan-China summit meeting in Belgium. Hosono, the former DPJ deputy secretary general, had arrived at the Beijing Airport that afternoon and had been whisked off to the Diaoyutai State Guesthouse where the Chinese government welcomes its special guests in the early evening. There, Hosono had met with State Councillor (with vice-premier status) Dai Bingguo, China's top foreign policy leader and a close aide to President Hu Jintao.

A year earlier, in December 2009, Ozawa Ichiro, the former DPJ secretary general, had led a group of about 140 Diet members on a visit to China which included meetings with President Hu and other leaders. Hosono had been in charge of liaising with the Chinese side before and during the trip, and it is likely that he maintained his contacts with China. But now in

STRAINED TO THE BREAKING POINT

September 2010, Hosono held no official post in the Party, nor had he ever served as a cabinet minister. As such, it was highly unusual for him to have been afforded a long meeting with Dai Bingguo, who was directly linked to President Hu.

The only way to explain the special treatment that Hosono received is to postulate that he had travelled to China as Kan's special envoy and was carrying a letter from the prime minister. After the meeting with Dai Bingguo, Hosono was asked whether he was a special envoy. To this, Hosono gave the quick reply. "That is not what it is." Asked if he had carried a letter from Kan, he stated he "couldn't answer" and refused to elaborate.

At about the same time, Kan was echoing the reply given by Hosono. "I am totally unaware of what he is doing," the prime minister said about Hosono's visit to China. As Maehara Seiji, the foreign minister, said, "A few days ago, I learned about the trip from other sources." But Maehara said with certainty, "The trip has nothing to do with the government." Asked whether Hosono had been entrusted with a letter, Maehara quickly denied it: "That's 100 percent negative."

Chief Cabinet Secretary Sengoku Yoshito also said in his press conference "I had heard about it indirectly." Thus, while admitting he had foreknowledge of the trip, Sengoku made sure to add the disclaimer, "The government has nothing to do with this. The government neither approved nor disapproved his trip to China."

But Sengoku had not revealed everything he knew. The truth was that immediately before leaving for China, Hosono had been called in by Sengoku. "We have the future to consider. Go to China with the intent to open up alternate channels [personal ties linking Japan and China]." Though none other than Sengoku had issued these instructions, he was now feigning ignorance with the disclaimer, "The government had nothing to do with Hosono's trip."

"I never told Hosono, 'Go negotiate and work this out.' There was such a difference in status [with Dai Bingguo and others] that Hosono wouldn't have been able to negotiate a deal even if he tried. I knew this."

As Hosono was leaving for China, it was clearly Sengoku who was pulling the strings behind the scenes. Sengoku explains the back-channel approach that there was never any plan to send Hosono to China as the prime minister's envoy or to entrust him with the prime minister's letter. The purpose of the trip was simply inter-party networking with the Chinese Communist Party as a means of strengthening the DPJ foundations. As a matter of fact, this purpose was clearly stated in Sengoku's press conference of October 5. "We want to develop relations for frank and direct discussions, including the younger people in the Party."

Sengoku recounts the developments that awaited Hosono's visit. "What a surprise! Hosono arrived in Beijing and was taken directly to Dai Bingguo by the International Liaison Department of the Communist Party of China. Hosono was then made to listen endlessly to statements of China's position. Hosono didn't buckle and spoke his own mind in rebuttal."

Whatever the original purpose of the trip may have been, it was clear that the Chinese side attached a certain significance to Hosono's visit and was reading between the lines to find the intent of the Japanese government. The result was the unusually grand reception afforded Hosono. Dai Bingguo had warmly welcomed someone who was no more than a foot soldier in the DPJ and had spent a considerable amount of time with him in the Guesthouse. It would be no exaggeration to say that this could be taken as an expression of the high expectations on the Chinese side. Hosono had been sent to China representing Sengoku, reputedly the sharpest mind in the DPJ and frequently referred to as the de facto prime minister. On the receiving side was Dai Bingguo, who had Hu's full confidence. In the context of Chinese thinking, it was clear that both Japan and China were signaling that they were ready to work together to improve the situation.

When Hosono's China visit became public knowledge on September 29, Sengoku responded in his press conference: "I have always been saying that the ball is in China's court." His point was to emphasize that improving bilateral relations depended on what the Chinese side was willing to do.

Sengoku's decision to release and deport the Chinese captain of the fishing vessel virtually unconditionally was already attracting strong criticism as weak-kneed diplomacy. On the other hand, the Kan Cabinet felt it needed to quickly improve relations with China in order to ensure APEC and other upcoming major diplomatic events went smoothly. However, China would not alter its basic position, which was to deny the facts of the incident and to demand apology and compensation from Japan.

Under the circumstances and given its position that "There is no territorial issue pertaining to the Senkaku Islands," Japan could ill afford to dispatch an envoy to China to take the initiative in improving relations. If it had done that, criticism of weak-kneed diplomacy would have certainly spilled over the borders and spread throughout Asia. It is notable that Maehara, the leading hawk in the Kan Cabinet, had met with members of the press on the evening of September 29 to shed a negative light on Hosono's China visit. "At the present stage, there is no need for us to take action," he said.

While carefully monitoring the various facts and developments that remained below the surface, Sengoku made the decision to dispatch Hosono to Beijing at this time. Just a few days earlier, Kan had made the decision to attend the ASEM summit conference to be held in Brussels, Belgium, on October 4 and 5. Hosono's visit was timed to take place before that.

Meeting the press at the Kantei, Maehara was asked about the significance and mission of Hosono's China visit, to which he replied, "I don't know whether it was Hosono's personal decision or a decision made by the DPJ. But what I can say definitely is that it was not a government decision." But members of the press would not let up and continued to pepper him with questions. "Did Hosono go to China to set the stage for a Japan-China summit meeting?" Raising his voice, Maehara said emphatically, "That is completely off the mark." Maehara would steadfastly continue to deny that the unexpected Hosono mission constituted dual-track diplomacy.

Next to meet the press was former Foreign Minister Okada Katsuya, who had now taken the post of DPJ secretary general. "The only thing I knew was that there was a possibility that former deputy secretary general Hosono might go to China. I first learned that he was in Beijing from media reports. In any case, I have always said that the DPJ had nothing to do with this trip." This flat-out denial of the Party's complicity in the Hosono visit was made with all due emphasis.

But Hosono was not alone on his visit to China. Rather, he was accompanied by Sugawa Kiyoshi, the former head of the Party's Policy Research Council. Sugawa was currently assigned to the Kantei by the DPJ as a special Researcher in the Cabinet Secretariat. Notwithstanding this fact, Okada was adamant in his denial of Party involvement. "The Party staff member who accompanied Hosono is now assigned to the Kantei. There is no sense here that he is a Party employee."

Okada then continued, "If there is a significant exchange of views in Beijing, I suppose we may talk to Hosono about it when he returns. But this whole thing is unrelated to the Party. So even if we talk to him, it would only be so we can know what happened."

Hosono himself was interviewed by the *Mainichi Shimbun* concerning his mission to China, the interview published in the paper's evening edition on October 15, 2010. "I had some old friends in the International Liaison Department," he said. "And I myself made all the decisions on going to China and who to go with. That is all there is to say." Hosono remained tight lipped and refused to add any details.

The question remains why the former and current foreign ministers,

Okada and Maehara, maintained a cool distance from the Hosono mission to China. The involvement of an independent consultant and China expert, Shinohara Tsukasa, provides an important hint to their cool stance. It was rumored that the ties between Sengoku and Shinohara went back to their university days when Sengoku was deeply involved in the All-Campus Joint Struggle League, the radical student movement known as Zenkyoto.

Born in 1950, Shinohara was known for such publications as *When You Make a Friend, Find a Chinese!* According to the CV that appears in his book, Shinohara graduated from the Chinese Literature Department of Waseda University and continued his studies at Singapore's Nanyang University and South Korea's Seoul University. He later participated in the establishment of several high-tech start-ups in Silicon Valley before moving to China at the end of the 1980s. His current occupation is listed as consultant to corporations seeking to establish themselves in China.

Shinohara is said to have played a behind-the-scenes role in promoting networking between Japan and China during earlier LDP administrations. It was in fact Shinohara who had arranged Hosono's China visit. As Shinohara later explained the situation in an interview with the TBS news program *News 23 Cross* that aired on December 6, 2010, "The media criticizes Sengoku for what it calls dual-track diplomacy. But I would say the media is barking up the wrong tree. The Ministry of Foreign Affairs had completely exhausted its channels. The only option left was to go to the private sector." Shinohara was not at all shy about admitting his involvement in Hosono's China visit. On his connection to Sengoku, Shinohara stated, "Sengoku and I go way back to our days in the student movement, and we have many friends in common."

"Japan was looking for a channel for negotiating with China and the Chinese were looking for a channel for negotiating with Japan. So the two sides' needs meshed." Shinohara said that both sides felt they had painted themselves into a corner and were looking for a way out. The Hosono visit materialized because the Chinese side and Sengoku at the Kantei were attuned to each other's state of mind and were prepared to take a step forward.

However, Sengoku denies Shinohara's statements. First, Sengoku claims he never met or knew Shinohara during his student days. Next, he explains that after the collision, "A certain person advised me that I should use Shinohara." Acting on this advice, Sengoku met secretly with Shinohara, which started the ball rolling for Hosono's visit to China.

At this stage, as previously noted, Sengoku did not harbor any grandiose expectations for the Hosono visit. However, when Hosono landed in

Beijing, he was surrounded by news teams from Japanese TV stations that were awaiting his arrival and was quickly whisked off to meetings with Dai Bingguo and other Chinese leaders. Sengoku introspectively recounts that watching these developments on television, "I thought to myself, 'We have been outdone by the Chinese.'" According to Sengoku, when Shinohara went on TBS after the Hosono visit to reveal what had gone on behind the scenes, "I made a point of not meeting with him [Shinohara] again."

Immediately before Hosono's China visit, Japanese diplomats were endeavoring to enter into high-level secret negotiations with China. But Sengoku was feeling increasingly frustrated with these diplomatic efforts and was close to concluding that Japan was "not equal to the task" of negotiating with China if such negotiations were to be carried out by diplomats who did not embody the political will of the DPJ. In his TBS interview, Shinohara echoed Sengoku's irritation with Japan's diplomatic exchanges with China during this period saying, "The Ministry of Foreign Affairs was very slow to understand. I believe they were very dense and insensitive."

It has already been noted that Sengoku was anxious that "the single charge of obstruction could end up overturning the bilateral relationship if it was not handled properly." Prodded by this anxiety, Sengoku maintained direct contact with Cheng Yonghua, the Chinese ambassador to Japan, and was looking for a way to release the Chinese captain of the fishing vessel. But the Chinese side showed no signs of easing its tough stance. The conclusion that Sengoku drew from this intransigence was that official diplomatic channels had become totally dysfunctional. Here again, Sengoku reverted to his own form of pragmatism and decided to use his own team to find way out of the impasse.

Mainichi Shimbun carried the following story on November 8, 2010. The meeting held at the Diaoyutai State Guesthouse between Dai Bingguo and his three Japanese visitors (Hosono, Sugawa, and Shinohara) lasted for seven hours. During this meeting, Dai Bingguo presented the Japanese side with two conditions for resolving the situation: (1) Japan must not release the video of the collision and (2) Okinawa Governor Hirokazu Nakaima must suspend his inspection of the Senkaku Islands. *Mainichi Shimbun* reports that Sengoku accepted these terms.

After these events, immediately preceding the ASEM summit conference, Sengoku had a direct phone conversation with Dai Bingguo on October 1. The two sides confirmed such principles as the significance of mutually beneficial relations based on common strategic interests and the importance of promoting bilateral exchanges. Having reached this understanding, Japan and China set out to accomplish the task of organizing a "hastily arranged summit meeting."

Even as he was preparing to leave Japan, Kan was still uncertain whether a meeting with Hu Jintao would materialize. To expedite matters, he instructed Sengoku, as previously agreed, to order his right-hand man, Deputy Cabinet Secretary Fukuyama Tetsuro, to negotiate secretly with the Chinese side. According to Sengoku, he and Fukuyama met with Ambassador Cheng Yonghua at the Imperial Hotel to find an acceptable way out. Fukuyama continued to attend these secret meetings until the day before he left for Belgium. Once in Belgium, Fukuyama remained in constant touch with his Chinese counterpart, Wu Jianghao, deputy director-general of the Department of Asian Affairs in China's Ministry of Foreign Affairs, to open the way and set the stage for the leaders of the two countries to meet.

"The situation did not allow us to take the initiative in requesting a summit meeting. The other side felt equally hemmed in. The point was that the impasse could not be resolved by working through normal diplomatic channels," says Fukuyama.

The two countries were set apart by two smoldering problems. One was the ban on the export of rare metals to Japan, and the other was the problem of Fujita Corporation, the middle-echelon Japanese general contractor whose four employees remained in custody in China. Fukuyama found himself stymied in his negotiations by three negative and contradictory factors. One was the pressure inside the Kantei to achieve "any sort of summit meeting, even if it is no more than a mere formality." The second was the increasingly vociferous criticism of the government that was coming primarily from the business community. Third was the public's expression of anger with China. Kan, Sengoku, and Fukuyama had concluded that these negotiations would not succeed if carried out by the diplomatic corps which, so to speak, came dressed in ceremonial garb. Thus, it would come down to a war of nerves with Fukuyama and his team in Belgium working on the one hand to restrain the Japanese side while working on the other hand to read the mind and attitude of the Chinese side.

"The question was whether we could just forget about rare metals, rare earths, and Fujita Corporation. The obvious answer was no, we could not." His mind made up, Fukuyama engaged in a series of politically led diplomatic negotiations. It was then that a ray of light broke through the darkness. In their speeches delivered at the ASEM plenary session, neither Kan nor Wen directly mentioned the Senkaku Islands. Both governments took this to be evidence of the absence of enmity on the other side. The two governments capitalized on this sentiment and, in what Sengoku liked to refer to as a "synchronicity of the state of mind," speedy progress was made toward preparing for the two leaders to meet outside of the banquet room. And all of this was achieved without either side seeming to have taken the initiative.

In Belgium, Fukuyama remained in constant touch with the prime minister by cell phone. In his final call to the prime minister before the meeting, Fukuyama said, "This is how far they have come." To this, Kan replied, "Let's do it." Without missing a beat, Fukuyama said, "In that case, meet him in the corridor." As a result, the meeting between Kan and Wen finally materialized with the two leaders seated on a couch in the corridor of the royal palace in Brussels.

As Fukuyama has explained, both sides were obsessed with the absolute need to avoid the impression that the summit had materialized as a result of a concession it had made. Although it was Japan that was negotiating with a nervous eye on the hostages China held, namely the rare metal exports and the Japanese company employees, Fukuyama recalls that it was the Chinese side that seemed to be feeling the pressure.

In a speech delivered at the United Nations headquarters in New York the previous month, Wen Jiabao had declared, "When it comes to sovereignty, national unity and territorial integrity, China will not yield or compromise." Having thrown down the gauntlet in New York, Wen—who was known as a Japanophile in China—could ill afford to be seen as agreeing too easily to a meeting with the Japanese. Such a show of weakness could very well cost him his political life. Notwithstanding this risk, Wen ultimately decided to meet with Kan.

That was the moment when the two sides finally succeeded in putting a lid on the fierce diplomatic battle between Japan and China that had been instigated by the collision—an impulsive act by a drunken Chinese captain at sea.

Last-minute Cancellation

"Japan ruined the atmosphere of the summit meeting. Japan must take full responsibility for this." These words negating the summit meeting between Kan Naoto and Wen Jiabao were spoken by Hu Zhengyue, China's assistant secretary of foreign affairs. The occasion was an ASEAN-related conference held in Hanoi, Vietnam, on October 29, 2010. Hu Zhengyue had gathered the Hong Kong media in one of the rooms in the hotel where the conference was being held to make a unilateral announcement on the cancellation of the meeting. On the receiving end of this ambush, Fukuyama, who had accompanied Kan on this trip, relates the details of the sudden and unexpected changes in the situation.

"The summit meeting was set for 6:30 p.m. With the clock running out, the Chinese side suddenly told us, 'The meeting cannot happen.' On the Japanese side, we wanted to act calmly and promote our mutually beneficial relationship based on common strategic interests. There was no change in our position."

Hu Zhengyue made the following argument. "Japan's diplomatic officials have conspired with another country to once again fan the flames of conflict over Diaoyutai [Chinese name for Uotsurijima]." In fact, two days before this, on October 27, Foreign Minister Maehara had met with Secretary of State Hillary Clinton at a Japan-US foreign ministers' meeting held in Hawaii. In the course of this meeting, it was reaffirmed that "Article V of the Treaty of Mutual Cooperation and Security applies to the Senkaku Islands." Hu's criticism was directed at this announcement.

That same evening, the Ministry of Foreign Affairs chief spokesman, Ma Zhaoxu, released a statement in Beijing concerning Clinton's affirmation that the Senkaku Islands came under the provisions of the Japan-US Security Treaty. "This is absolutely unacceptable," he said.

But the pushback did not stop there as Ma Zhaoxu unilaterally continued his criticism of Japan. "Even as the ASEAN Summit Meeting was being held, the Japanese side used the media to spread statements violating China's sovereignty and territorial integrity." He then went on to comment on the Japan-China foreign ministers' meeting that had been held on October 29 between Maehara and Chinese Foreign Minister Yang Jiechi. He said, "Japan has made untrue statements and has distorted China's position on upholding the principles that are the shared understanding of the two countries."

According to foreign ministry officials who were travelling with Maehara, the Chinese side had taken issue with an article written by France's AFP which included a statement attributed to Maehara. "The two countries have agreed to resume negotiations for provisions on the development of gas fields in the East China Sea." As this was clearly contrary to the facts, the Japanese foreign ministry immediately contacted AFP to demand a correction.

When the two foreign ministers met in Hanoi on October 29, both sides started with statements of territorial claims in the Senkaku Islands. On the matter of the development of gas fields, Maehara did request a resumption of treaty negotiations, to which Yang Jiechi responded, "We want to first prepare the necessary environment." Next, Maehara asked for an explanation about moves toward drilling in the Shirakaba Gas Field (Chinese name: Chunxizo Gas Field) shown by the Chinese side. Yang avoided this question with the comment, "It is exactly as we have explained in the past."

Be that as it may, the meeting extended far beyond the originally scheduled 30 minutes. Finally, after 80 minutes of talks, the two foreign ministers parted after confirming that they would each "report to their superiors on arranging for a summit meeting." The message that Maehara conveyed to the prime minister after his meeting with Yang was, "The discussion was very constructive and good. The atmosphere also was good."

"Reports have circulated that an agreement was reached on the issue of the gas fields, but this is not fact-based. It would be regrettable if the summit meeting were to be cancelled because of unfounded media reports," stated Fukuyama while still in Hanoi. By implication, he was expressing his frustration and dissatisfaction with China's emotional response. At the same time, Fukuyama revealed that Prime Minister Kan had responded to the news of the postponement of the meeting by telling those around him, "Let's respond to this in a calm manner." Fukuyama had not forgotten to choreograph Kan's statement to point out to the world that Japan was making a conscious effort to remain calm.

In the cabinet reshuffle, Kan had decided to appoint Maehara to head the Ministry of Foreign Affairs. As this decision was being made, Fukuyama asked the prime minister if he was sure Maehara measured up to being entrusted with diplomatic relations with China. "Are you sure you want to appoint Maehara?" he asked. "He was the minister with jurisdiction when the Coast Guard made the arrest off the Senkaku Islands. Then there are all the things that happened when we were in the opposition. Appointing Maehara under these conditions may further strain our relations with China."

Fukuyama's premonition had unexpectedly proven right, and now in Hanoi, he was feeling he had been sucker punched. "I really can't figure out what [China] is thinking," he said squeezing the words out of his mouth.

In the scenario envisioned by Kan and Fukuyama, Hanoi would serve as a follow-up to the Brussels meeting that had Kan and Wen Jiabao on the same couch. The second meeting, it was hoped, would establish the tone for improving Japan-China relations. This then would become a stepping stone to the mid-November APEC Summit Meeting in Yokohama. Anticipating that President Hu Jintao would be present in Yokohama, the scenario would reach its climax in a Kan-Hu summit. This is why China's "last minute cancellation" in Hanoi was such a shock to Kan, Maehara, and Fukuyama. Outwardly they feigned composure, but inwardly they could hardly contain their bewilderment and frustration.

The following morning, October 30, China completely reversed itself. According to Fukuyama, China suddenly indicated that it would be amenable to a ten-minute conversation between Kan and Wen Jiabao to be held in the conference hall on the site of the East Asia Summit Meeting. Fukuyama describes the meeting saying, "It was a very natural setting." The two leaders agreed that "it was too bad" the meeting scheduled for the previous day had not materialized, and proceeded to agree on three further points: to strengthen private-sector exchanges, to promote mutually beneficial relations based on common strategic interests, and to make opportunities for engaging in leisurely talks."

As the leaders of the 16 countries participating in the East Asian Summit Meeting were streaming into the conference hall, Wen Jiabao turned to Kan and said, "It was unfortunate what happened." Kan was conversing with Sultan Bolkiah of Brunei when Wen approached the two, shook hands with Sultan Bolkiah, then extended his hand to Kan. The prime minister immediately said, "It is too bad we were unable to meet," to which Wen responded, "I feel the same. Let's find an opportunity to have a proper discussion."

What was behind the choreography of Wen taking the initiative and approaching Kan? It is very likely the Chinese side was aiming to counter the impression that China was finding excuses to refuse a summit meeting. France's AFP had accepted that its earlier report on the "Maehara statement" at a Japan-China foreign ministers' meeting regarding joint development of the gas fields in the East China Sea, which the Chinese side had seen as a problem, had been wrong, and in its correction, AFP clearly admitted that the "Japanese side had not stated that an agreement had been reached." The release of this retraction had helped China soften its position.

Even more importantly, China's unilateral cancellation in Hanoi endangered the path toward improved relations that had been arranged in Brussels. It was clear that, left unattended, this situation would cast a dark shadow over President Hu Jintao's visit to the Yokohama APEC Conference and the summit with Kan. If these warning lights were not turned off, Japan-China relations would sink further into the abyss, and this was not what China wanted.

"Various things have happened, but there is absolutely no change in our mutually beneficial relationship based on common strategic interests. I am certain we will continue to enjoy meaningful and friendly relations." That is what Kan said in the press conference that followed his conversation with Wen, and there was no mistaking the sense of relief that could be seen in his face. Kan chose to put a positive spin on the relations with China that had proven to be so troubling and perplexing. "I don't believe the minor problems that are occurring now are decisive problems in light of what has occurred in the past. If both sides approach these issues calmly, it is entirely possible to achieve further progress in Japan-China relations in terms of both our economic and our cultural ties." Kan was sending a strong signal to his Chinese counterpart.

China had cancelled a formal meeting between the leaders of the two countries at the last minute. But for its own reasons, it had stepped forward the next day with an idea for a conversation. What was to be made of these dramatic shifts in stance? By this time, Japan had completed all criminal procedures pertaining to the Chinese captain of the fishing vessel collision incident, culminating in a final disposition consisting of release without indictment. Fukuyama hypothesizes that, "The settlement [suspended indictment] was probably very difficult for China to take."

From the Chinese perspective, suspended indictment meant that Japan's judicial procedures had been duly consummated as a nation under the rule of law. In other words, it implied that "Japan's territorial rights had been preserved and procedures for the exercise of power had been duly completed" (Fukuyama) with respect to the Senkaku Islands. For China, which claimed the Senkaku Islands were integral to its sovereign territory, this was not an acceptable outcome. Faced with this intolerable prospect, China's national psychology had been thrown off balance. There is a very real possibility that this is what triggered the strange behavior of cancelling the summit meeting at the last minute.

How did the international community view the Japanese and Chinese responses to the collision incident? The predominant view, says Fukuyama, was that "China was acting barbarically in its diplomacy." Fukuyama points out that, "A clear picture was emerging. What China had been doing with Vietnam and the Philippines around the Spratly Islands, it was now trying to do with Japan." China had definitely damaged its own image in the eyes of the world, and it was now feeling the need to restore and rehabilitate its international standing. Wen Jiabao may have been driven to his sudden reversal by this mounting pressure.

STRAINED TO THE BREAKING POINT

Looking back on those days, Fukuyama, to whom Japan's behind-the-scenes diplomacy had been entrusted from Brussels to Hanoi, was increasingly certain that this was what was going on in China.

"We should return to conditions that prevailed in June before the collision." This is what Kan emphasized in his meeting with President Hu Jintao in Yokohama on November 13, 2010. Three months before the collision, Kan had met with Hu Jintao in Toronto, Canada, and it was in this meeting that the basic principle of a mutually beneficial relationship based on common strategic interests had been confirmed. Kan was harking back to those halcyon days in an effort to highlight the need to mend Japan-China relations.

The week preceding this meeting, both Japan and China had been thrown into a fresh round of confusion. The Coast Guard had a video of the collision off the coast of the Senkaku Islands, and the prosecutors' office which had suspended indictment believed that the images provided "evidence proving the guilt" of the Chinese captain of the fishing vessel. In an unexpected turn of events, this video was uploaded on YouTube and made available to the world. Furthermore, a mere three days before the summit meeting in Yokohama, the Coast Guard officer who had wrongfully released the video admitted to what he had done. In Japan, this had triggered a storm of protest directed at Kan and increasingly boisterous calls for the prime minister to resign by way of taking responsibility for this.

Held against the backdrop of these untoward developments, the summit meeting between Kan and Hu Jintao was afforded a mere 22 minutes, including the time taken for interpretation. Such were the restrictive conditions under which the meeting was held.

To begin the meeting, Kan had clumsily extended his hand to Hu Jintao. Obviously nervous and afraid of misspeaking his lines, Kan kept his eyes riveted to the notes that he held. To observers, it appeared as though Kan was making a determined and conscious effort to avoid eye contact with Hu.

"I heartily welcome you to the APEC Summit Meeting. In truth, Japan and China are separated by no more than a narrow stream." The welcoming words spoken by Kan were little more than routine and banal, to which Hu Jintao responded with an equally commonplace and banal, "Thank you for your invitation. Let us now talk about improving and developing the relations between our countries." It was the safe thing to say. But once these words had been uttered, Hu sat back with tightly pursed lips and kept the same stern visage throughout the entire meeting. To even the most casual observer, it was obvious that there was no chemistry between the two leaders. It was as though the atmosphere of the meeting faithfully replicated the strained state of bilateral relations.

Sengoku had sent Hosono to Beijing virtually as the prime minister's envoy and had thereby succeeded in finding a path to resolving the situation. Speculating on the future of Japan-China relations in the twenty-first century, Sengoku opined, "In terms of economic, social, and cultural exchange, Japan-China relations have risen to a level that cannot be compared to where we were five years ago. I believe exchanges of various types at various levels will, in the long run, create an unassailable foundation for our bilateral ties."

In his role as an aide to Sengoku, Fukuyama had been a witness to all that the Kan Cabinet had done to cope with the incident and he had endeavored tirelessly behind the scenes to achieve a resolution. In summarizing and critiquing the entire incident that started when the Chinese fishing vessel rammed the Japan Coast Guard patrol ship, Fukuyama says, "[In Japan,] we were criticized for being weak-kneed. But actually [from the Chinese perspective] Japan had taken a very strong and drastic step [by arresting the Chinese captain of the fishing vessel and sending him to the public prosecutors]. It is here that a critical gap was emerging in the Japanese and Chinese consciousnesses."

This gap was unresolved when the Noda Cabinet followed the Kan Cabinet into office, and this was the situation when the Noda Cabinet made the decision to nationalize the Senkaku Islands—a decision that would have an enormous impact on Japan's diplomacy and national security policy in the twenty-first century. What had been an invisible gap between Japan and China was now growing unnoticed into a vast chasm that neither side could control.

CHAPTER
2

The Bombshell Announcement

Tokyo Governor Ishihara Shintaro declaring his intent to purchase the Senkaku Islands
in a speech in Washington, DC
Kyodo

There was nothing abrupt or unpremeditated about the April 2012 announcement that Ishihara Shintaro made in the United States. This chapter examines the origins of Ishihara's positions on the United States and China from the perspective of his behind-the-scenes activities.

Impact of the Ishihara Statement

"I have decided that the Metropolitan Government of Tokyo will purchase the Senkaku Islands."

This was a totally unexpected announcement by Tokyo Governor Ishihara Shintaro on April 16, 2012. His venue was the Heritage Foundation, an influential think tank headquartered in Washington, DC Facing his audience of nearly a hundred people, Ishihara was spouting his thoughts in his all too familiar bravado style. He argued forcefully on the need for nuclear simulations, a position that presupposed Japan's acquisition of nuclear weapons. The speech proceeded along lines that only served to bolster Ishihara's well-established reputation. But as if to say that wasn't enough, Ishihara used the last few minutes of his speech to unveil his plan to purchase the Senkaku Islands.

Ishihara explained the reasoning behind the plan. "China has started to say that it will end Japan's effective control. These statements cannot be countenanced. Leaving things the way they are now is far too dangerous." Ishihara continued his heated rant. "We are proposing to purchase the islands so that the Japanese people can properly protect the territory of Japan. Does anyone have a problem with that?" Here, he was falling back on his default position as a patriot to justify the proposed action.

The Senkaku Islands are five small islands and a number of rocks located approximately 70 kilometers north of the Yaeyama Islands in Okinawa Prefecture. Aside from Taisho-jima, the other four islands (Minami-kojima, Kita-kojima, Uotsurijima, and Kubajima) were at this time owned by individuals residing in Saitama Prefecture and leased to the national government. In past times, the islands were populated by several hundred Japanese. But today, the islands are completely uninhabited.

Beginning in 1885, Japanese missions investigated the islands on multiple occasions and confirmed that China's Qing Dynasty did not control them. Following these actions, a cabinet decision to incorporate the islands into Japanese territory was signed in January 1895. In April of the same year, China ceded "Taiwan and the Pescadores group" to Japan in the Shimonoseki Treaty. According to the Ministry of Foreign Affairs, the Senkaku Islands were not included in the areas ceded to Japan under this treaty.

At the end of the Second World War, the Senkaku Islands, together with Okinawa, were temporarily placed under the administration of the United States. When Okinawa was returned to Japan in 1972, all of the Senkaku Islands were also returned to Japan. The Senkaku Islands were subsequently governed by Japan without incident. The entire picture began to change in 1968 when it became known that the seabed around the Senkaku Islands was possibly rich in petroleum resources. Coming into the 1980s, China and Taiwan began to claim territorial rights to the Senkaku Islands. Throughout these developments, Japan maintained the position that "no territorial issue exists in the Senkaku Islands." There has been no change in this position to the present.

The same day that Ishihara made his bombshell announcement, Chief Cabinet Secretary Fujimura Osamu made the following comment in his regular press conference. "We are not aware of the facts. The government has been taking various opportunities to contact the owner. If the reports are true, perhaps there will be some consultation in the future." By implication, this statement was acknowledging a matter of critical significance. That is, already at this time, "The possibility of the government's purchasing the Senkaku Islands, in other words nationalization, was not zero."

The Democratic Party of Japan (DPJ) suffered a devastating defeat in the general election held at the end of December 2012, making way for the transfer of power back to the Liberal Democratic Party (LDP). After the transfer had been completed, Fujimura agreed to an exclusive interview with *Mainichi Shimbun* on January 24, 2013. In the course of this interview, Fujimura touched on the nationalization of the Senkaku Islands. "The government has been engaged in behind-the-scenes negotiations with the owner of the islands since the closing days of the Koizumi administration."

"Regarding the purchase of the Senkaku Islands, the file was handed over to us when the Noda Cabinet came into office in September 2011. We learned that behind-the-scenes negotiations had been moving forward since the closing days of the Koizumi administration," Fujimura explained. In light of the developments that predated the transfer of power to the DPJ, Fujimura explained that the Noda Cabinet decided to form a special section (office) within the Cabinet Secretariat to continue negotiations with the owner of the islands and to gather information on properties that could be deeded to the owner in exchange for the Senkaku Islands. This was to go forward while liaising with the Foreign Ministry.

An official from the Cabinet Secretariat briefed Fujimura in detail on past negotiations and other matters related to the Senkaku Islands. Fujimura thereupon presented a summary of this information to Prime Minister Noda. Details of the exchange that took place between the two at this time are presented later in this chapter.

Responding to the bombshell announcement by Governor Ishihara, another key figure in the DPJ spoke up on the same day. This was Hirano Hirofumi, minister of education, culture, sports, science and technology (MEXT). Hirano was a confidante of Hatoyama Yukio, the first DPJ prime minister, and had served as Hatoyama's chief cabinet secretary. "That idea did come up during my term as chief cabinet secretary. However, nothing materialized at the time. But the Senkaku Islands are an inherent part of the territory of Japan and were owned by an individual. Therefore, discussions on what should be done from a national security and territorial perspective have continued to this day. What Governor Ishihara said can be seen as part of that general discussion."

Thus we have the testimony of both Fujimura and Hirano that the government was engaged in behind-the-scenes discussions with the owner of the Senkaku Islands well before Governor Ishihara's bombshell announcement. This awareness surfaced in the press conference held immediately after the Ishihara statement and was condensed in the words, "The government has been taking various opportunities to contact the owner."

When he commented on the Ishihara announcement, Foreign Minister Gemba Koichiro took a more orthodox approach that was in line with standard diplomatic protocol. "The Senkaku Islands comprise territory inherent to Japan. In terms of both history and international law, there is no doubting the truth of this fact. Japan effectively controls the Senkaku Islands."

Gemba, however, was firm in denying Ishihara's criticism that "the government's current stance [on territorial security] is dangerous." Gemba took the occasion to refute the claim directly, "That is absolutely wrong." There is no question that Gemba felt compelled to take a strong stand because Ishihara had been extremely vocal and caustic in his criticism of the Foreign Ministry. As the head of Japan's foreign policy establishment, Gemba simply could not ignore the criticism. As time would show, Ishihara and the foreign policy establishment headed by Gemba would soon become embroiled in a clash of interests and objectives on the treatment of the Senkaku Islands.

On April 18, 2012, Prime Minister Noda Yoshihiko stood before a special session of the House of Representatives Budget Committee convened for the purpose of deliberating foreign affairs and national security. Questioned on the subject of the Senkaku Islands, Noda said "We will ascertain the true intent of the owner and consider all options without prejudice." Basically, his statement accorded with that of Fujimura in not explicitly denying that nationalization was a possibility. Noda still seemed to enjoy a certain level of political confidence and composure at this time. Things appeared to be under control—the file had been handed down from previous administrations, due process had been followed in the Kantei to deal with the issue, and the government was in contact with the individual who held title to the islands. It did not matter what Ishihara was saying. At the end of the day, the government had the upper hand, and nothing would change that. Noda's words and actions indicated that this was in fact how he viewed the situation.

Ishihara had taken the initiative and announced the Tokyo Metropolitan Government intended to purchase the islands. In response to this, Noda had said, "We will gather information on his [Ishihara's] intent and will work calmly toward a decision on the matter." During this period, the Kantei was making a conscious effort to "work calmly toward a decision" on the Senkaku Islands in collaboration with some high-ranking Foreign Ministry officials. This approach would be carried forward and incorporated into the basic policy that the government would later establish on the nationalization of the Senkaku Islands. The key phrase would be "peaceful and stable maintenance of control" of the Senkaku Islands.

The purchase plan announced by Ishihara in Washington featured the purchase of three islands: Uotsurijima, Kita-kojima, and Minami-kojima. The two remaining islands were excluded from the plan. Taisho-jima was already owned by the government and Kubajima was being used by the US military as a firing range.

"Ideally, the government should purchase the islands, but it won't. Therefore, Tokyo is stepping up to protect the Senkaku Islands." Ishihara had struck a dramatic pose. In his heart, Ishihara was somewhat confident he could emerge victorious. What gave him this confidence was the promise that he had already extracted from the individual who held title to the islands. Kurihara Kunioki, the Saitama Prefecture resident who owned

three of the Senkaku Islands, had in the course of behind-the-scenes negotiations said that he would "sell the islands to the Governor of Tokyo."

After his Washington speech, Ishihara had met with the press and
admitted that he had been in secret negotiations with the owner of the
islands since the end of the previous year. "An agreement in principle has
been reached with the owner. Our attorney is now pursuing detailed negotiations with the owner." This is how Ishihara described the situation. He
also touched briefly on the sentiments of the owner, who had previously
adamantly rejected all offers to buy the islands. Referring to a death in the
owner's family, Ishihara explained that the "situation has changed." In a
sharp departure from his norm, Ishihara refused to elaborate.

Negotiating with the Owner

The negotiations between Kurihara Kunioki, the owner of the islands, and
Governor Ishihara were facilitated by a secret go-between: Santo Akiko, an
LDP member of the House of Councilors.

Santo had become acquainted with Kurihara in functions held by the
Tokyo Chapter of the Junior Chamber International (JCI), where they were
both members. In the years that followed, Santo was appointed director of
the Science and Technology Agency in December 1990. This appointment
made her a member of the second cabinet formed under Prime Minister
Kaifu Toshiki. Later, she teamed up with Kurihara to form the Shoheikai,
an association of prominent individuals born during the Showa Era (1926–
1989). It was with Santo's help that a connection was established between
Ishihara and Kurihara in the fall of 2011. The relationship deepened
quickly, and the two became close enough to meet in person to discuss the
purchase of the Senkaku Islands.

Prior to this, Kurihara had been repeatedly approached by various
administrations, organizations, and individuals but had always refused
to sell. However, his attitude began to change in September 2010 when a
Chinese fishing boat ran into a Japan Coast Guard patrol ship off the Senkaku coast. By this time, Kurihara was already quite old. Santo recalls that
whenever they met at a Shoheikai function around this time, he would say,
"Maybe the time is approaching for me to sell to the government."

"If that is how you feel, I want to buy the Senkaku Islands."

Made aware of Kurihara's change of heart, Santo began to look around
for a high-quality counterpart with enough influence to cement the deal.
Governor Ishihara was not the first name that had come to her mind. Santo's first candidate was the youthful politician and mayor of Ishigaki City,

Nakayama Yoshitaka. He was an up-and-coming politician born on Ishi-gaki Island, Okinawa Prefecture, the closest municipality to the Senkaku Islands. Nakayama had attracted national attention by bringing conservative politics to Ishigaki's traditionally progressive government. Santo went ahead and arranged a meeting between Nakayama and Kurihara in January 2011. The secret meeting took place in an undisclosed location in Tokyo with Kurihara bringing his close aide who was in charge of his finances.

Nakayama made an earnest case for purchasing the islands, but there were some troubling problems from Kurihara's perspective. First, Nakayama seemed to be very young. Second, he was still in his first term as mayor. Finally, any deal that the mayor made would require coordination with the Ishigaki City Assembly in a process that remained nebulous and highly uncertain.

According to Santo, Kurihara cited all of these reasons in reaching his conclusion. "This man does not yet have the necessary power and authority to be entrusted with the islands."

Hearing of Ishihara's announcement in Washington, Mayor Nakayama had rushed to hold his own press conference and make sure that he remained in contention. "I welcome this idea. It would be desirable for the islands to be owned jointly by Tokyo and Ishigaki City. I look forward to speaking to Governor Ishihara when he returns." It would appear from this statement that the two had separately met with Kurihara through Santo and had come to a secret understanding on the purchase of the Senkaku Islands.

In his press conference, Nakayama had emphasized his total support for the Ishihara plan. He was speaking on behalf of the municipal government entity located closest to the islands. "The Senkaku Islands are isolated islands that mark the boundaries of our national territory. From the perspective of defending our waters and our territories, it is better for the islands to be owned and managed by the national government, a prefectural government, or some other local government entity rather than by an individual." This expression of support reflected the talks that had been moving forward below the surface. Further confirmation would later be provided by Osaka Mayor Hashimoto Toru, who relates that, as Ishihara's political partner and collaborator, he had prior knowledge of Ishihara's plan to purchase the Senkaku Islands.

"This is true to Ishihara's style. Such a plan would never cross the average politician's mind. Obviously, there are some problems, such as diplomatic issues, but nobody but Governor Ishihara could arrive at this decision and take action." Hashimoto was effusive in his praise of Ishihara.

After his unsuccessful meeting with Nakayama, Kurihara told Santo, "I think very highly of Governor Ishihara Shintaro. I have read all of his books." As a young conservative member of the LDP, Ishihara had formed a political group that he named Seirankai. Back in those early days, Ishihara had met with Kurihara's mother and directly pleaded with her to sell the islands to a group of conservative Diet members. It seems Kurihara had a clear memory of the meeting with Ishihara and the unusual level of energy and enthusiasm that Ishihara exuded as a young politician.

"This is what my mother said at that time. 'Politicians are not to be trusted. Now is not the time to sell.' But if she were living today, I believe she would say, 'If you are going to sell, sell to Governor Ishihara.'"

Kurihara muttered his thoughts as if he were speaking to himself. But as soon as the words were spoken, Santo took action, placing a call to Ishihara's oldest son, Ishihara Nobuteru, who in due course would run for the LDP presidency. "I want you to convey a message to your father." When he heard the words that Kurihara had muttered, Ishihara wasted no time in signaling his interest. "That's great news!" These exchanges took place in the early summer of 2011.

With Santo acting as the go-between, Ishihara and Kurihara met on September 1, 2011. It was the second meeting for the two, the earlier one having taken place several decades earlier. Santo had explained that she was bringing Ishihara with her to the Kurihara home in Omiya City in Saitama Prefecture to "offer incense for your late mother." While this was little more than a slightly veiled pretext, it did provide adequate cover, for Ishihara had been acquainted with the late mother and had attended her funeral in October 2007.

Kurihara Hiroyuki, Kurihara Kunioki's younger brother by five years, has written a book entitled *Senkaku shoto urimasu* [Senkaku Islands for sale] (Koseido Publishing). In this book, he explains that the family's first meeting with Ishihara occurred nearly 40 years ago, "in 1973 or so." On that occasion too, Ishihara had come to the Kurihara home in Omiya at the introduction of a mutual friend. Recalling that meeting, the younger Kurihara writes. "This is what my mother said. 'I agree to meeting with you, but only once.' After the meeting, she had this to say to the visitor. 'I appreciate what you have said. But under no condition am I willing to sell.'"

Ishihara came to the meeting with a Buddhist rosary in hand and offered incense before the family altar. Ishihara and Kurihara then sat down to talk. For Ishihara, the meeting provided an unexpected reunion with a woman that he had known many years ago. She turned out to be the daughter of a man who had worked under Ishihara's father at the Yamashita Steamship Company. As children, the two had been neighbors. Ishihara recognized her and said with a warm smile, "What wonderful memories this brings back!" Ishihara was in the best of spirits and shared this story with Santo when they took their leave. "My father wanted my brother, Yujiro, to marry her."

The two principals, Ishihara and Kurihara, accompanied by Santo as the go-between, would thereafter meet in secret on a number of occasions. In addition to the three, Ishihara's son Nobuteru, with his sights firmly set on the LDP presidency, would join the group almost every time.

Fast-forward to the closing days of 2011 and a French-Italian restaurant in Tokyo's Ginza district. Ishihara and his son were hosting the dinner. Santo was present as always, and Kurihara was accompanied by his trusted aide. Ishihara broached the subject of the sale of the islands. Santo relates how the two principals tip-toed gingerly around the subject as they tried to gauge each other's position.

Ishihara: "Mr Kurihara, I think it's about time. Why don't you sell?"
Kurihara: "When the time is right, I will consider."
Santo: "The time is already right."
Kurihara: "I like both of you and I value our friendship, but . . ."

So far, Kurihara had continued to signal his indecision. But as they parted, Ishihara extended his hand. Kurihara took the extended hand and the two shook hands. Santo interpreted this handshake to have been a tacit confirmation that a gentleman's agreement had been reached.

Kurihara was well known as a businessman and major landowner in Saitama Prefecture. According to Santo, the family harbored a deep distrust of the government because large portions of its holdings had been confiscated during and after the war. Santo testifies that while the family was not against selling the Senkaku Islands, the prevailing sentiment was, "Yes, we would like the government to purchase the islands, but we cannot trust the current government."

As previously explained, at this point in time, Kurihara held title to three of the five Senkaku Islands. These were Uotsurijima, Kita-kojima, and Minami-kojima. Beginning in April 2002, the islands were leased to the Ministry of Internal Affairs and Communications and managed by the government, this lease renewed annually. In preparation for the December 2011 Ginza meeting, Ishihara and Santo had carefully investigated the

Kurihara family's financial situation and had concluded that a "fair purchase price" for the three islands would be somewhere in the vicinity of 1.5 billion yen (Santo). Notwithstanding these exhaustive preparations, Ishihara had failed to come away from the secret year-end meeting with a firm commitment to sell.

When Ishihara learned that Chief Cabinet Secretary Fujimura had mentioned the possibility of nationalization after Ishihara's Washington speech, this did not seem to affect the governor's confidence. In fact, throughout this period, there was no change in his bullish tone. "Who knows when the government can get around to making up its mind! On the other hand, our transaction will soon be consummated."

"Instead of all its dilly-dallying, [the government] should have acted swiftly [to make the purchase]. The owner [of the islands] came to me because he could not trust the government."

This statement underscores the confidence Ishihara felt as a result of his meticulous courting of Kurihara. The courting game predated Ishihara's bombshell statement by many months and Ishihara sensed that by now he had won the owner's full trust. On the other hand, there are some indications that Ishihara was not fully convinced that the islands would be sold to him. This is borne out by the fact that Ishihara continued to contact Kurihara for confirmation until the last minute before his departure for Washington. Ishihara's attempts to get a firm yes went on until moments before he boarded his plane.

Why the Heritage Foundation

"Come on, what will it be? I am about to board my flight. You know I want to make the announcement."

Before departing for Washington, Ishihara repeatedly called Santo from the airport to inquire about the owner's final decision. In television and other interviews that she gave after Ishihara's bombshell statement, Santo explained that Ishihara and Kurihara had reached a gentleman's agreement by the end of 2011. However, even as he was boarding his flight to Washington, Ishihara had not yet received a firm commitment from Kurihara. As time ran out, Ishihara called Santo to say, "I want you to contact Kurihara directly and get a final answer."

What was behind Ishihara's growing impatience? The fact was that things had not proceeded smoothly after the year-end Ginza meeting, and clouds had been gathering over the gentleman's agreement since the beginning of 2012. Early in the year, there was a death in the Kurihara family. Citing this, Kurihara contacted Santo to say he wanted to take the verbal agreement "back to square one." Santo found this strange and said to herself, "Does this man really want to get into a contest of strength with Ishihara?" But she continued faithfully in her role as intermediary.

Santo recalls the difficulties she faced as intermediary. "On the one hand, there was this very unusual person, Kurihara. On the other hand, there was Ishihara, famous for his short fuse." At one point, Ishihara became totally exasperated and blurted out emotionally. "Let's just say that our discussions [on the purchase of the Senkaku Islands] never happened!" On this occasion, it was Ishihara's son, Nobuteru, who saved the day. Pulling the despondent Santo aside, he told her, "Never mind what my father is saying. You know that he really wants to get this done." Prodded by Nobuteru's pleas, Santo recomposed herself and continued her contact with the Kurihara family.

A little while before this incident, Ishihara had confided in Santo. "Arrangements have been made for me to give a speech in America. What I want to do is to announce that we are going to purchase the Senkaku Islands." Ishihara had said the same thing to a political ally, Sonoda Hiroyuki, secretary general of the Sunrise Party of Japan. The two would later join forces to found the Party of the Sun before ultimately merging with the Japan Restoration Party.

"I am going to announce the purchase of the Senkaku Islands. This is going to attract a great deal of attention." Ishihara could barely contain his excitement. On the other hand, Sonoda did not bother to mask his doubts. "So you think it's going to work out for you." To this, Ishihara confidently retorted, "You just watch me!" These comments reveal how emotionally invested Ishihara was in his upcoming trip to the United States and particularly in his scheduled speech in Washington.

Ishihara had chosen the Heritage Foundation as the venue for his bombshell announcement. Among the many think tanks headquartered in Washington, the Heritage Foundation ranked as the most right-leaning of all conservative Republican think tanks. This obviously was a conscious choice. Ishihara could have selected the bipartisan Center for Strategic and International Studies (CSIS) if he were interested in reaching such noted pro-Japan security experts as the former special assistant to the president, Michael Green (senior director for Asian affairs at the National Security Council). On the other hand, if his primary aim had been to reach out to the Obama administration and the Democratic Party, he could have opted for the Brookings Institution with its long and distinguished history. But

Ishihara had selected the Heritage Foundation to deliver his announcement. Here was a think tank that was not shy about its ideological leanings and was known for its hardline stance on China.

How then was the speech arranged? The answer is provided by Bruce Klingner, who has held such positions as Defense Intelligence Agency (DIA) and CIA analyst on the Korean Peninsula, and later senior fellow in Northeast Asian affairs for the Heritage Foundation. According to Klingner, Ishihara's speech was arranged by Walter Lohman, director of the Heritage Foundation's Asian Studies Center.

Lohman had previously served as an Asian affairs expert for the Senate Committee on Foreign Relations and had moved to the Heritage Foundation in 2006 as senior research fellow for Southeast Asia, Australia, and New Zealand. During his Senate staff years, Lohman had first served as an advisor to Senator Jesse Helms of North Carolina, who gained a reputation in the 1990s as an "ultra-right" member of the conservative Republican caucus. He had also served Senator John McCain, the maverick Republican senator from Arizona who ran for president in the 2008 election. In both instances, Lohman had worked with key senators who were hardliners when it came to US policy on China.

Ishihara was the leading hawk in Japanese politics, and Klingner and Lohman were just the type of American experts that he would take a liking to. Following careful behind-the-scenes orchestration, Ishihara would ride into the bastion of American conservatism and anti-Chinese sentiments to announce the Tokyo Metropolitan Government's intent to purchase the Senkaku Islands, which would fit snuggly into the overarching conservative strategy of Chinese containment.

While it would be possible to find and arrange evidence in support of some kind of conspiracy theory, it is far more likely that the truth is completely different. "We had no idea what he was going to say," Klingner avers. Though they had arranged the event, the two Americans had not been privy to Ishihara's purpose or the details of his presentation.

In a meeting with Ishihara in Tokyo, Lohman had been told, "I want to deliver a speech in Washington. Can you arrange it for me?" But according to Klingner, Ishihara had been tight-lipped and revealed no more. The bombshell that Ishihara dropped in Washington triggered a storm whose gales swept over Japan as well as the United States. But of all the people who were in the audience that day, no one was more surprised than Klingner and Lohman.

According to newspaper reports, sources close to Ishihara stated at the time that the speech had been delivered at the request of the Heritage Foundation. As for why Ishihara had chosen the Heritage Foundation, the sources had explained, "It is a conservative think tank with many people who take a hard line on China. Also, it is has an influential voice."

Contrary to these newspaper reports, Klingner notes that the suggestion for the speech came from Ishihara himself. Newspaper articles appearing after the speech state sources close to Ishihara as saying, "The idea is to pressure the Japanese government by making the appeal that our ally, the United States, stands behind this proposal. This external pressure may move Japan to act." What emerges from this is a picture of Ishihara carefully pre-planning every aspect of his bombshell announcement—everything from the venue and timing to the anticipated effect of the announcement.

In Ishihara's mind, the Heritage Foundation speech provided the perfect opportunity to announce his plan to purchase the Senkaku Islands. There is no doubt that Ishihara did in fact succeed in pushing the Japanese government off dead center and bringing the Senkaku problem to the world's attention.

"Why would the United States possibly oppose the Tokyo Metropolitan Government's plan to purchase the Senkaku Islands? That would be unthinkable."

Ishihara was bragging to the reporters who surrounded him after the speech. He was effusive in describing the proposed use of the islands. "We could create some effective fishing reefs and develop the marine resources in the area." But he also showed a degree of flexibility in his stance. "We will put our heads together and we will consult the government whenever that's necessary."

Notwithstanding his confident tone, the plan proposed by Ishihara had two weaknesses. First of all, he had not been able to extract anything more than a vague oral promise from Kurihara, the owner of the islands. The second problem was obvious to anyone with training in national security. What happens after the purchase? Ishihara was asked what he would do if Chinese battleships menacingly approached the islands after the purchase. His response was shockingly simple. "We would leave that to the government."

First Meeting

"Hey, you know, I've never met Noda. I need you to set up a face-to-face with this fellow." It was now April 22, 2012, a week after Ishihara's announcement in Washington. The awkward order spoken with its familiar undertone was directed at Nagashima Akihisa, DPJ member of the House of Representatives.

Since wresting the reins of government away from the LDP in a historic election win in September 2009, the DPJ was already fielding its third prime minister by April 2012. The man currently in the Kantei was Noda Yoshihiko. Officially a high ranking government official with round-the-clock access to the Kantei, Nagashima Akihisa was serving as the prime minister's advisor for foreign affairs and national security.

Among the people characterized as liberals in the DPJ, Nagashima distinguished himself with his emphasis on the Japan-US alliance and his well-established ties with former Deputy Secretary of State Richard Armitage, former Special Assistant to the President Michael Green, and many others. With this background, Nagashima had come to be known as one of the leading US experts among Japanese politicians. Because of his realistic approach to foreign relations and national security, there was a long-standing feeling in the LDP that "Nagashima is the type of person that should run on the LDP ticket." (Ishiba Shigeru, LDP secretary general)

One of the reasons for this was that Nagashima had previously served as an aide to Governor Ishihara's son, Ishihara Nobuteru, in the House of Representatives. After studying in Washington, Nagashima had studied at the Council on Foreign Relations (CFR) under Michael Green, who would later become special assistant to the president. All the while, Nagashima was eyeing a career in politics and at one time had actually considered running for office as an LDP candidate. But due to the turns and twists of fate, this dream never came to fruition. Instead, he eventually came to the attention of the DPJ as it was eagerly looking for new talent.

Up to this point, the Nagashima story is relatively well known in the political corridors of Nagata-cho. Far less known is the life-long friendship that Nagashima enjoyed with his former boss's younger brother—Governor Ishihara's second son, Yoshizumi, the weather forecaster and popular television personality.

Both Nagashima and Yoshizumi had received all of their schooling, from kindergarten through university, at Keio. From earliest childhood, Nagashima had played kick-the-can and hide-and-seek in the Ishihara yard and on the Shonan beaches. One day as they were playing hide-and-seek in the house, Nagashima was running around looking for Yoshizumi when he came to a tightly closed closet door. He pushed open the door with all his might, but all he found inside was a *daruma* doll with one blank eye that had never been painted in. The doll harked back to the Tokyo gubernatorial election of 1975 when Ishihara had run against the incumbent, Minobe Yokichi, and lost. The blank eye, meant to be painted in to fete the election win, spoke eloquently of the trauma of defeat in the political arena. Stepping into the darkened closet, Nagashima felt as a young child that he had "seen something he was never supposed to see."

It was drawing on this lifetime association with Nagashima that Ishihara had barked out his crisp order to arrange an immediate face-to-face with the top leader of the Japanese government, Prime Minister Noda. Albeit he was the governor of Tokyo, Ishihara's tone would have normally earned a rebuke and a speedy rejection. But in light of his long history with the Ishihara clan, this was not a request that Nagashima could easily ignore.

"I wonder what he wants to discuss with the prime minister." This question pinged Nagashima's consciousness for a fleeting moment after he hung up. Yet it was not that he had no idea what Ishihara had in mind. Actually, Nagashima had a pretty good inkling what Ishihara wanted to see Noda about.

Two possibilities immediately came to mind. First, of course, was the purchase of the Senkaku Islands by the Tokyo Metropolitan Government. But Nagashima was betting on the second possibility, which he thought was Ishihara's real agenda. Ever since the gubernatorial election, Ishihara had been hinting at "the election promise I have not yet kept," this in reference to the joint military and civilian use of the US military base at Yokota (in Tokyo's Fussa City). Even after he was appointed advisor to the prime minister, Nagashima had continued to actively participate in study groups and seminars organized by the Tokyo Metropolitan Government on transitioning Yokota Air Base to joint military and civilian use. What further supported his hunch was the fact that Prime Minister Noda was now preparing to leave for Washington on an official visit that would give the DJP its first full-fledged summit meeting with the United States.

Nagashima acted immediately to contact Noda. "It would be a real headache if he wants to talk to you about the Senkaku Islands. But most likely, the topic is going to be Yokota. I confirmed this with people around him and am quite sure of it." Given this explanation, Noda agreed to meet Ishihara at the Kantei. The meeting was set for April 27.

When the two met, Ishihara acted exactly as Nagashima had predicted. He immediately brought up the subject of the Yokota Air Base and his political commitment to joint military-civilian use. Ishihara reviewed the history of the case, explaining how the matter was brought up in Japan-US bilateral talks during the Koizumi administration and how it was ultimately tabled. The meeting lasted a mere 15 minutes. But during this short session, Ishihara managed to thoroughly lambast the Foreign Ministry. In closing, he entreated Noda to bring up the subject of joint use of Yokota Air Base in the upcoming summit meeting in Washington.

After the meeting, Ishihara was asked by the press how the prime minister had reacted. Ishihara explained, "I feel he understood very well." He then went on to state that he "had not uttered a word" about the purchase of the Senkaku Islands. This explicit statement left no room for speculation that the Senkakus had come up in their meeting.

The Yokota RAPCON

The US military base at Yokota functions as an extremely important strategic base. Not only is it home to the United States Forces in Japan (USFJ) Command, the nerve center of the Japan-US alliance, but it also houses the Fifth Air Force Command, which is part of the US Pacific Air Forces. Moreover, the US Air Force 374th Airlift Wing is also based in Yokota.

More than 10,000 US military personnel and their families reside on the base and in Fussa City and surrounding areas, creating a sizeable American community. According to the Fussa Municipal Government, Yokota Air Base's 3,300-meter runway records 13,000 to 16,000 landings per year. Peacetime landing frequency is considerably lower than that at the US airbases located at Misawa in Aomori Prefecture and Kadena in Okinawa Prefecture, and anti-base campaigns by local residents have been muted in recent years.

The origins of Yokota Air Base go back to 1940 when it was first developed as an auxiliary facility to the Imperial Japanese Army Tama Airport. At the start of the Allied occupation, Yokota was quickly requisitioned by US Forces and was renamed Yokota Air Base in June 1946. This immense military installation currently occupies about 714 hectares and is sprawled over portions of the municipalities of Fussa, Musashi-Murayama, Hamura, Tachikawa, Akishima, and Mizuho, all located within the boundaries of the Greater Tokyo area.

The peacetime face of Yokota Air Base can be deceptively calm and tranquil. But in case of any military contingency in the Korean Peninsula and other parts of the Asia-Pacific region, Yokota Air Base will play an extremely critical role as the relay hub in the transport of personnel and materiel to the hotspot. It is notable that USFJ Command is located at Yokota Base and not at Kadena, which is equipped with F-22 Raptors, the latest in stealth fighters, or at Misawa, which was secretly tasked during the Cold War to be trigger-ready with F-16 fighters equipped to carry air-launched tactical nuclear weapons. The location of USFJ Command at Yokota is clearly related to contingency scenarios for the Far East.

The idea of opening Yokota Air Base to joint military and civilian use stood as one of Ishihara's long-standing campaign promises that he has often repeated in gubernatorial elections. In fact, in the governor's June 1999 policy speech, Ishihara included demanding the joint military and civilian use of Yokota as one of his principal policy commitments.

Ishihara saw joint military-civilian use as a temporary measure and a stepping-stone toward the full repatriation of Yokota Air Base at some future time. It was in May 2003 that this cherished political objective came closest to being realized. Those were the days when Koizumi Junichiro, the maverick leader who came out of the LDP's Seiwakai to which Ishihara himself once belonged, was prime minister. Koizumi had presented the joint-use proposal to President George W. Bush, with whom he had nurtured a close relationship, and had requested the president consider the idea favorably.

"Alright. We will consider the possibility." This was President Bush's response to Koizumi at the meeting at the Bush ranch in Crawford, Texas. Koizumi's proposal had been prefaced with "We appreciate the fact that Yokota Air Base is performing a critically important function." Koizumi then continued, "Because it is so close to the center of Tokyo, we are wondering whether it would be possible to make greater use of the facility through some form of joint use with civilian aviation."

On the surface, this was a very simple and straightforward exchange. But the president's response was highly significant in the context of the Japan-US alliance because no previous US administration had agreed to look into the possibility of allowing the joint use of Yokota Air Base. At around the same time, the Bush administration was examining various options for the transformation of US military forces, which involved re-thinking the deployment of US forces throughout the world with an eye to reducing defense spending in the post-Cold War environment. Koizumi's proposal sought to position the joint use of Yokota Air Base as part of this global initiative.

About six months prior to this meeting, Ishihara had visited the United States on October 7, 2002, to meet with Richard Armitage, the doyen of the Republican Party's Japan experts, who was serving as deputy secretary of state. The purpose of the visit was to directly petition Armitage and to make the case for the joint use of Yokota Air Base. However, all that Armitage was willing to say on this occasion was, "This is an issue that should be discussed between our two governments." The response was just sufficient for Ishihara to save face, but Armitage would go no further and did not give any concrete assurances on moving the proposal forward.

Still, that did not stop Ishihara. Upon returning to Japan, he expressed his gratitude to the plenary session of the Tokyo Municipal Assembly in the following words. "I wish to thank the Assembly for its special consideration. Notwithstanding the fact the Assembly was in session, with your understanding and cooperation, I was able to fulfill my objective of visiting the United States." He continued, "Work on the most massive tunnel begins with a tiny hole made with a small chisel. You have to drill that first hole. I can say with certainty that I was able to register [joint military-civilian use of Yokota] as a formal issue for discussion between Japan and the United States." His words conveyed a strong confidence that the matter would move forward.

During this same period, Administrative Vice-Minister of Defense Moriya Takemasa was actively endeavoring to further strengthen the Japan-US alliance, which to his mind included the possibility of fundamentally re-defining the alliance. Moriya, who stood at the top of Japan's defense establishment, was widely referred to as the "emperor of the Defense Agency." Moriya was committed to rectifying, as far as possible, the distortions that marred the one-way-street nature of the alliance and to calling on the United States to further reduce the burden shouldered by Japan.

Shortly after these events, Moriya would become deeply involved in the realignment of US forces in Japan with the full backing of Prime Minister Koizumi. In the process, Moriya would formulate a number of proposals in rapid succession. These included plans to move the Futenma Air Station to Henoko and plans to move night-landing practice (NLP) from the Atsugi Naval Air Facility to Iwakuni Air Station in Yamaguchi Prefecture.

It was in the fall of 2004 that Moriya received a top-secret order from Prime Minister Koizumi. The message was conveyed to him by Iijima Isao, executive secretary to the prime minister. The instruction was straightforward. "Go and meet with Ishihara." Acting on his instructions, Moriya visited Ishihara in the governor's office. The high ceiling in the luxuriously appointed office took up two floors in the high-rise that housed the Tokyo Metropolitan Government. Moriya felt overwhelmed as he was led in. What immediately caught his eye was a scale-model that occupied a corner of the office. The carefully constructed model was a representation of Yokota RAPCON (Radar APproach CONtrol), the airspace above Tokyo that the US military air-traffic controllers continued to control more than 60 years after the end of the war.

The jurisdiction of US military air-traffic controllers stationed at Yokota Air Base covers the airspace above Tokyo and eight adjoining prefectures—Tochigi, Gunma, Saitama, Kanagawa, Niigata, Yamanashi, Nagano, and Shizuoka—and extends to a maximum elevation of approximately 5,500 meters.

As long as the Yokota RAPCON remains under the control of the US military, any civilian aircraft intending to enter this airspace must seek permission first. As a result, Japan Airlines (JAL), All-Nippon Airways (ANA), and all other major airlines fly detours to avoid the Yokota RAPCON, although this costs them extra in terms of both fuel and flight time.

Moriya undertook his own investigation with in-depth interviews with JAL, ANA, and other major civilian carriers. What he found was that each of these companies could save approximately 10 to 20 billion yen annually in fuel expenses if they did not have to avoid the RAPCON corridor.

As in the case of Yokota, the US military was also operating the Kadena RAPCON from its Kadena Air Base in Okinawa, with the jurisdiction of US military air-traffic controllers extending to almost all of the main island of Okinawa. But the US had already agreed to return this airspace to Japan by the end of 2007. Encouraged by this precedent, Moriya was secretly preparing to prod the United States to agree to a complete reversion of the Yokota RAPCON. Koizumi's order to meet with Ishihara had been conveyed to him just as he was beginning to move his project forward.

Regaining the airspace over Tokyo had important symbolic value for Japan in that it would sweep away a conspicuous vestige of the American occupation and spell the end of the postwar-era psychology. Convinced of the seminal significance of the reversion of this airspace, Moriya was feeling overwhelmed by emotion as he examined the scale-model of the Yokota RAPCON. Moriya commented on how wonderful the model was and spoke from his heart as he shared his thoughts on how he was going to "regain the Yokota RAPCON, or the airspace over Tokyo, and bring Japan's postwar to an end." But Ishihara's response was surprisingly simple in its intensity. What Moriya heard was, "I want to see a commercial airport at Yokota."

"I am thinking about building a commercial airport at Yokota. The Foreign Ministry insists the US military will not accept the plan, but I know they have agreed to let us send staff to the United States to talk with the

Department of Defense. I just don't understand why the Foreign Ministry is so meek." The gist of this exchange is recorded in Moriya's book, *Futenma kosho hiroku* [Record of the negotiations on Futenma] (Shincho Bunko), showing here again that Ishihara never missed a chance to express his frustration and disappointment with the Foreign Ministry.

Moriya was openly empathetic. "No other independent country in the world has unconditionally ceded the control of the airspace over its capital city to an ally . . . I believe this point has to be conveyed to the US government and a demand made for the return of the Yokota RAPCON."

But somewhere in his heart, Moriya was feeling that the meeting had been oddly anti-climactic. Ishihara was not the zealous patriot he had imagined him to be—at least not on the subject of Yokota. At the end of the meeting, Moriya stated, "The Yokota RAPCON will have to be returned to Japan, even if the goal is merely to achieve joint military-civilian use." Moriya closed with this comment. "Please move forward with your plan. As for me, I will concentrate on RAPCON."

The two continued their discussions after this first meeting. From time to time, Ishihara would phone Moriya for advice, and occasionally invite Moriya to his office. The one constant in all of these exchanges was Ishihara's unmitigated criticism of the Foreign Ministry. Then, at the end of one of their meetings, Ishihara turned to Moriya and said, "I am counting on your continued support."

On May 17, 2011, Ishihara appeared on a livecast discussion program hosted by Tahara Soichiro and distributed through the video sharing website *Nico Nico Douga*. Ishihara quickly homed in on one of his favorite subjects—the Yokota RAPCON. "Yokota's air-traffic control zone covers a huge area and goes as far as Niigata. Japanese airplanes cannot fly in this zone. Returning to Japan from Europe, you fly over Russia and the next thing you know you are flying over the Sea of Japan. Logically, the plane should then head straight for Narita Airport. But no, it has to make a detour that takes it all the way around to Japan's Pacific coast. I can't believe how stupid this is. But most Japanese don't seem to care."

Recalling the impression that he gained from his direct exchanges with Ishihara, Moriya declares, "I didn't feel the zeal of a patriot out to regain the airspace over Tokyo. What I did observe was the representative of the citizens of Tokyo committed to delivering better administrative services to his constituents. That's what I sensed."

Along with talking with Ishihara, Moriya was also trying to find out what the US military was thinking. For this, he had tapped a retired Japan

Air Self-Defense Force officer with strong ties to the US Air Force. What he wanted to know was the US military's real position on the Yokota issue. Interestingly enough, the feedback indicated that the American side was not adamantly opposed to returning the Yokota RAPCON. According to Moriya, it turned out that one of the reasons the US military was reluctant to return the Yokota RAPCON was its distrust of Japan's civilian air controllers. In other words, the American side was prepared to move forward on reversion if jurisdiction were to be turned over to uniformed controllers with Japan's Air Self-Defense Forces. It seems the US military was quietly setting the stage for a transfer of authority on these terms.

"It is acceptable so long as priorities are strictly observed in case of a contingency" was the bottom line that was ultimately delivered to Moriya. Armed with this knowledge, Moriya made his move to include the Yokota RAPCON issue in Japan-US discussions conducted within the Defense Policy Review Initiative (DPRI) framework. But as he had already told Ishihara, his mind was singularly set on regaining air-control jurisdiction in the airspace over Tokyo. Joint use of the Yokota Air Base was not central to his thinking.

Prime Minister Koizumi had sent Moriya to meet with Governor Ishihara in 2004. As Moriya had inferred at the time, numerous Japan experts in the United States began to flash green lights on the question of joint military-civilian use of the Yokota Air Base in the years that followed.

The Center for New American Security (CNAS), a new think tank created in 2007 by Democratic Party national security and foreign relations experts, is a case in point. One of the leaders of the initiative was Kurt Campbell, assistant secretary of state for East Asian and Pacific affairs during President Obama's first term. In October 2012, CNAS published a report entitled *Yokota: Civil-Military Use of US Bases in Japan.*

The report took a very clear position urging the US government to accept joint military and civilian use of Yokota Air Base. It also discussed the critical shortage of airport facilities in case of a contingency in the Asia-Pacific region. With this in mind, the report made the argument for developing an environment conducive to receiving Japanese government permission to use civilian airports in times of need, concluding that the United States should pursue a win-win outcome that would benefit both countries.

Paul Giarra, one of the authors of the report, was a proponent of the Nye Initiative formulated during the mid-1990s. Led by Assistant Secretary of Defense for International Security Affairs Joseph Nye, who then headed the Japan Section reporting directly to the secretary of defense, the Nye

Initiative sought to re-define the parameters of the Japan-US alliance in the post-Cold War era.

According to Giarra, his direct involvement in the Tokyo Metropolitan Government's plan to transition Yokota Air Base to joint military-civilian use went back about five years. Giarra dated his involvement to his introduction to one of Governor Ishihara's advisors, Takase Tamotsu, Kyoto Sangyo University professor emeritus and currently advisor to the Tokyo Metropolitan Government. The two first met at the Hudson Institute and found that they were kindred spirits. Thereafter, Giarra and Takase engaged in a broad range of discussions and exchanged policy notes and position papers. The first published result of this exchange was a CNAS report released in October 2012.

"The issue should be negotiated within the broad framework of the Japan-US alliance." This is what Giarra said in a speech delivered at a seminar held on March 27, 2008. The subject was joint military and civilian use of the Yokota Air Base and the venue was the Committee for the Study of Joint Military and Civilian Use (chaired by Sugiyama Takehiko, president of Hitotsubashi University) established by the Tokyo Metropolitan Government. The position Giarra took was unambiguously in favor of joint use. "The top priority should be assigned to joint use of bases by the US forces and Japan's Self-Defense Forces (SDF)." With an eye to China's growing military power, Giarra expressed the strong hope that joint military and civilian use of Yokota would lead the way in strengthening joint Japan-US air power.

Giarra looked to Takase as the real driving force in achieving joint military-civilian use of the Yokota Air Base. Takase had been a close associate of Wakaizumi Kei, Prime Minister Sato Eisaku's envoy in the secret talks that were conducted parallel to the negotiations for the return of Okinawa.

Appearing on the May 17, 2011, livecast with Tahara, Ishihara shared a Takase story. "The Pentagon really hates me. This story comes from Takase, who worked with Wakaizumi in the behind-the-scenes negotiations for the return of Okinawa. I have asked Takase to stay on as a professor at the Tokyo Metropolitan University. He was laughing when he told me this story. After a few drinks, the Pentagon people told me what they were really thinking. That whole thing about the Yokota Air Base was started by that Ishihara guy!"

Giarra, the point man in Japan-related policies, shared the observation that he saw no trace of Moriya and Wakaizumi's nationalism in Takase or the other Tokyo Metropolitan Government officials. "From beginning to end, they had a very business-like attitude and never manifested any nationalistic sentiment. If they had been nationalistic, I would not have gotten involved in this project."

Giarra has maintained his contact with Team Ishihara that had been put together to deal with the Yokota issue. The comment that he made concerning his contacts in the Tokyo Metropolitan Government is consistent with the "oddly anti-climactic" feeling that Moriya had in his first meeting with Ishihara.

Discussions on the joint military-civilian use of Yokota Air Base continued on the American side and culminated in a study commissioned in the summer of 2012 by Congress and the Department of Defense and conducted by the Center for Strategic and International Studies (CSIS). The resulting report contains the following passage.

"The governor of Tokyo would like to have some civilian use of Yokota AB for private executive jets or cargo . . . There are operational complications that come with such dual use arrangements, but the political and strategic payback could be considerable for the United States . . ."

The report was put together by Michael Green, former special assistant to the president (senior director for Asian affairs at the National Security Council and CSIS senior vice president for Asia and Japan Chair). Commenting on the joint military-civilian use of Yokota Air Base, Green said, "We have adopted a more flexible stance on this issue, and we are prepared to accept it in part."

Green, Giarra, and Patrick Cronin, the former CSIS vice president who had played a central role in drafting the CNAS report, had one important point in common: all three had worked under Assistant Secretary of Defense Joseph Nye during the Clinton administration and had served as members of a skunk-works team of Japan experts tasked with formulating proposals for reinforcing the Japan-US alliance.

In his April 3, 2009, press conference, Governor Ishihara had emphasized his commitment to transitioning the Yokota Air Base to joint military-civilian use. "When the time is right, I myself will go to the United States to convey the message from Tokyo. I believe this will open the way to restarting the discussion." Ishihara was not shy about broadcasting his intent to continue pressuring the American side.

But by this time, the presidency had changed from George W. Bush to Barack Obama. While Prime Minister Koizumi had established a degree of rapport with President Bush, President Obama was a complete unknown. During the press conference, Ishihara's normally bullish attitude seemed to be clouded by a sense of uncertainty. "The person with final authority over the Yokota issue appears to have been nominated but has not yet been confirmed by the Senate. We are not at a stage where we can propose the start of negotiations."

In May 2006, the Japanese and US governments jointly issued a final report stating that their review of this issue would be completed by March 2010. However, discussion of joint use of the Yokota Air Base came to a virtual standstill after the release of this report. Up until then, Ishihara had relentlessly criticized the Ministry of Foreign Affairs. But for the sake of achieving his objective, Ishihara outwardly toed the line that Japan is united on this matter. Notwithstanding these professions of unity, there is no doubt that Ishihara's long-standing frustration with Japan's foreign policy establishment was mounting.

It did not take long for Ishihara's frustration to find a new target that, like the Yokota Air Base problem, had been shelved and ignored (the words of former Deputy Chief Cabinet Secretary Nagahama Hiroyuki) for years and years by successive administrations. That new target was none other than the Senkaku Islands.

A Pacific Charter

On April 30, 2012, three days after meeting with Ishihara at the Kantei, Noda was at the White House.

This marked the first time for a DPJ leader to be stepping into a full-fledged summit meeting with a US president. Noda appeared uncharacteristically euphoric. Three years had passed since the last formal Japan-US summit meeting in Washington. For Noda who was constantly referring to the critical importance of the Japan-US alliance as the cornerstone of Japanese diplomacy, this was certainly the highlight of his political career.

Sitting next to President Obama, Noda trotted out a metaphor designed to flatter his counterpart. "In my style of leadership, I'm like a point guard in basketball—not too flashy, but I get things done and deliver results." He then suggested that Obama was the power forward in this game. The president was smiling.

Noda had arrived in Washington the day before the summit meeting to attend a gathering where he would express the gratitude of the Japanese people for the assistance extended by the United States following the Great East Japan Earthquake of March 11, 2011. "I will lead the way in tilling the soil and watering the plants to ensure the Japan-US bilateral relationship blossoms with the most beautiful flowers." Noda had compared the bilateral alliance to flowers that required constant care and attention. This was in fact a favorite rhetorical device employed by Harvard's Professor Nye, the Democratic Party's leading Japan-hand, and other Japanese and American national security experts. Noda had prepared meticulously for his visit.

During their talks at the White House, the two leaders exchanged views on a number of subjects. Noda brought up such issues as the North Korean problem and dealing with China as an emerging power. On the economic front, Noda was interested in discussing Japan's participation in the negotiations for the Trans-Pacific Partnership Agreement. Including the time taken for lunch, the meeting lasted nearly two hours. Participants from the American side included Secretary of State Hillary Clinton and Secretary of the Treasury Timothy Geithner, a clear indication of the high expectations that the Obama administration had for Noda.

The meeting closed with a joint statement by Noda and Obama entitled "A Shared Vision for the Future" that featured a commitment to "expand cooperation and further strengthen the alliance." While affirming the progress made in reviewing the realignment of US forces in Japan, Noda made no reference to the relocation of Futenma Air Station to Henoko.

Although he mentioned Futenma in the joint press conference that followed the meeting, Noda was not willing to go any further than to say, "We will work toward an early solution in line with past developments." In responding to a question from the press, Noda was clearly attempting to minimize the issue. ". . . our two countries will cooperate in the context of a deepening bilateral alliance towards the realization of the optimum US force posture in the region and the reduction of the burden on Okinawa, and we will continue to work for an early resolution of this issue." This down-playing was intentional and was designed to distance the Noda administration from the Futenma problem that had set the Japan-US alliance adrift under the two DPJ administrations that preceded him.

"I believe that the Japan-US alliance is the cornerstone of Japanese diplomacy. I am extremely pleased to be able to release a joint statement." Newspaper articles report that this was the first sentence that Noda uttered at the summit meeting. The joint statement released that same day contains the following short paragraph set apart from the rest of the text. "Japan and the United States pledge to fulfill our roles and responsibilities by utilizing the full range of capabilities to advance regional and global peace, prosperity and security. Our cooperation and dialogue extend to all levels and areas of government and the private sector." It would be no exaggeration to say that these words contained a distillation of the credo of a prime minister born to a father who served in the Self-Defense Forces, a prime minister who was wont to repeat that "the Japan-US alliance is the cornerstone," and a prime minister who was unabashed in presenting himself as a pro-US politician.

The Japan-US Security Treaty had passed an important milestone in 2010—the fiftieth anniversary of the revision of the original treaty. The two governments had taken the opportunity of this anniversary to begin behind-the-scenes discussions on further developing the Japan-US alliance in the twenty-first century. What the two sides were considering was a robust framework for the future that would be unveiled and advocated at the top levels of government. But plans would soon be derailed by the lingering effects of the damage done by Prime Minister Hatoyama Yukio, the first DPJ prime minister to take the reins of power. On the issue of US forces in Okinawa and the relocation of Futenma Air Station, Hatoyama had advocated, "Relocating to another country if at all possible or at least relocating to a site outside Okinawa." While committing to realizing an equal Japan-US relationship, Hatoyama had signaled that he was amenable to building an East Asian community that did not include the United States. The impact of these and other statements led to the postponement of the forward-looking message that had been originally intended.

Recalling the thoughts and emotions that flooded his mind as he prepared for the Japan-US summit meeting, Noda says, "What I really wanted to do in Washington was to announce a Pacific Charter patterned after the Atlantic Charter that the United States and Britain announced after the start of the Second World War."

The Atlantic Charter was a joint declaration drafted by US President Franklin Roosevelt and British Prime Minister Winston Churchill in their meeting at the Atlantic Conference held in August 1941. The two original signatories called on other countries of the world to adopt this Charter that advocated eight basic policies and principles as a foundation for the postwar world order. Among them were the renunciation of territorial aggrandizement, freedom of choice of form of government, global economic cooperation, freedom from fear and want, freedom of navigation, and disarmament of aggressor nations. These would later be incorporated into the United Nations Charter. What Noda had in mind was a Pacific version of this Atlantic Charter. The lofty aspiration that Noda secretly cherished was to sit down with President Obama in Washington and hammer out a document with similarly far-reaching ramifications.

It is well known that when they announced the Atlantic Charter, Roosevelt and Churchill had already foreseen the coming confrontation between the Soviet Union and the countries of the West. In other words, they were cognizant of the inevitability of what was to become the Cold War dividing East and West. If the same conceptual framework were to be applied to Noda's Pacific Charter, there is no doubt that China would stand today where the Soviet Union stood then.

Noda outlined the process and features of his Pacific Charter in these words. "To start with, Japan and the United States would engage in thorough and rigorous discussions on trade, investment, freedom of navigation, and national security. This would be followed by a call to the Association of Southeast Asian Nations (ASEAN) to join the partnership leading to the establishment of a large framework. Once in place, China would be drawn into the framework. This is roughly what I had in mind."

Various elements of Noda's concept can be found throughout the joint statement that emerged from this summit meeting. For instance, toward the beginning of the joint statement, there is a reference to the roles and responsibilities to be fulfilled by the two nations. In the area of national security, the joint statement makes explicit reference to the development of Japan's dynamic defense force and to strengthening cooperation between Japan's SDF and the US military in surveillance and warning operations. The document also provides for enhancing the ability to respond to contingencies in the region.

Regarding this dynamic defense, which also appears in the appendix to the statement, consideration was given to joint exercises by SDF and US forces in the US territories of Guam and Tinian in the North Mariana Islands and to joint use of facilities aimed at strengthening warning, surveillance, and patrol activities. Both were designed to address China's ambitious naval expansion in the vicinities of the Nansei Islands and elsewhere in the East China Sea.

The Noda-Obama joint statement had its precedents in the 2001 joint statement by Prime Minister Koizumi Junichiro and President George W. Bush. But in the Noda-Obama summit meeting of April 2012, the Japanese side was initially hoping for a joint declaration, a document of greater weight and import than a joint statement. Noda would have to go all the way back to 1996 to find a Japan-US joint declaration. Formally entitled the "Japan-US Joint Declaration on Security," the 1996 document had been signed by Prime Minister Hashimoto Ryutaro and President Bill Clinton and sought to define the Japan-US alliance in the post-Cold War era.

Thus, a Noda-Obama joint declaration would have had all the more historical weight. There is no doubt that Japan's pursuit of a joint declaration in the 2012 summit reflected Noda's hope to hammer out something like a Pacific Charter.

Making the best of the situation, the Japanese diplomats appended the word "vision" to the joint statement—presumably to assign it greater weight, placing it in line behind the 1996 Japan-US Joint Declaration on Security signed by Prime Minister Hashimoto after the end of the Cold War and the 2006 joint communiqué signed by Prime Minister Koizumi after the 2001 terror attacks in the United States. The essential portions of the Noda-Obama joint statement are:

The US-Japan Alliance is the cornerstone of peace, security, and stability in the Asia-Pacific region. This partnership has underwritten the dynamic growth and prosperity of the region for 60 years.

The strength of this Alliance, which was demonstrated during the Great East Japan Earthquake of 2011, is founded on the close bonds between our two nations and our people. These bonds will continue to anchor and sustain our partnership.

Japan and the United States share a commitment to democracy, the rule of law, open societies, human rights, human security, and free and open markets; these values guide us in our joint efforts to address the global challenges of our time.

The US-Japan partnership continues to be defined by our enduring commitment to the maintenance of peace. . .

Japan and the United States pledge to fulfill our roles and responsibilities by utilizing the full range of capabilities to advance regional and global peace, prosperity and security. . .

(We) seek to further enhance our bilateral security and defense cooperation. . . We will pursue our respective commitments, including the development of Japan's dynamic defense force . . . and the US strategic rebalancing to the Asia-Pacific with its efforts to achieve a more geographically distributed and operationally resilient force posture in the region. Our updated US force realignment plan will further enhance the Alliance's ability to respond to a variety of contingencies in the region.

In the joint press conference that followed the summit meeting, President Obama took the opportunity to reiterate his expectations for China as a responsible member of the international community, saying, "We do believe that as China continues to grow, as its influence continues to expand, that it has to be a strong partner in abiding by international rules and norms." Obama also emphasized that "the United States is once again leading in the Asia Pacific." Then, with an eye to China's growing military influence, he included an explicit reference to "America's defense posture in the Asia Pacific with forces that are more broadly distributed, more flexible, and more sustainable." These statements aside, there is no reason to think that Obama had any inkling at this time that Ishihara's statement of intent to purchase the Senkaku Islands would muddy the waters for his own China policies.

The same can be said of Noda, as can be surmised from the following exchange that took place during the summit meeting. The issue on hand was a tripartite strategic dialogue involving Japan, the United States, and China. Deputy Secretary of State Jim Steinberg and other top Obama administration officials felt that the time was not yet ripe for this type of dialogue. Notwithstanding this negative assessment from the American side, Noda had directly petitioned Obama saying, "This is something I want to do."

During the joint press conference, Noda echoed Obama's words and emphasized that the two leaders were on the same page. "China's development is an opportunity for the international community and for Japan . . . China has to be a strong partner in abiding by international rules and norms." Convinced of the critical importance of the Japan-US alliance as the lynchpin of Japan's diplomacy, Noda had seized this moment to make the strongest possible case that the Japan-US alliance remained robust and unshakeable under a Japanese government led by his DPJ.

The White House, on the other hand, had in fact been somewhat shaken by a comment that Noda had made during the summit meeting. This comment came in the closing moments of the meeting that immediately preceded the press conference. As he had promised Ishihara, Noda brought up the issue of joint military-civilian use of Yokota Air Base. "I have received a request from the governor of Tokyo . . ." Noda looked straight at Obama as he enunciated the request that the two governments get together to once again consider the issue of the joint use of Yokota Air Base.

Daniel Russel (National Security Council senior director for Asian affairs) and the other presidential aides who were present at the meeting did not attempt to hide their surprise. Noda's proposal had caught everyone off guard because Yokota had not been brought up anywhere in the working-level discussions that preceded the summit. As Ishihara had feared, the Foreign Ministry had blanked Yokota out from all the preliminary discussions with the American side.

While Russel and the others were wondering, "Why bring this up now?" Nagashima, who had accompanied the prime minister, jumped to the rescue with a quick-witted explanation. "We would like this issue to be considered in the context of strengthening the Japan-US alliance." Thanks to Nagashima, the awkward moment passed without incident.

As previously noted, Noda considered his visit to the United States the highlight of his political career. There was no mistaking the excitement and sense of elation that imbued all of Noda's words and actions. For instance, during the joint press conference, Noda proudly declared, "This is the first official visit to the United States by a Japanese prime minister in the bilateral context since the change of government took place in Japan." Painfully aware of developments that had allowed the alliance to stray off course during the earlier DPJ administrations, Noda appeared to be praising himself when he exclaimed, "The Japan-US alliance has reached new heights." At the banquet hosted by Secretary of State Clinton, Noda again took the opportunity to emphasize his pro-US leanings. "Born the son of an SDF officer, I grew up with a very real and personal sense of how the Japan-US alliance stands as our foundation."

It is unclear why Noda would take the considerable political risk of bringing Yokota up in the summit meeting. After all, nothing more than a verbal had been exchanged with Ishihara. In explaining his decision to broach the subject with Obama, Noda notes, "To be honest, there was no time left in my meeting with the president. But I figured that perhaps I would need the governor's cooperation at some future juncture." In other words, Noda was motivated by the desire to put Ishihara in his debt.

Noda had not yet envisioned a future scenario that would pit him directly against Ishihara over the purchase of the Senkaku Islands. Nagashima speculates on what may have been going through Noda's mind that day. "I would say the prime minister was trying to be considerate. He didn't want to disappoint Governor Ishihara."

As discussed above, the CNAS—a think tank with close ties to the Obama administration—soon thereafter came out with a report urging the Japanese and US governments to adopt the joint military-civilian use of Yokota Air Base. Following the publication of this report, there was a growing feeling among the prime minister and his aides that joint use would "certainly contribute to strengthening the Japan-US alliance." (Nagashima)

Reconsidering the situation from this point of view, Nagashima explains that Noda's proposal "was not necessarily about keeping his word or currying favor with Ishihara."

In Washington to announce his intent to purchase the Senkaku Islands, Governor Ishihara had said, "I think the government should purchase the islands. That would actually be better because it would really infuriate the Chinamen. But the Foreign Ministry is already shaking in its boots." Depending on how these words are interpreted, it is possible to infer that Ishihara was goading Noda and his Democratic Party.

However, as testified by Fujimura, the government had been intermittently negotiating with the owner of the Senkaku Islands, Kurihara Kunioki, since the closing days of the Koizumi administration. According to Fujimura, these negotiations for the purchase of the islands were moving forward, albeit very slowly and with little in the way of results. While the LDP was still in power, the government had actually prepared a property in Aichi Prefecture to be proffered in barter for the Senkaku Islands. Fujimura recalls that Kurihara personally inspected the property that was on offer about a year before Noda took office.

Fujimura explains that it was Ishihara's bombshell statement in Washington that brought these behind-the-scenes developments to the fore and accelerated the process. "After the Noda administration came into being, the administrative officer from the Cabinet Secretariat who had been handling Senkaku issues briefed us on past developments and the current status."

After Ishihara's announcement on the intended purchase of the Senkaku Islands, a Cabinet Secretariat administrative officer briefed Fujimura on the status of the negotiations to purchase the islands. In turn, Fujimura reported the information to Noda. At the end his report, Fujimura turned to the prime minister and asked, "What should we do?" Appearing to be less than fully convinced, Noda responded, "What a headache. I wonder what would happen if we just let Tokyo buy the islands."

While this was going on, Nagashima was busy trying to set up a meeting between Noda and Ishihara. As for what Ishihara wanted to discuss, Nagashima was "quite sure it was Yokota." But this did not mean that the Senkaku possibility had not crossed his mind. Actually, Noda himself was worried that the Senkakus were the real reason Ishihara was requesting a meeting with him.

But Ishihara did not make even the slightest mention of the Senkaku Islands during his meeting with Noda. As a politician who had now climbed to the pinnacle of power, Noda may have sensed that this omission was an indication of a hidden problem.

"By the way, what is your thinking on the Senkaku problem?" Noda directed his question to Nagashima, who had arranged the April 2012 meeting with Ishihara. Nagashima responded to the straightforward question with an equally straightforward answer that reflected his frank and sincere nature. "It makes more sense for the government to purchase the islands than for the Tokyo Metropolitan Government to buy them." Nagashima recalls what Noda then said without a moment's hesitation: "Yes, it does"

Roughly six months after the summit meeting in Washington, Noda stepped into his last summit meeting with the newly re-elected President Obama on November 20, 2012. The meeting was held in Phnom Penh, Cambodia, and lasted for about 30 minutes. Touching on the friction with China that had rapidly escalated following the nationalization of the Senkaku Islands, Noda explained, "We will focus on the big picture and remain calm, and we will endeavor to ease the tension through continued discussions." It is reported that Obama expressed his understanding.

The discussion then turned to Japan's participation in the Trans-Pacific Partnership (TPP) negotiations. The atmosphere became more relaxed when Noda indicated that Japan was prepared to accelerate the pace of preliminary consultations on specific topics of mutual interest, including automobiles, insurance, and beef, in preparation for the negotiations. Taking a positive stance on Japan's participation, Noda assured Obama, "There has been absolutely no change in our commitment since our [November 2011] decision to join the talks." He then shared the following allegory with Secretary Clinton who was travelling with The president. "The relationship between Japan and the United States is like the Beatles. The US is John Lennon and Japan is Paul McCartney. Without both of them, there can be no Beatles and there can be no music."

Noda had frequently used this allegory in Japan when addressing the politically explosive issue of Japan's participation in the TPP, and had been able to quell the worries of his audience by comparing the members of the Beatles to Japan and the United States. "Japan is Paul McCartney [composer of the Beatles' most successful pieces]. Can you imagine the Beatles without Paul?" Noda was using his favorite allegory to guide public opinion toward his position, which was that Japan needed to play a leading part in the TPP negotiations.

According to Noda, when he shared this with Obama and Clinton, they both laughed out loud and agreed with him. Commenting on the summit meeting, Noda declared, "We were able to confirm . . . the present-day significance of the Japan-US alliance and where Japan-US relations should be headed in the longer term." And throughout his tenure, Noda continued to emphasize the importance of the United States as the foundation of Japan's national security policies. Obama's unaffected laughter that day testified to the fact that the president had accepted and welcomed Noda's stance toward to the United States.

It was widely rumored that Ono Yoko had poisoned and destroyed the legendary partnership between John Lennon and Paul McCartney. Perhaps Noda would soon be extending his allegory to include Governor Ishihara in the role of Ono Yoko—the spoiler who was sowing the seeds of discord in the Japan-US alliance with demands for joint military-civilian use of Yokota and the nationalization of the Senkaku Islands.

Clandestine Operations

Anti-Japan demonstrations in Suzhou, China (September 15, 2012)
Kyodo

Hoping to catch up with Ishihara, who had taken the lead with his announcement at the Heritage Foundation in April 2012, Prime Minister Noda Yoshihiko gathered his staff in a secret meeting at the Kantei. While moving to establish contact with the owner of the islands, Noda also launched a series of maneuvers targeting China.

The Secret Meeting

The venue was the Kantei and the date was May 18, 2012—one month after Governor Ishihara's announcement at the Heritage Foundation. Prime Minister Noda had called his closest aides to a secret meeting. Present were Chief Cabinet Secretary Fujimura Osamu, Deputy Chief Cabinet Secretary Nagahama Hiroyuki, Special Advisor to the Prime Minister Nagashima Aki-hisa, Vice-Minister of Foreign Affairs Sasae Kenichiro, and Assistant Chief Cabinet Secretary (later Vice Minister of Foreign Affairs) Kawai Chikao. Some of the participants had entered the Kantei surreptitiously to avoid being spotted by the media covering the prime minister's movements.

During this meeting, Noda ordered the participants to take concrete steps toward nationalizing the Senkaku Islands. Everyone on this "Team Noda" was surprised by Noda's words. This even included Nagashima, who could easily be labeled the most committed advocate of Senkaku national-ization among them.

From his perspective, Nagashima saw the nationalization of the Sen-kaku Islands as a sure prelude to two conflicts. One would be the external conflict with China, and the other an all-out internal face-off with Tokyo Governor Ishihara Shintaro who had already very publicly announced his intention to have the Tokyo Metropolitan Government purchase the islands. Nagashima instinctively knew that Noda had calculated and accepted all the diplomatic and internal political risks before coming to this decision. The thought that went through Nagashima's mind was that this was a very gutsy decision, but he remained silent. The same evening, still on his adrenaline high, Nagashima wrote in his journal, "Deeply impressed by the prime minister's unwavering determination."

But what was actually going through Noda's mind was not exactly what Nagashima had imagined. During the meeting, Nagashima and others had argued that "nationalization by the government would be much more rea-sonable than purchase by the Tokyo Metropolitan Government." There was no strong opposition to this argument, even from Foreign Ministry

Vice Minister Sasae. This had led Nagashima to conclude that the prime minister had "arrived at a decision on nationalization." Some others present at the meeting also interpreted the prime minister's words as meaning he was presenting the group with his firm decision. However, Noda himself recalls that he had not yet arrived at a final decision and felt the best way forward was to steadily reinforce Japan's effective control by carefully and vigilantly adding to the list of *faits accomplis*.

In other words, Noda's telling indicates that he believed the possibility of purchase by the national government needed to be examined but that the final decision on whether or not to go through with this scenario would be postponed until the last possible moment. In the interim, the government would vigilantly monitor developments. There were three specific points that Noda needed to keep an eye on from an overall perspective.

The first point was the Tokyo Metropolitan Government, and in particular Governor Ishihara, who enjoyed a considerable lead in the race to acquire the Senkaku Islands. Second was China's reaction, given its obsessive commitment to maintaining the status quo as regards the Senkakus and the overt and covert pressures it was continuing to exert on the situation. The last point related to how the Obama administration would respond to nationalization, a matter that could not be easily predicted. On the one hand, Secretary of State Clinton had declared, "Article V of the Security Treaty applies to the Senkaku Islands." On the other hand, the administration's stated position on Japan-China relations was, "The United States makes it a rule not to intervene in territorial disputes." Among these three points, Noda was especially worried about Ishihara and what he might do as he advanced at full speed toward his publicly stated goal of acquiring the Senkaku Islands.

Immediately after instructing his aides to examine the possibility of nationalization, Noda had turned to Nagashima and said, "This will have to be explained to Governor Ishihara." He then ordered Nagashima to contact Ishihara. Noda saw himself stepping into a three-front war, and it would be no surprise if he had decided to keep vigilant watch over his most formidable adversary. Noda wanted to have advance notice of Ishihara's movements and to block him off as much as possible.

"Ultimately, the islands should go to the government." Noda had a very clear memory of the words that Ishihara had uttered after announcing his plan to purchase the Senkaku Islands. But Ishihara had gone out on a limb and had bragged in public. It did not seem likely that he would now suddenly step aside and defer to the government. With that in mind, Noda decided that it would be wiser to provide Ishihara with thorough and detailed explanations on what the government was doing rather than to ignore Ishihara in pushing the nationalization project forward. Moreover, Noda calculated that if the nationalization project were to proceed properly and without incident, Ishihara could actually decide to leave the ring without putting up a fight.

Acting on his instructions from Noda, Nagashima moved immediately to set up a meeting with Ishihara. "If at all possible, I have something I want to tell him first thing on Monday." But scheduling the meeting was not easy. As was well known, Ishihara did not schedule meetings with outsiders during the first part of the week. But Nagashima persisted and, with some help from others, was finally able to secure a slot in the governor's schedule for May 24, which was still six days away.

Nagashima was alone and nervous as he rode to the Tokyo Municipal Government building with the task of informing Ishihara of the government's plans to acquire the Senkaku Islands. But the governor was in full battle mode from the start, and his first words were: "So the national government plans to get in the way, does it?"

In setting up the appointment, Nagashima had used a ruse. "I would like to speak to you about Yokota Air Base," he had said. But the moment Ishihara saw his face, he yelled out, "It's about the Senkakus!" Nagashima's original intent was to probe Ishihara on his intentions by indirectly sounding him out. But now that his cover had been blown, Nagashima changed his tactics and decided to go for a frontal attack.

Ishihara: Do you mind telling me what the government intends to do with the islands?

Nagashima: We are considering it now. We are very nervous [thinking about what the Tokyo Metropolitan Government might do]. Be that as it may, personally, I believe it would be better for the government to buy the islands.

Ishihara: [Without a moment's hesitation] Of course it would! But we have already received 900 million yen in donations from the public. With all this good will, you can understand that I just can't back down. But that doesn't mean you have to defer to me or to be a gentleman about it. Don't worry. I'm not going to say, 'The government stole the islands from me.' You don't have to worry about that."

Nagashima was thinking to himself, "This is my lucky day!" Ishihara was not saying it had to be the Tokyo Metropolitan Government that buys the islands come hell or high water. Perhaps Ishihara would step down without making a fuss if the government made steady progress toward sealing the acquisition. Perhaps this would turn out to be much easier than he had thought.

Lost in these pleasant mental calculations, Nagashima was suddenly yanked back to reality. Two of Ishihara's aides had jumped into the conversation. One was Hyodo Shigeru, Ishihara's old yachting friend who now held the post of special secretary to the governor. The other, having the same job title, was Takai Hideki. It was as though they were there to finish what the governor had left unsaid. "If the government is buying, you have to offer a decent property to make it an equal-value exchange. You can't get away with an offer of land in some isolated location."

The two aides continued their unsolicited remarks. As Nagashima remembers the meeting, the aides alluded to various proposals that had been made to the landowner by previous administrations. "At the very least, you will have to construct some kind of facility [on Senkaku Islands]." That pushed Ishihara to jump in with his own rant against Nagashima. "When Abe [Shinzo] was deputy chief cabinet secretary, the government had the nerve to propose a trade with land located somewhere deep in the mountains. I didn't realize bureaucrats could be so cheap." Noticing that Ishihara, too, had started to sound warnings, Nagashima made no objections as he didn't want to ruin the atmosphere in the room, which once seemed amenable to the government buying the islands. He shortly took his leave with this brief comment. "I was deeply moved [by Ishihara's thinking]. I will confirm things [with Noda] and come back to see you again."

Nagashima hurried back to the Kantei to deliver his report. After mulling over the report, Noda called Deputy Chief Cabinet Secretary Nagahama Hiroyuki and ordered him to immediately enter into negotiations with the landowner. This was the turning point for Noda. By June, the Noda administration's nationalization process was in full acceleration mode. The process started with Ishihara, then moved on to the owner, and finally to China.

The Lease Agreement

"The central government, not the Tokyo Metropolitan Government, should be responsible for acquiring the islands. In my days as deputy chief cabinet secretary in the Koizumi Cabinet, we seriously discussed purchasing the islands in the Cabinet Secretariat. I was in favor of an outright purchase. But after a lot of twists and turns, we settled on leasing the islands in 2002."

These were the words of Abe Shinzo recorded in an interview with *Sankei Shimbun*. The interview, dated May 12, 2012, revolved around the purchase of the Senkaku Islands and had been given when Abe was former prime minister. Concurrent with this interview, Noda and Nagashima on one side and Ishihara on the other were trying to figure out what the other side was thinking.

As previously noted, Fujimura Osamu, the Noda Cabinet's former chief cabinet secretary, had also given an interview concerning government plans for acquiring the Senkaku Islands. In this interview with the *Mainichi Shimbun*, Fujimura had said, "The government has been engaged in behind-the-scenes negotiations with the owner of the islands since the closing days of the Koizumi Cabinet." Fujimura's explanation was basically consistent with Abe's comments. Ishihara's caustic remark to Nagashima on how cheap bureaucrats were also had its origins in the same setting.

Abe was technically correct in stating that negotiations between the government of Japan and the Kurihara family, which owned the islands, went back to the days of the Koizumi Cabinet. However, a closer inspection of the exchange between the two sides casts some doubt on the accuracy of Abe's "we seriously discussed purchasing the islands." The fact is that several knowledgeable people have strongly and directly taken issue with Abe's characterization. One of these is Fukuda Yasuo, Abe's immediate superior and the key official in the Koizumi Cabinet. According to Fukuda, the nationalization of the Senkaku Islands was "never once seriously discussed" by the Koizumi Cabinet.

During this period, the top administrative officer in charge of Senkaku-related matters was Deputy Chief Cabinet Secretary Furukawa Teijiro. According to Furukawa, the Koizumi Cabinet's counterpart in negotiations was not Kurihara Kunioki, the owner with whom the Noda Cabinet was to negotiate, but rather Kurihara's mother, who was still living at the time. Furukawa recalls, "At that time, the owner's attitude was, 'I am willing to lease you the islands, but under no circumstance am I prepared to sell to the government.' She was very clear about this."

This is borne out by the book written by Kurihara Kunioki's younger brother, Hiroyuki. In his book *Senkaku shoto urimasu* [Senkaku Islands for sale], Hiroyuki recounts how a group of conservative politicians from the

Seirankai group formed by Ishihara Shintaro met with his mother in 1973 or so to discuss purchasing the Senkaku Islands. At the end of this meeting, Hiroyuki's mother told the politicians, "I appreciate what you have said. But under no circumstances am I willing to sell."

Furukawa avers that, given the position taken by the owner, the idea being considered in the inner circles of the government was "basically, to sign a lease agreement." Furukawa explains that purchasing the islands, or nationalization, was not on the table. Nevertheless, it is easy to imagine that all options were being carefully examined on the administrative level, including everything from outright purchase to leasing. Ishihara had mentioned the idea of an equal-value exchange with property located elsewhere. This too must have been one of the options that the government considered. Be that as it may, ultimately only two options remained on the table, and these were the options that reached Furukawa's desk. The first featured the ceding of surface rights to the government for a period of about 50 years. The second was entering into a straightforward lease agreement.

Furukawa recalls that the top echelons of the government, led by Prime Minister Koizumi, Chief Cabinet Secretary Fukuda Yasuo, and Deputy Chief Cabinet Secretary Abe Shinzo, were satisfied to see the administrative staff "carry the work forward solemnly and in accordance with procedure." Furukawa states that there was no indication that the political side intended to intervene in the process to exercise political leadership. Finally, Furukawa explains, there was no deep discussion of title transfer under the Koizumi Cabinet. Instead of advancing in the direction of a real estate transaction, which title transfer implies, the Koizumi Cabinet settled on pursuing a lease agreement.

A property lease agreement involves the payment of an agreed amount of money by the lessee (in this case, the government of Japan) to the lessor (the Kurihara family), in exchange for which the lessee gains the right to use the property in question. Even after a lease agreement has been signed, of course, the lessor retains the right to sell the property to a third party. On the other hand, if the lessee registers the lease, the lessee can then retain its claims on the property even after it has been sold. As a matter of fact, the agreement signed by the government and the Kurihara family at that time contained a clause prohibiting the sale of the property to any third party.

Furukawa had several objectives in pursuing this line of action. The basic goal was to safeguard the three islands (Uotsurijima, Minami-kojima, and Kita-kojima) that were then privately owned. Specifically, by registering its lease, the government would be able to take legal action against any third party that might trespass or erect a structure on the islands without permission. In case of such violations, the government would be able to petition the courts for a temporary injunction against the trespasser or for the removal of the structure. Furukawa and others believed that this legal standing not only would allow the government to take rigorous action in case of trouble with China but also would allow it to uphold the basic principle in case of an internal or domestic violation.

Furukawa's account of developments is affirmed by Fukuda. "We received the explanation that this was intended to prevent undue actions by third parties, as well as by the landowner, and we accepted this advice in a purely businesslike manner."

The lease agreement for the Senkaku Islands was duly concluded between the government and the owner in April 2002. However, this agreement did not become public knowledge until it was leaked nearly a year later in an article on the front page of the *Yomiuri Shimbun* on January 1, 2003.

It has been learned that the government of Japan has leased three of Okinawa's Senkaku Islands, an inherent part of Japanese territory where China and Taiwan are also claiming territorial rights. The three islands, including Uotsurijima—the largest of these islands—are owned by a private individual and have been leased by the government for about 22 million yen annually. The lease was registered last October. It is believed the intent of the lease is to ensure stable government control and management of the islands by blocking their sale and barring any third party from landing on them. There is no precedent for the government leasing private property in connection with territorial issues. The move to strengthen government control may be said to be an indication of the government's determined stance on the Senkaku issue.

Actually, this was not the first time the government had leased the Senkaku Islands from a private owner. Of the five islands comprising the Senkaku Islands, Taisho-jima is government property. However, Kubajima, the remaining island, is owned by a private individual. Since being returned to Japan by the United States in May 1972, Kubajima has been leased to the director of the Naha Regional Defense Facilities Administration Bureau (currently the Okinawa Defense Bureau). The lease has been renewed annually.

Kubajima, the northernmost of the Senkaku Islands, is located approximately 27 kilometers northeast of the Uotsurijima, the largest of the five islands. With a circumference of 3.5 kilometers, Kubajima covers an area of about 0.9 square kilometers. Along with the other four islands, Kubajima was incorporated into Japan following the Cabinet decision of 1895. This island was placed under US administration for a number of years after the war but was returned to Japan concurrent with the 1972 reversion of Okinawa.

Following reversion, Taisho-jima and Kubajima were used as firing and bombing ranges by US forces in Japan. This arrangement was based on a bilateral agreement in which the Japanese government committed to providing the islands for use by the US. To make this possible, the government initially leased Kubajima from its owner for a period of 20 years. When the lease expired in 1992, a new lease agreement was concluded with the owner.

At some point around the mid-1970s, US forces stopped conducting military exercises in Kubajima. However, because the bilateral agreement remained valid in 1992, the government again leased the island for 20 years. Unlike the other three islands leased from a private owner, the government did not register its lease in the case of Kubajima because the island presented a special case given its status as "training ground for US forces."

When Ishihara announced his intention to have the Tokyo Metropolitan Government purchase the Senkaku Islands, his plan covered only three islands—Uotsurijima, Kita-kojima and Minami-kojima. Kubajima and Taisho-jima were excluded from the planned acquisition because of their special circumstances.

Act Resolutely

Furukawa Teijiro, who stood at the center of the Koizumi Cabinet as its chief administrative officer, repeated his request on numerous occasions within the government while working to conclude the lease agreement with the landowner. "Whatever you do, please no grandstanding on the Senkaku issue. Just act resolutely. That is all we need to do."

In line with this basic policy of acting resolutely on the Senkaku issue, the Koizumi Cabinet decided that it was essential these privately owned islands be leased and managed by the national government. This basic approach was put to the test by an incident that occurred exactly two years after the government leased the Senkaku Islands.

The incident occurred on March 24, 2004, at a little past 7:00 a.m. Arriving on the scene in what was thought to be a Chinese fishing boat, seven individuals landed on Uotsurijima and were seen waving what appeared to be the Chinese flag. On the same day, the landing was reported on a Chinese website known as the Patriot's League Network. The site, operated by a group of young people who claimed that the Senkaku Islands belonged to China, carried a flash report that Chinese activists had landed on Uotsurijima. This was the first landing by Chinese individuals since an October 1996 landing by Hong Kong activists, and the first landing by individuals from the Chinese mainland.

That morning, Vice-Minister for Foreign Affairs Takeuchi Yukio called Chinese Ambassador Wu Dawei to the Ministry of Foreign Affairs to lodge a protest. "Uotsurijima is an inherent territory of Japan, and this action is extremely regrettable. The situation is serious and demands immediate action. We demand that appropriate action be taken." Takeuchi went on to state, "The Japanese government shall deal with this case strictly in accordance with the applicable laws and ordinances."

"This is the sovereign territory of Japan, and we expect China to act accordingly." So said Prime Minister Koizumi to the press that noon. Chief Cabinet Secretary Fukuda Yasuo followed up with a statement given at his regular press conference the same day. "From the perspective of both history and international law, there is no doubt that the Senkaku Islands are the inherent territory of Japan. The illegal landing is very regrettable." As Koizumi had noted, the Okinawa Prefectural Police arrested all of the Chinese activists for violation of the Immigration Control and Refugee Recognition Act (illegal entry). This was the first time that foreign nationals landing on the Senkaku Islands had been arrested by Japanese authorities.

That evening, Koizumi met with the press for a second time. "Although this is an unprecedented case, it will be handled according to the law. This is only natural for a nation governed by the rule of law." In making this statement, Koizumi was once again emphasizing that the actions taken by Japan were fully justified.

Why did the Koizumi Cabinet go so far as to arrest the Chinese activists under the Immigration Control and Refugee Recognition Act? This decision was doubtless influenced by the basic act-resolutely policy that Furukawa and the administrative staff who had signed the lease agreement for the Senkaku Islands in 2002 had been advocating. The policy was not aimed solely at underscoring Japanese sovereignty in the Senkaku Islands. It had the additional objective of demonstrating to the whole world that Japan was a nation governed by the rule of law, as was the United States and other advanced countries, and to contrast this with China's rogue behavior.

The seven Chinese activists arrested by the Okinawa Prefectural Police categorically denied the charges during questioning, claiming that "[the islands] belong to China and therefore there was no illegal entry." If the Japanese police authorities had not arrested the seven, China could have interpreted this as Japan's abdication of its claim of sovereignty. Similarly, having claimed this as its sovereign territory, if Japan had failed to take resolute legal action against illegal entry, this omission would have given rise to a serious logical contradiction in Japan's position.

It was against this backdrop that this incident culminated in the first arrest of foreign nationals landing on the Senkaku Islands. However, there was no presupposition of arrest in the thinking or actions of the Japanese government.

According to media reports at the time, a vessel sailing under the Chinese flag was first spotted approaching the Senkaku Islands before 7:00 a.m. on March 24. The vessel was discovered by a patrol boat from Japan's 11th Regional Coast Guard Headquarters as it entered Japan's territorial waters east of Uotsurijima. The patrol boat observed as seven people left the fishing vessel, got into two rowboats, and rowed to the island where they landed. Meanwhile, the fishing vessel exited Japan's territorial waters and left the seven stranded on the island. That evening, Okinawa Prefectural Police officers landed on the island by helicopter and arrested the seven. The thinking was that this illegal entry and occupation situation should not be allowed to go on.

The Japanese government had previously compiled an Arrest Manual for use in cases involving unauthorized landing on the Senkaku Islands by one or more foreign nationals. The manual stipulated the following procedures. First, Coast Guard patrol ships would warn foreign nationals or vessels entering the territorial waters around the Senkaku Islands. If the warning was ignored, patrol boats would approach the vessel. In certain cases, patrol boats would force the vessel to stop by blocking its passage, and would seize the vessel if necessary. In case any individuals succeeded in landing on the islands, they would immediately be returned to their vessel and forcibly deported. If deportation proved difficult, action would be taken with the possibility of arrest by immigration or police officers for violation of the Immigration Control and Refugee Recognition Act.

"They managed to sneak by. [The Chinese activists] landed using rowboats and we missed them." This is how Chief Cabinet Secretary Fukuda explained in a press conference the same day why the activists had not been stopped before landing. Past incidents and the government's existing guidelines stipulated that intruders should be stopped before landing and forcibly returned to their vessel in the event they succeeded in landing. While these principles certainly applied to the case on hand, the fishing vessel that had brought the intruders had vanished from the scene, which meant there was no vessel to which the individuals could be returned. Ultimately, nothing could be done but to arrest the seven. As Fukuda had said, the intruders had managed to sneak past Japan's patrol.

Following the arrest, the government immediately began to deliberate on the best way to handle the seven Chinese activists in their custody. The initial deliberations were convened by Futahashi Masahiro, who had succeeded Furukawa as deputy chief cabinet secretary and chief administrative officer of the Cabinet. Those called to the meeting held in the Kantei included Yabunaka Mitoji, director-general of the Ministry of Foreign Affairs Asian and Oceanian Affairs Bureau, and Segawa Katsuhisa, director general of the National Police Agency Security Bureau.

Newspaper articles describe the situation as follows. Information from the Okinawa Prefectural Police indicated that the arrested activists had engaged in destruction of property on Uotsurijima, and that they had denied the charges against them saying, "Diaoyu is the sovereign territory of China, and therefore our landing cannot be illegal entry." In light of these developments, the prevailing atmosphere in government circles was, "While it may not lead to indictment, it is probably necessary to send the activists to the prosecutors."

What is the standard procedure for legal action against foreigners who have illegally entered or are illegally residing in Japan? In most cases, even if they are arrested and indicted, violators are deported immediately after a court ruling has been rendered. In other words, from Japan's perspective, there is no difference in the outcome even if violators are indicted. On the other hand, if considerable time were to pass before a court ruling was rendered, the thorn in the side of Japan-China relations would only fester. Taking into consideration the political factor of diplomatic relations with China, it would make sense to avoid the time-consuming legal procedures of indictment and trial. The smarter solution would be to transfer the seven trespassers to the Justice Ministry's Immigration Bureau, where they would be forcibly deported without delay. It was easy to predict that the deliberations would come to this conclusion.

While keeping a close eye on China's response to the arrest of the activists,

Koizumi said, "We want to handle this case in a way that will not pose an obstacle to overall Japan-China relations." Meanwhile in Beijing, Japan's charge d'affaires ad interim, Harada Chikahito, was called to the Chinese Ministry of Foreign Affairs on the afternoon of March 25. Commenting on Japan's arrest of the seven Chinese activists, First Assistant Foreign Minister Dai Bingguo conveyed the Chinese government's protest saying, "This is a serious violation of China's territorial sovereignty and the civil rights of its citizens." Calling for assurances of their safety, Dai Bingguo demanded that the seven arrestees be immediately and unconditionally released.

Harada responded, "Any violation occurring within the territory of Japan is dealt with in accordance with the applicable laws and regulations. This is natural for a nation governed by the rule of law." As the top officer in charge of China's foreign policies, Dai Bingguo played a key role in the Hu Jintao administration and wielded immense influence over Chinese policy toward not only Japan but also the United States. He answered Harada's rebuttal with an ominous warning. "Responsibility will be entirely on Japan's head if the situation gets complicated and there are serious consequences."

Even prior to the incident, Japan-China relations had been rapidly cooling following Koizumi's visit to Yasukuni Shrine. Mutual visits by the leaders of the two countries had already been suspended by this time. Relations were further frayed by Koizumi's statements on the Yasukuni issue during Diet deliberations. Appearing before the House of Representatives Budget Committee, Koizumi had chosen the following words to comment on the enshrinement of Class-A war criminals in Yasukuni Shrine. "It doesn't bother me. But I am not in a position to say anything about this." These comments infuriated the Chinese side. Bilateral relations would sustain further damage if Japan were to adopt a hardline position on the activists. If the arrests were to be culminate in prosecution and indictment, there was no doubt that Chinese protestations would gather steam and Japan-China relations would deteriorate from "cool" to "stormy."

The next phase in dealing with the arrested activists unfolded on March 26, 2004, two days after the initial incident. Since the activists had been arrested under the Immigration Control and Refugee Recognition Act, the Okinawa Prefectural Police handed them over to the Naha District Immigration Office of the Fukuoka Regional Immigration Bureau in accordance with the provisions of Article 65 of that law. The transfer was completed on the afternoon of March 26, at which point the Immigration Office made an immediate determination of illegal entry and moved to deport the activists. Deportation procedures were completed by evening and the seven activists were place aboard a China Eastern Airlines flight departing Naha for Shanghai.

Article 65 stipulates that a person taken into custody for illegal entry may be handed over to the immigration authorities within 48 hours of arrest if the person is not suspected of any other criminal offense.

Initially, Niioka Kuniyoshi, director of the Okinawa Prefectural Police Security Department, had made the following statement at a press conference. "We suspect these individuals may have committed other violations in addition to illegal entry." This referred to reports that the Chinese activists had damaged the lighthouse erected by Japanese rightists on Uotsurijima. Niioka had hinted that the police intended to send the activists to the prosecutors in order to investigate what they had done while on the island. But this course of action had been derailed by the response received from the Ministry of Justice stating, "If there is no evidence establishing a specific individual as a suspect in a specific violation, this constitutes 'no suspicion.' Consequently, the provisions of Article 65 would apply." Niioka explained that Article 65 was ultimately applied to the case in line with the advice received from the Ministry of Justice. However, it is obvious that a political decision had been rendered in light of the importance of diplomatic relations with China.

After the Chinese activists were deported, Koizumi made the following statement at a press conference. "The matter shall be handled appropriately and in accordance with the law. At the same, this problem should not be allowed to have a negative impact on Japan-China relations. Therefore, a decision should be made from an overall perspective. This is our basic policy, and I have instructed the competent government offices to act accordingly." In this way, Koizumi took it upon himself to emphasize that "political considerations" had played a role in the final decision that was reached.

On March 25, the day after the incident, an opposition party member had loudly called for the government to maintain a hardline position on China. It was as though this Diet member had foreseen that the Koizumi Cabinet would seek to settle the matter based on "political considerations." "The Diet must adopt a resolution to send a perfectly clear message that this is the sovereign territory of Japan. Anything less is bound to be misinterpreted." The speaker was none other than Noda Yoshihiko, who was then the chairman of the DPJ Diet Affairs Committee. Noda would later occupy the office of prime minister and ultimately make the decision on nationalizing the Senkaku Islands.

This exchange had taken place in the March 25 meeting of the directors of the House of Representatives Security Committee. An LDP hardliner had suggested a resolution be passed affirming that the Senkaku Islands belong to Japan. Noda had spoken out in support of this suggestion.

"Stay calm, stay calm! The important thing is to stay calm. Let's stay calm." Following the arrest of the Chinese activists and China's vociferous protests, Chief Cabinet Secretary Fukuda had repeated the phrase "stay calm" four times. His call for restraint was directed not only at Noda but also at everyone involved on both the Japanese and Chinese sides. In January 2013, recalling the events of March 2004, Fukuda commented on the Noda Cabinet's nationalization of the Senkaku Islands. He was implicitly critical of Noda: "The Chinese side was probably blindsided. They must have been thinking 'How can they be doing this?'"

The Lighthouse and the Shrine

In March 2002, the Koizumi Cabinet had concluded an agreement for leasing the Senkaku Islands, and in March 2004, Chinese activists had landed on the islands. A straight line can be drawn linking these two events to the series of tumultuous Senkaku-related developments that emerged during the latter half of the 1990s. One person cast a long shadow over these events—none other than Ishihara Shintaro. In the fall of 2012, he would directly ignite the fireworks that followed his announcement in the United States that he planned to purchase the Senkaku Islands.

To fully verify this nexus of events, it will be helpful to turn back the clock to the second half of the 1990s and review what was happening then.

The first stop comes in mid-July 1996. It became known at this time that a Japanese rightist group using a small fishing boat had landed on Kita-kojima and erected a solar-powered lighthouse. A second landing by Japanese rightists occurred two months later, this group erecting a similar lighthouse. It had been eight years since a rightist group had last erected a lighthouse in the Senkaku Islands in 1988. As was widely expected, China strongly protested the actions.

After the erection of the second lighthouse became known in mid-September, Anami Koreshige, Japan's charge d'affaires ad interim in Beijing, was called to the Chinese Ministry of Foreign Affairs. Awaiting him at the Ministry of Foreign Affairs was Director General of the Department of Asian Affairs Wang Yi (currently minister of foreign affairs). Wang protested, "We consider this to be a grave violation of the territorial sovereignty of China." The protest was repeated two weeks later at the United Nations Headquarters in New York when Japanese Foreign Minister Ikeda Yukihiko met with Chinese Vice-Premier and Foreign Minister Qian Qichen. "The Japanese government failed to take due measures against the activities of the group and failed to stop them," Qian said in his criticism of the Japanese government. The erection of lighthouses had met with strong responses not only from China but also from Hong Kong and Taiwan. When a group of Hong Kong activists attempted to land on the Senkaku Islands, one member of the group had lost his life.

The rightwing organizations that had erected the lighthouses in 1996 filed applications with the Japan Coast Guard for their formal recognition and approval under the Navigation Aids Act. The government's response was that it was not in a position to restrict or order the removal of the lighthouses because they stood on "private property." On the other hand, if the government were to approve the lighthouses, the Chinese side could interpret this as government involvement in their construction. When a similar application had been submitted in 1989 for a lighthouse that had been erected on Uotsurijima, the government had reserved judgment and effectively refused to accept the application.

Ikeda's response to Qian Qichen in New York was informed by these past developments. After first affirming that the Senkaku Islands are the sovereign territory of Japan, Ikeda addressed the question of approving the lighthouses. "The government has had absolutely no involvement in the lighthouses, and we will be very cautious in treating any application for recognition and approval." The implication of his statement was that the government's policy was to refuse approval.

"These actions do not reflect the intent of the Japanese government. The ministries and agencies concerned have been consulted on this matter. In consideration of international relations and the safety of Japanese nationals living abroad, a decision was reached from a broad perspective on whether the government should formally recognize the lighthouse. The decision is to defer and reserve judgment on this matter. This decision does not affect Japan's position on its territorial rights in the Senkaku Islands. This decision will be conveyed to China and others through diplomatic channels."

Ikeda made this statement at a press conference following the Cabinet meeting of October 4, 1996. By stating that the government would "reserve judgment" on the lighthouses built by rightwing organizations, Ikeda was formally announcing that the government would not recognize the light-houses. Following this announcement, the leader of the rightwing orga-nization responsible for erecting the lighthouses held a press conference on October 17 at the Foreign Correspondents' Club in Yurakucho, Tokyo. Speaking to the press, Seinensya Chairman Eto Toyohisa said, "The primary aim is to ensure the safety of navigation in the East China Sea. If the govern-ment is claiming territorial sovereignty [of the Senkaku Islands], it should build lighthouses to ensure the safety of navigation in its territorial waters."

Around the same time, Prime Minister Hashimoto Ryutaro met with Tang Jianxuan, assistant to the Chinese Minister of Foreign Affairs. The meeting with Tang, known as China's leading Japan expert, was held at the Kantei. During the meeting, Hashimoto let slip the behind-the-scenes story of how the Japanese government came up with the solution of not recognizing the lighthouses. "We are going to continue trying. However, as a nation under the rule of law, we are bound by the framework of the law. We would like you to understand that there are things we can do and things that we cannot do."

Approximately a year later, four Japanese sailing from Ishigaki Island in Okinawa Prefecture landed on Uotsurijima in the Senkaku Islands. The group was led by Nishimura Shingo, a New Frontier Party member of the House of Representatives. This was at 8:20 a.m. on May 6, 1997. Accord-ing to media reports, the group landed on the island with cameras, video equipment, and Japanese flags. Nishimura had received moral support from an individual who looked on from aboard a ship that had anchored nearby and flew the British flag—one Ishihara Shintaro.

"A political group has built us an excellent lighthouse. When the order was being placed, I introduced them to the Hydrographic Department [of the Ministry of Transportation]. There were two or three problems that had to be fixed. Finally, the Seinensya constructed an excellent lighthouse." This is how Ishihara described developments at his press conference on May 11, 2012, at the Tokyo Municipal Government building. He went on to vent his anger at the Foreign Ministry and how it had mishandled the situation.

> I don't know with whom or with what country the ministry was try-ing to curry favor. What we know is that they refused to formally register the lighthouse. The government went along with that and allowed it . . . The Ministry of Foreign Affairs is apparently more con-cerned about China than it is about the life and safety of our com-

patriots and others who navigate in those waters. The apprehension associated with the possible response by some other country outweighs everything else. This kind of response does not deserve to be called diplomacy.

After the landing, Nishimura's office released the following comment to justify the landing. "The purpose of the landing was to inspect the Senkaku Islands situation and to observe the status of patrol activities. It is only natural Diet members should inspect the territories of Japan." Needless to say, Prime Minister Hashimoto did not take the announcement at face value. "The owner [of the Senkaku Islands] rejects any landings on the island. No one, not even a member of the Diet, has the right to blatantly ignore the owner's wishes."

This is how Hashimoto expressed his displeasure at a press conference in the Diet on the same day. On the following day, May 7, 1997, Chief Cabinet Secretary Kajiyama Seiroku went a step further. "It is illegal to do something like this when the owner has explicitly banned landings. Also, it is undesirable from the perspective of how this will be seen abroad." As a key member of the Hashimoto Cabinet, Kajiyama went so far as to label the landing "illegal."

At a press conference in the Diet in the evening of May 7, Nishimura responded with blistering criticism. "The Chinese government issued a statement [on the landing] to say that its territorial sovereignty had been violated. What did the Japanese government do? It criticized me and trivialized it by making this a matter of private ownership. It is clear the government lacks the will to stand up to China and to assert territorial sovereignty."

Linked to the Senkaku landing, Nishimura issued a series of questions seeking clarification of the government position. The government issued the following response to Nishimura.

The government once again emphasized its basic position, which is that the Senkaku Islands are the inherent territory of Japan and are effectively controlled by Japan. Next, it stated that illegal landings and other acts by foreign nationals violate the Immigration Control and Refugee Recognition Act. In the event of such violations, it is the government's policy to remove violators by appropriate means. The government shall not respond in any manner that affects or abandons the nation's sovereignty.

Nishimura attempted a second landing on Uotsurijima in September 1997 but failed. The navigational range of the pleasure boat he had chartered was limited, and patrol boats from the 11th Regional Coast Guard were on hand to warn him against landing. In the end, Nishimura gave up. Approximately two years after this failed attempt, Nishimura was a Liberal Party member of the House of Representatives serving as the parliamentary Vice Minister of Defense. In an interview with the *Weekly Playboy* magazine, Nishimura addressed the question of the nuclear arms race between India and Pakistan. Prefacing his comment by saying that this was merely his personal opinion, Nishimura said, "Maybe it would be better for Japan to exercise the nuclear option. The Diet should probably deliberate whether or not to go nuclear." Taking responsibility for his comment in the ensuing uproar, Nishimura resigned his post as parliamentary vice minister of defense.

Three years after Nishimura's landing, the issue flared up again. At the end of April 2000, it became known that the rightist organization, Seinensya, had constructed a small Shinto shrine on Uotsurijima. According to reports, the small shrine was only 50 centimeters tall and 35 centimeters wide. Unlike the construction of the lighthouses that preceded it, the building of a shrine was directly linked to Japan's own religious tradition of Shinto and was definitely intended to directly underscore Japan's claim of sovereignty.

The Seinensya went so far as to announce, "In part, the shrine is meant to memorialize the island inhabitants who starved to death during the war. Going forward, we plan regular visits to pay homage at the shrine. Our policy is to eventually post several priests on the island on a permanent basis."

China responded as soon as newspapers reported the shrine's existence. Late the same evening, China's Ministry of Foreign Affairs spokesperson released an emergency statement that voiced severe criticism of what it called the "violation of China's sovereign territory." The spokesperson stated that China had forwarded an inquiry to the Japanese government through diplomatic channels demanding an explanation of the facts related to the construction of the shrine. At the same time, the Chinese government demanded appropriate measures be taken to prevent landings by "rightwing activists."

Faced with this new development, China started criticizing Japan for having abandoned the responsibility it had taken on as a party to the Japan-China consensus on the Senkaku problem. How was Japan to interpret the terminology used by China? The consensus that the Chinese side was trumpeting was understood to refer to what Deng Xiaoping, China's supreme leader, had proposed in the late 1970s, which was to "leave it to future generations to resolve." As to the claim that Japan had "abandoned its responsibility," this was interpreted as pointing to the Japanese government's failure to thwart landings by rightwing organizations.

The seven Chinese activists who landed on Uotsurijima in the spring of 2004 did do some damage to the small shrine and the lighthouse. This is why the Okinawa Prefectural Police were considering charges of destruction of property after arresting the activists. However, as previously noted, the Koizumi Cabinet decided to immediately deport the activists from an overall perspective. The Seinensya protested loudly, claiming that the decision had weakened Japan's effective control of the islands. The group then petitioned the government for permission to land on the Senkaku Islands again in order to repair the property that had been damaged.

Yachi Shotaro, advisor to the Cabinet and assistant chief cabinet secretary (formerly vice minister of foreign affairs and later secretary general of the National Security Secretariat and special advisor to the Cabinet) recounts the developments that followed the conclusion of the lease agreement for the Senkaku Islands by Deputy Chief Cabinet Secretary Furukawa Teijiro and others. Yachi says that the Koizumi Cabinet responded to the Seinensya by saying, "The government will be responsible for repairing the damaged property." Finally, hoping to bring the matter to a close, the Koizumi Cabinet conveyed its policy that it would not permit a landing.

However, the Seinensya would not let up. It claimed that it should be allowed to undertake the repairs because the shrine "had a religious significance that differentiated it from the lighthouse." Yachi responded to the rightwing organization by stating, "It is possible to pray and pay homage from a boat offshore." This seemed like an ingenious idea for settling things peacefully, and it was clear the government was bending over backwards to avoid negatively impacting Japan-China relations.

In November of the following year, Nishimura was arrested by the Special Investigations Division of the Osaka District Prosecutors Office on charges of violating the Attorney Act. The case involved the law firm Nishimura operated as a qualified attorney and his illegal name lending to a former employee of the firm who was acting as a lawyer without a proper license. Following his arrest, Nishimura disappeared from the national political stage. Concurrent with Nishimura's retirement from public life, the repeated near misses with Senkaku landings that threatened to disrupt Japan-China relations disappeared for a time.

But Nishimura would make a comeback before long. Nishimura ran in the December 2012 House of Representatives election on the Nippon Ishin no Kai, a political party led by Ishihara, ticket and was elected from the Kinki District's proportional representation bloc. He thus returned to the Diet following a three-year absence and was soon back in the news with a gaffe that he made at a party meeting on May 17, 2013. "Japan is crawling with Korean prostitutes," Nishimura had said. This was enough to earn him immediate expulsion from the party.

The clock now moves back to the late spring of 2012, or about the time that Deputy Chief Cabinet Secretary Nagahama Hiroyuki was meeting Kurihara for the first time. Sent on this mission by Prime Minister Noda, Nagahama was beginning to sense a subtle change in the landowner's attitude. He thought to himself, "Both seller and buyer are getting serious about making a deal."

The meetings were held at various locations, such as hotels in Saitama near the Kurihara family home. Nagahama was accompanied by several others, including Assistant Chief Cabinet Secretary Kawai Chikao, who had been seconded to the Cabinet Secretariat by the Foreign Ministry. The team met repeatedly with Kurihara and his aides as both sides tried to probe the other's position.

"This issue of nationalizing the Senkaku Islands has been raised and shelved repeatedly by the past administrations like a never-ending loop." This was a frequent complaint that Nagahama heard from Kawai and the other administrative staff members of the team. On the other hand, Nagahama never once heard Kurihara say, "I won't sell to anyone but Ishihara." Nagahama found this meaningful. Based on his extensive business experience as an executive at Bandai Company and Itochu Corporation, Nagahama was beginning to feel that, "This real estate transaction is going to happen."

Nagahama recalls, "For Kurihara, letting the islands go was not about selling a piece of property for a certain sum of money. It was more like selling a piece of his beloved homestead. With that in mind, I tried to put myself in his place. 'How has this person become entangled in this affair?' This is the question that I kept asking myself."

As the person negotiating with the seller, Nagahama committed himself to two principles that he maintained throughout the negotiations. First, he did not allow his public persona as deputy chief Cabinet secretary and aide to Prime Minister Noda to interject itself in the negotiations. Similarly, he put a lid on all personal views and feelings that he held. Thus he handled the negotiations for the nationalization of the Senkaku Islands purely as a real estate transaction. Second, he endeavored to foster a personal relationship with Kurihara. His experience in the private sector had taught him that this was a fundamental prerequisite for all successful business and transactional relations.

After several secret meetings, Kurihara began to warm to Nagahama. Kurihara told stories from the history of the Senkaku Islands and shared pictures from his own youth. Nagahama showed genuine interest in what Kurihara and his aides related. "So that is what was happening in those years," Nagahama would repeat. His sixth sense was telling him with increasing confidence, "Sooner or later, we're going to close this deal."

But Nagahama was mindful that his relationship with Kurihara was only three months old at best, whereas Ishihara's history with the Kurihara family went back decades. He was also painfully aware that other prominent people were also involved. Therefore, while sensing that "Sooner or later, we're going to close this deal," he also knew that there were certain truths that he would never be able to unravel. For Nagahama, there was always something he felt he could not know about Kurihara until the very end.

"We're going to close this deal" may have been an objective assessment. But as Prime Minister Noda's aide with a personal interest in promoting nationalization, Nagahama constantly warned himself against the pitfall of subjective thinking and the allure of wishful thinking.

"I can't deny that there was an element of wishful thinking in my mind. After all, the statements Governor Ishihara made had a way of making you believe that the government must buy the islands or at least the government should buy the islands."

Nagahama recalls the meeting that he and Nagashima had with Ishihara at the Tokyo Metropolitan Government building. During the discussions, Ishihara had mentioned constructing a moorage or similar facility on the Senkaku Islands. He had commented that it would not be a problem if China were to respond harshly and back its threats up with a show of force. Remembering what Ishihara had told him, Nagahama felt the full weight of the importance of nationalizing the Senkaku Islands, not as a negotiator in a real estate transaction but as a politician. Nagahama recounts what was going through his mind at that time.

"I certainly felt the pressure. I had been told, 'Go make it happen.' Naturally, I was telling myself, 'I have to get this agreement signed.' If I wanted to worry, this was going to impact our relations with China and our own national interests. But I decided to look at it in very simple terms: My mission is to purchase this piece of property. I remained focused on the deal."

Exit Strategy

"Obviously, the right way of going about it is for the state to purchase the islands. I admit that my approach is not the right way, but with all the donations that have poured in, I can't back down."

Thus spoke Ishihara Shintaro on June 1, 2012. The site was the imposing Governor's Office in the Tokyo Metropolitan Government building. Two men sat meekly facing the governor, leaning forward to ensure they did not miss a single syllable that left the governor's lips. One was Nagashima, charged by Prime Minister Noda Yoshihiko to lead the negotiations with Ishihara and the Tokyo Metropolitan Government. The other was Nagahama, responsible for the negotiations that were already underway with the owner of the Senkaku Islands, Kurihara Kunioki.

During the meeting, Nagashima and Nagahama informed Ishihara that behind-the-scenes negotiations had already started with the owner who held title to the islands. "Tokyo Metropolitan Government can buy the islands and turn around and transfer them to the government. I am willing to enter into a secret codicil like that."

Nagahama recounts that Ishihara mentioned this possibility in their meeting. In fact, in his press conference held the same day, Ishihara did state, "We would be willing to hand the islands over to the government." To this day, the Tokyo Metropolitan Government website contains the following record of the press conference held that day.

Question: Are you suggesting that Tokyo's plans to purchase the islands can be suspended and the whole matter put in the hands of the national government?

Ishihara: If the national government makes a clear statement of intent, I am always prepared to cooperate with the government's efforts to act on behalf of the will of the people. That includes the donations that we have received.

Watching the exchange between Ishihara and Nagashima from the sidelines, Nagahama felt that Ishihara was taken aback by the information that the government was in negotiation with the landowner. In the first moments of the meeting, Ishihara had looked at Nagahama and Nagashima as if to say, "Who the hell are you?" But Ishihara's expression gradually changed to a look of surprise. "So, you have already made that much progress with Kurihara?" Nagahama says that Ishihara's surprised reaction could not be missed.

Nagahama continues, "Ishihara must have been thinking that various Liberal Democratic Party (LDP) administrations had tried on multiple occasions and failed. So he concluded he would have to do it himself. You got the sense that he wanted to say, 'There is no way you can succeed where others have failed. Just stay out of my way!' That's the way it came across."

Noda was briefed on the meeting and the various statements Ishihara made. After reviewing the report, Noda issued a second secret order to Nagashima. "Go back to the governor and find out what he is really thinking." When Nagashima contacted Hyodo Shigeru, the governor's special secretary, he was told, "Priority should be given to whichever party can complete the procedures faster."

The Tokyo Metropolitan Government had formulated the following scheme for purchasing the islands. First, the Tokyo Metropolitan Assembly would approve the purchase in its December session. The next milestone would come on March 31, 2013, the date the lease agreement between the government and landowner would expire. The actual agreement for the purchase of the islands would be concluded at this time.

In light of this schedule, Nagashima theorized that what Hyodo meant was, "If the national government moves quickly, that would make it very difficult for the Tokyo Municipal Government to consummate its plans and purchase the islands."

In his meeting with Nagashima, Ishihara had said he would not back down because of the donations that had poured in from the public. But there were indications that the decision to collect donations had been made without Ishihara's approval and arrangements had moved forward without his knowledge. Evidence for this can be found in the words and deeds of Vice-Governor Inose Naoki, who would go on to become the 18th Governor of Tokyo as Ishihara's handpicked successor. (Inose later resigned as governor in December 2013.)

"The purchase will be made using the Tokyo Municipal Government budget. But the budget expenditure can be held down by soliciting donations from Tokyo residents, or perhaps even from people throughout Japan." Inose's statement was made in an interview with the Nippon Hoso Kyokai (NHK) immediately following Ishihara's April 16, 2012, Washington announcement that he planned to purchase the Senkaku Islands. In his book *Kaiketsu suru chikara* [Problem-solving power] (PHP Business Books),

Inose explains that this brief mention triggered a deluge of donations from the public. Inose went on to explain the justification for the proposed purchase of the islands by Tokyo Metropolitan Government based on the following argument.

> The private owner of the islands is old, and the inheritance question will come up sooner or later. If the islands were to be sold as private property, there is no telling who the next owner might be. The islands that are now being leased by the government for 24.5 million yen per year may be plunged into a dark realm of greed and personal gain. There is a rumor that someone in China is offering 30 billion yen for the islands. If the Tokyo Municipal Government becomes the owner, the ownership question will certainly stand on much firmer ground.

There is no indication that Ishihara and Inose had discussed what Inose would say in his NHK interview. The fact is that in various media appearances Inose has implied that the idea of collecting donations was his. After the speech in Washington, Ishihara gave the press the following explanation. "We have an agreement in principle with the owner. Negotiations are moving forward between the owner and our attorneys." Asked about the cost of the purchase, Ishihara responded, "I can't say. It is not that expensive." Throughout the entire exchange, Ishihara did not make any mention of donations from the public.

An interesting commentary comes from Sonoda Hiroyuki, secretary general of the Sunrise Party of Japan and Ishihara's confidante on Senkaku-related matters. "I don't think the idea of donations had occurred to Ishihara." However, this is contradicted by Santo Akiko, the LDP member of the House of Councilors and go-between for Ishihara and the owner of the islands, Kurihara Kunioki. Santo says she, Ishihara, and his son Nobuteru secretly discussed the idea of calling for donations to purchase the Senkaku Islands in early 2011.

The scheme that the three had initially come up with was primarily intended to bring the problem of the Senkaku Islands to national attention. Awareness would be raised and a national fund drive would be launched. It was hoped this would culminate in a national expression of "we will defend the nation ourselves." Santo has testified that these discussions had advanced to the point where she was making plans to ask her supporters to contribute seed money.

The plan never saw the light of day. What derailed it was the Great

East Japan Earthquake of March 11 that year. The nation was shocked at the destruction, and donations began streaming into the hard-hit Tohoku region soon after the earthquake. Under the circumstances, Ishihara and Santo concluded charitable giving should be concentrated on Tohoku. In other words, the idea of crowdfunding totally disappeared from Ishihara's mind at this time. Santo recalls the exchange. "Given the devastation of the earthquake, the feeling was it was a very poor time for us to launch our fund drive."

Kurihara was now beginning to show more interest in selling. With an eye to the change in Kurihara, Ishihara conveyed this short message to Santo. It was as if he had made up his mind. "Don't worry about it. I am going to have Tokyo buy them." But many hurdles still remained at this point. For instance, the three islands of Uotsurijima, Kita-kojima, and Min-ami-kojima were under lease to the government. Much remained to be done before the Tokyo Metropolitan Government could formally acquire the islands.

First of all, under the terms of the lease, the owner was barred from selling the islands to "any third party" (in this case, the Tokyo Metropolitan Government) during the duration of the lease. The agreement also contained a clause stipulating, "No one shall be allowed to land on the islands without the prior consent of the government."

Being a part of Okinawa Prefecture, the Senkaku Islands were located outside the administrative jurisdiction of Tokyo and would effectively constitute a detached enclave if purchased by the Tokyo Metropolitan government. Here, the Ministry of Internal Affairs and Communications had taken the position that there is nothing in the Local Autonomy Act that would restrict or prevent enclaves. Be that as it may, the immediate problem was that under the provisions of the lease agreement, the Tokyo Metropolitan Government would need the government's permission to survey the islands. The bottom line was that Ishihara and the Tokyo Metropolitan Government would have to wait until the lease expired, which would happen the following spring.

Another major sticking point was the price to be paid for the islands. According to the Tokyo Metropolitan Government rules and regulations, any purchase of real estate requires prior assessment to confirm that the proposed acquisition is appropriately priced. This in turn requires onsite surveys. Ordinances stipulate the presentation of the transaction price to the Council on Property Prices panel of experts, which examines and affirms that the proposed purchase price is justified. Furthermore, the acquisition of any property "exceeding 200 million yen and 50,000 square meters" must be submitted to the Tokyo Metropolitan Assembly for approval. Needless to say, the Senkaku Islands would fall under this rule.

As previously noted, Ishihara could not give a clear answer when the press in Washington asked about the details of the plan to purchase the Senkaku Islands, including the cost of acquisition. At least at this time, Ishihara was vulnerable on such questions as the cost of the acquisition, the source of funding, and various procedural matters.

However, there is another way of looking at these weaknesses, for they ultimately allowed Ishihara to retreat with honor when the time came for him to make his final decision. They allowed him an exit strategy falling back to his fundamental position that, "The islands really should be purchased by the central government, not by Tokyo."

Inose was full of confidence as he boasted, "I expect donations to come in from Tokyo and all over Japan. Donations will enable us to reduce the budgetary requirement." This was on the evening of April 17. It is unclear what Ishihara was thinking at this point, but Inose turned out to be right. Donations started pouring in from all over Japan to support the purchase of the Senkaku Islands. The idea had triggered an explosion of interest and donations quickly accumulated in the Senkaku Islands Fund.

On April 25, 2012, only nine days after Ishihara's Washington announcement, the *Sankei Shimbun* reported, "About 3,500 comments were received during a four-day period, with about 90 percent favoring the plan [for the Tokyo Metropolitan Government to purchase the Senkaku Islands]." The article quoted Inose as saying, "The nationwide excitement is a manifestation of the public's keener awareness of the significance of the Japanese archipelago and our national territory, an awareness that has been growing since the Great East Japan Earthquake." Ishihara was also quoted as saying, "I am very encouraged. I believe this reflects the people's concern and their love of their country."

Two days later, on April 27, Ishihara announced that a "dedicated unit will be launched on May 1" to prepare for the purchase of the Senkaku Islands in 2013. The unit was to have one person with department-chief status and two with section-chief status. It was the start of a full-blown effort to prepare for permission to land on the islands. At the same time, Ishihara announced that a special bank account had been established for the donations that were flowing in.

Ishihara also commented on the onsite survey of the islands, a necessary procedure for determining and approving the purchase price. This of course would involve landing on the islands. "I think landing on the Senkaku Islands will take place after we sign a provisional contract with the landowner." Asked what he would do if the government refused to issue a landing permit, Ishihara responded, "If the government rejects our application, we will keep applying until we get the permit. The Tokyo Metropolitan Government is just trying to protect the Senkaku Islands, and there is no reason for the government to not allow us to land." The forceful words that Ishihara uttered were meant to be a warning to the Noda Cabinet.

Even then, Ishihara could not give a straightforward answer when asked about the possibility of the national government stepping in to purchase the islands. His response was consistently ambiguous and open to interpretation. "We are moving forward because we know the government won't throw its hat into the ring. If the government is prepared to buy, I am always ready to step aside. After all, it is the central government that should be buying the islands."

About two months later, on June 22, Ishihara announced that he wanted to remain governor until plans for the purchase of the Senkaku Islands were more or less finalized. As previously noted, by this time, Nagashima and Nagahama had already informed Ishihara that the government had started negotiations with the landowner.

Concurrently, there was much talk among those close to him that Ishihara was going to from a new "Ishihara Party" and use this as a vehicle for moving out of the governor's office and back to the national Diet. As for the donations that were pouring in from all over Japan, the amount received totaled 1,228 million yen as of the previous day.

Ishihara's words on this occasion showed that he was seemingly wavering between his own political ambitions and the goodwill (donations) the public had exhibited. "What we said we would do has really resonated with the public. Look at the response! It is impossible for us to give up midway."

In the course of this press conference, Ishihara also revealed that he had had a chance to dine with Kurihara Kunioki's younger sister, who held title to Kubajima. He expressed his enthusiasm for undertaking a consolidated purchase of the islands. "Tokyo will acquire all four islands under one consolidated agreement, and we will defend them for the sake of the country. That is what we have to do." When asked about Taisho-jima, an island already owned by the national government, he did not mince words, commenting, "They had better take good care of it." The tug-of-war with the Noda Cabinet had already begun, although it remained veiled from the public eye. Indeed, it seemed that in choosing his words, Ishihara was purposely burning the honorable retreat bridge that he might have to use as his exit strategy.

By this time, the government was negotiating in earnest with the islands' owner, Kurihara Kunioki. Deputy Chief Cabinet Secretary Nagahama Hiroyuki had received his instructions from Prime Minister Noda and had put together a team that included Assistant Chief Cabinet Secretary Kawai Chikao, an administrative officer who had been seconded by the Foreign Ministry. Several meetings had been held with Kurihara, and Nagahama and his team were now trying to determine whether Kurihara was prepared to sell to the government.

"The best solution would be for the central government to purchase the islands. But I want you to show some deference to Governor Ishihara so he doesn't lose face." According to multiple government sources familiar with the details of the meetings, Kurihara repeated this statement on several occasions in the course of the negotiations. In effect, he was calling on the government to give a little. But what exactly did Kurihara mean by showing deference to Governor Ishihara? This was, it turned out, a call for the government to erect some new structure on Uotsurijima as a demonstration of Japan's effective control.

"Could you at least build a moorage? That's not too much to ask, is it?" It is reported that Kurihara asked this question in his negotiations with Nagahama. Ishihara was known to be a yachting aficionado, and the idea of building a moorage in the Senkaku Islands was dear to his heart. After announcing the plan to purchase the islands, Ishihara had from time to time referred to building a moorage as a symbolic step that would reinforce Japan's effective control. If the national government were to purchase the islands predicated on a behind-the-scenes promise to build a moorage after the islands had been nationalized, that would certainly allow Ishihara to lower his banner and make an honorable exit. In other words, this would create a second door that Ishihara could use in his exit strategy.

But it was a sticking point for the national government. One of the reasons it had entered the negotiations in the first place was that the government wanted to block Ishihara from loose cannoning and building new structures to project Japan's effective control. For the government, the ultimate objective of nationalization was the "maintenance of peaceful and stable management." There was no way that Kurihara's demand for deference to Governor Ishihara could be reconciled with this key government objective. The two positions were at loggerheads from the start and would remain so to the end.

At around the same time, Nagashima and Nagahama were feeling growing pressure from the competition. "The Ishihara side is making an all-out effort to catch up." The two speculated on what was energizing Ishihara. One idea that crossed their minds was that Ishihara was committed to the Senkaku Islands as a "patriot." The second had to do with his personal political ambitions and schemes. It was rumored that Ishihara was preparing to form a new political party to serve as his vehicle for doing something big on the national political stage. Furthermore, Nagashima and Nagahama had received reports that Ishihara was privately telling his inner circle. "If the Senkaku Islands lead to war with China, so be it." "Territory comes before business or the economy." To top things off, Ishihara was boasting, "Even if it comes to war with China, that's not one Japan will lose."

Unbeknownst to the government, the Tokyo Municipal Government and Kurihara had been making steady progress in their behind-the-scenes negotiations. By now, both sides had appointed lawyers to actually negotiate the purchase price. Deputy Chief Cabinet Secretary Nagahama Hiroyuki, who had been appointed by Prime Minister Noda to lead the government team, recalls, "We had absolutely no idea they had gotten that far."

Now began a series of miscalculations that would soon dog Ishihara. A very subtle and barely perceptible change was taking place in Kurihara's words and behavior. Earlier, Kurihara had averred, "If I sell, it has to be to Governor Ishihara." But something was changing, and the first to notice was Santo Akiko, the Diet member who was serving as an intermediary between Ishihara and Kurihara. As previously mentioned, both sides had appointed lawyers to represent them in the negotiations on the purchase price. Santo explains that Kurihara began to grow increasingly suspicious and distrustful of the Tokyo Metropolitan Government. "He started to say that he didn't like the lawyers that Tokyo had appointed. Until then, he had repeatedly said, 'If I sell, it has to be to Governor Ishihara.' So, I felt quite confident and secure until then."

Santo recalls that she advised Kurihara not to meet with Prime Minister Noda's negotiating team headed by Nagahama. At the same time, she anxiously watched as the administrative and legal aspects of the negotiations were delegated to the proxies, lawyers and real estate appraisers appointed from both sides.

According to Santo, from the beginning of the negotiations, Ishihara and his team had estimated that Uotsurijima and the two other islands could be purchased for "roughly 1.5 billion yen." Although this was a considerable sum, Kurihara was feeling increasingly frustrated by the assessment standards that the Tokyo Metropolitan Government was applying to the transaction. "This is going to lead to an unacceptably low price," Kurihara worried.

As a patriot focused on the big picture, Ishihara was essentially uninterested in the details of the transaction. The same certainly did not apply to his staff and lawyers, who were ever-mindful that the purchase would have to undergo scrutiny by the Council on Property Prices and be approved by the Assembly. Hence, the staff and lawyers were inevitably focused on the details. Ishihara and Kurihara had really hit it off and had excitedly discussed "registering the beautiful Senkaku Islands as a World Heritage Site." Santo says that the two men had come to an understanding—a "gentlemen's agreement." Perhaps the excitement and luster of this understanding could not survive the dour bureaucratic details that had to be worked out. Santo's interpretation of these developments is that Kurihara's growing distrust was not aimed at Ishihara himself but that he was increasingly suspicious of the Tokyo Metropolitan Government and its bureaucracy.

Turning to Prime Minister Noda and his team of surrogates, Nagahama was moving forward with due speed in his efforts to convince Kurihara. On June 1, 2012, Nagahama had met with Ishihara to inform him of the government's intentions. Less than one week later, on June 7, Nagahama had informed Kurihara that the government had made up its mind to purchase the islands. Next on Nagahama's agenda was the task of extracting a statement of intent from Kurihara. However, at this point, Kurihara was still talking about helping Governor Ishihara save face. He remained evasive and would not give a firm commitment to the government side.

"Ishihara was very confident that the owner would never sell to the national government. But the truth was that the owner was beginning to waver." Noda was receiving detailed reports on the negotiations from Nagahama and his team and was beginning to sense a change in Kurihara's attitude. Noda did not miss the positive atmosphere that was emerging in the talks. While concentrating on reading Kurihara, the landowner, the Kantei was taking bold yet careful steps forward. Each step they took brought them closer to the final prize.

Nagashima recounts the tension that infused the Prime Minister and his aides at this juncture. "This is what we were thinking at the time. Just one word from the landowner that he would not sell to the government would immediately be 'Game over' for us." The Noda camp was engaged in a psychological battle whose outcome could not be predicted. However, it was just about this time that the Noda camp got a rare piece of good news from a totally unexpected source.

"If the government is going to purchase the islands, the deal can be done at whatever price the landowner names." This message of support had come from the Ministry of Finance, led by Administrative Vice Minister of Finance Katsu Eijiro, who was being touted as "the first powerhouse vice minister of finance in a long time." Noda had secretly instructed the Ministry of Finance to consider the budget options available for financing the purchase of the islands, and it was on June 28 that the top officials of the Ministry presented their brilliantly crafted solution. "The purchase of the Senkaku Islands can be financed using the contingency funds budgeted for the Cabinet." The message had been conveyed to Noda through the Ministry's administrative channels.

One month later, as previously instructed by Chief Cabinet Secretary Fujimura, the Ministry of Land, Infrastructure, Transport and Tourism (MLIT) issued its "real estate price" for the purchase of the three Senkaku Islands (Uotsurijima, Minami-kojima, and Kita-kojima). The price presented by MLIT came to 2 billion yen, which was significantly higher than the 1.5 billion yen that Ishihara and the Tokyo Metropolitan Government had in mind. According to government officials, the "final price" that the government had come up with was based on a "special property valuation formula" that was used in assessing the value of new land created through reclamation for the construction of new airports.

If a purchase agreement were reached, normal procedures would have required the government to put a supplementary budget together providing for the 2 billion yen purchase price and get it passed by the Diet. This in turn would entail intense debate with the LDP that was hoping to return to power, and Noda would have been forced to cross swords with the opposition. This would certainly create an opening for Ishihara to regain lost ground. In the worst scenario, there was no guarantee that the landowner would not change his mind in the din of battle.

Noda was hemmed in. It was then that the Ministry of Finance had come forward with its "reward" to Noda, the former finance minister who had made the bold political decision to raise the consumption tax rate. According to a high ranking ministerial official familiar with the details of the case, the position of Vice Minister of Finance Katsu and the other top officials at the Finance Ministry was that they "were not giving the matter any special consideration." The Cabinet's (general purpose) contingency fund stands as a non-earmarked budget item that allows the government to cover emergency expenditures related to natural disaster relief and other unexpected events. The decision to draw on this reserve fund is a political one left solely to the discretion of the government in power. In this sense, the Finance Ministry was simply providing technical advice.

The fiscal 2012 general budget contained two non-earmarked contingency items. A total of 350 billion yen was allocated to the "general reserve fund." Another 900 billion yen was allocated to the "reserve fund for economic emergency response and regional revitalization." This second reserve item was designed to be used for stabilizing the economic environment in case of sudden adverse developments in the economy.

Be that as it may, the green light on accessing the Cabinet general reserve fund came as a great relief to Noda and his team, mired as they were in a war of nerves with Ishihara and the Tokyo Metropolitan Government. There is no doubt that the go-ahead to use the Cabinet contingency fund appeared as a "knight in shining armor." Upon receiving the good news, Noda had become even more convinced that, "We have to take the shortest possible route." This was a watershed moment, the moment in which an important step had been taken toward nationalizing the Senkaku Islands.

A Quiet Approach

It was June 5, four days since Nagashima and Nagahama had first told Governor Ishihara the government had started negotiating with the landowner. Noda called Chief Cabinet Secretary Fujimura Osamu and Nagashima to the Kantei. No one else was present as Noda reiterated his thoughts on the path to nationalizing the Senkaku Islands. He then issued an instruction. "I want you to run some simulations on what impact nationalization might have on our relations with China."

Acting on this instruction, Nagashima invited several top officers from the Chinese Embassy in Tokyo to a dinner meeting. He was hoping to get a feel for the Chinese thinking and to gather hints on how China would respond to nationalization. At the same time, he began quietly contacting Japan's leading Sinologists and national security experts. Among them was Kokubun Ryosei, National Defense Academy president and former Keio University professor. Nagashima actively briefed these experts and sounded them out on all possible scenarios and reactions if the national government purchased the Senkaku Islands. Nagashima was making his best effort to wrap his head around the implications of a purchase.

A wide range of simulations were undertaken to predict how China would react to the nationalization of the Senkaku Islands. The discussions pointed to a consensus on what constituted China's bottom line. "No matter what it takes, the Tokyo Metropolitan Government cannot be allowed to get its way on this." Japanese Embassy personnel in Beijing were similarly mobilized to support Foreign Minister Gemba Koichiro in a top-secret diplomatic effort to sound out the Chinese side. The feedback was basically the same as the expert opinions collected by Nagashima: "Ishihara would be a disaster."

China was quick to stop the export of rare metals to Japan in the wake of the 2010 incident in which a Chinese fishing boat rammed a Japan Coast Guard patrol ship. But that was not all. As described in an earlier chapter, China had resorted to the outrageous action of taking several employees of Fujita Corporation, a middle-echelon Japanese general contractor, into temporary custody. The string of China's radical responses eventually led to an outpouring of international criticism led by the United States. As criticism mounted, Professor Joseph Nye of Harvard University, well known in the United States and China as both a Japan expert as well as a China expert, commented that "China blew it" in its reaction.

At about the same time as Nagashima was meeting with his experts, Vice Minister of Foreign Affairs Sasae Kenichiro was meeting with his Chinese counterparts in a hotel on the banks of Lake Yamanaka in Yamanashi Prefecture. Sasae was one of the few people who had been read into the details of the Noda Cabinet's plan to nationalize the Senkaku Islands, and he was sitting across the table from Vice Minister of Foreign Affairs Zhang Zhijun. The Japan-China Strategic Dialogue was currently in its 13th round, following on the 12th round that had been held the previous December. According to official Japanese government announcements, the two vice ministers confirmed bilateral cooperation on problems related to North Korean nuclear and missile tests and discussed measures related to the prevention of maritime disputes in light of the 2010 collision involving a Chinese fishing boat off the coast of the Senkaku Islands.

In a related move, Zhang Zhijun met with Foreign Minister Gemba at the Ministry of Foreign Affairs in Tokyo. "When problems occur, it is important both sides respond calmly," Gemba is reported to have said in this meeting. Zhang responded somewhat cryptically, "We had an in-depth exchange of views." What did Zhang mean by an "in-depth exchange of views?" The reference was to the informal discussions that were carried out in "overtime" after the formal portions of the talks had ended. The fact was that the two sides had clashed bitterly over the Tokyo Metropolitan Government plan to purchase the Senkaku Islands.

A number of diplomatic sources, both Japanese and Chinese, have commented on what took place on the banks of Lake Yamanaka. After dinner, several people from both sides came together in a private setting. Alcohol flowed and suddenly the two sides were caught up in a strident debate. Perhaps the debate had been helped along by the drinks that had been imbibed. Zhang Zhijun spoke up strongly against Tokyo's plan to purchase the islands, saying that such an action had to be stopped because it would undermine the very foundation of Japan-China relations. Sasae and his cadre of Foreign Ministry officials responded with this straightforward question. "From an overall perspective, which do you think is more desirable: for Governor Ishihara to acquire the islands and do as he pleases [e.g., building a moorage or other facilities], or for the government to buy the islands and work toward maintaining peaceful and stable management? In your estimation, which would be better?" It is reported that the Japanese side went on to hint at the possibility of nationalization and to seek China's understanding.

The Noda Cabinet had by now settled on the basic position that it would maintain in the event of nationalization. "This is no more than a domestic transfer of title and has absolutely nothing to do with such diplomatic matters as sovereignty and territorial rights." Given the commitment to this basic position, there was significant risk associated with Japanese diplomatic personnel mentioning the Senkaku issue in talks with China. The fact that the exchange had taken place in an informal setting did not effectively reduce this risk. The Japanese position was that this was strictly a domestic matter involving the transfer of real estate title, but the fact that the Ministry of Foreign Affairs was explaining the matter to the Chinese side as an external matter was in itself a serious self-contradiction. What would have happened if the Chinese side had capitalized on this inconsistency? Japan's commitment to diplomatic accountability could well have collapsed.

However, as previously mentioned, no one knew at this point how the entire matter would be resolved. Even Prime Minister Noda was uncertain of the direction things would take and what the ultimate conclusion would be. How serious was Governor Ishihara about purchasing the islands? Would the landowner ever agree to sell to the national government? If Ishihara were to make the purchase, would he really construct a moorage or some other structure to underscore Japan's territorial claims? And if he did, would this throw Japan-China relations into unprecedented turmoil?

All of these questions remained unanswered. Nor was there any clarity on whether the plan being pushed forward was second worst or second best. Notwithstanding all this uncertainty, Japan's foreign policy officials provided the Chinese side with full explanations on the background to the nationalization of the Senkaku Islands and endeavored to convince their counterparts to accurately convey the Noda Cabinet's intent to the leadership in Beijing.

The Japanese side felt it was on very thin ice. Extreme caution was exercised in sounding the Chinese side out and in how the Japanese position was explained. But why this extreme caution? The answer can be found in how China had responded to Ishihara's announcement that he intended to purchase the Senkaku Islands. On that occasion, the Chinese side had almost instantly hardened its attitude.

"It is very important our core interests and matters of high concern be accorded proper respect." This is how Wen Jiabao broached the subject when he met with Prime Minister Noda in Beijing's Great Hall of the People on the evening of May 13, 2012. The statement was meant to deliver a strong warning to Japan for its treatment of the Senkaku Islands. Each word uttered by Wen Jiabao conveyed the extreme sense of dissatisfaction and vigilance that had emerged on the Chinese side since Governor Ishihara had announced, roughly a month earlier, that the Tokyo Metropolitan Government intended to purchase the Senkaku Islands.

Noda did not shy away from responding in kind. During the hour-long meeting, Noda emphasized that the Senkaku Islands "are the integral territory of Japan." But he did not stop there. China's heightened level of maritime activity around the Senkaku Islands and elsewhere have heightened Japanese feelings on this, Noda countered. Throughout the meeting, Noda showed that he was not going to back down and was prepared to give as good as he got.

The meeting followed an unusual format. The first portion featured a meeting of a select few, which was followed by a plenary session involving all the participants. Pointing to the first portion, Wen Jiabao emphasized, "In the smaller meeting, we engaged in a frank exchange of views on very important matters. The mutual trust between our two countries must be increased, and our bilateral relations should follow a sound and stable path of development." Noda responded, "It is undesirable for the overall framework of Japan-China relations to be affected by this problem." Thus, there were some indications of a willingness to narrow the distance between the two sides.

The May 13, 2012, meeting marked the first time the Japanese and

Chinese leaders had met since Ishihara announced his plan to purchase the Senkaku Islands. The atmosphere was unmistakably heavy and awkward. For example, the unthinkable occurred when the Japan-China-South Korea summit had to delay its joint declaration one day. What is more, the joint declaration completely left out all mention of the key topic of the summit meeting, which was the issue of North Korea, and what the three leaders had agreed to do to stop North Korea from further affronts, including nuclear weapons tests.

The summit was unusual in other ways as well. Chinese President Hu Jintao met alone with South Korea's President Lee Myung-bak, but his meeting with Noda at the Great Hall of the People became a "tripartite meeting" with President Lee also in attendance. Deputy Chief Cabinet Secretary Saito Tsuyoshi provided the following explanation on whether there was an exchange between Hu Jintao and Noda on bilateral matters. "There was some discussion on this. But it was difficult to schedule time just to discuss the bilateral relationship." The point being made was that the Japanese side had requested a one-on-one meeting with China but that the request had been rejected.

All of this culminated in what appeared to be the orchestrated coverage given to the meeting between Noda and Wen Jiabao in the Chinese media. China Central Television and the state-run Xinhua News Agency both reported that Wen Jiabao had referred to the Senkaku Islands problem in parallel to the Xinjiang Uyghur Autonomous Region, a region noted for its separatist and independence movement from China's central government, demanding that Japan "respect China's core interests and matters of high concern."

China's "core interests" were defined in a whitepaper entitled *China's Peaceful Development* published in September 2011. According to this document, China's core interests include national sovereignty, national security, territorial integrity, national unity, the general stability of the national political system and society, and the fundamental assurance of sustained economic and social development. These principles are interpreted by the United States, Japan, and others to essentially denote the "absolute rejection of independence for Taiwan, Tibet, and other regions." The Chinese stance prior to the statement attributed to Wen Jiabao was that the Senkaku Islands issue did not infringe upon China's core interests.

What the Chinese media reports did was to convey a highly nuanced message suggesting that what Wen Jiabao had said in his meeting with Noda established an "equivalency between the Senkaku Islands and China's core interests." In other words, the media had manipulated its reports to equate "matters of high concern" (Senkaku Islands) with "core interests" (Taiwan, Tibet, Uyghur, and other regions), which comprise the highest priority for the leadership of the Chinese Communist Party in safeguarding and perpetuating its political system. In doing so, the media had given the impression that territorial issues related to the Senkaku Islands had been elevated to the status of a "core interest."

Chief Cabinet Secretary Fujimura Osamu reacted to this immediately stating, "At no time during the meeting did Premier Wen Jiabao make any statement linking the Senkaku Islands to core interests." Made on the day following the meeting between Noda and Wen Jiabao, Fujimura's statement flatly refuted the "equivalency between the Senkaku Islands and China's core interests."

For China, "core interests" connotes the "absolute rejection of any form of compromise." The reason China had acted as if it were expanding this to include the Senkaku Islands was clear to all observers. This was obviously meant as a stern warning to the Noda Cabinet as it mulled its response to Governor Ishihara's plan to acquire the Senkaku Islands.

Noda himself has commented on the exchange with the Chinese side. "This would apply to Wen Jiabao as well, but [Foreign Minister] Yang Jiechi also voiced various complaints." This proved to be only the first salvo, as Yang Jiechi thereafter took every opportunity to harshly criticize Japanese government actions related to the Senkaku Islands.

During the 2008 Beijing Olympics, Hu Jintao had invited US President George W. Bush to view a basketball game. Also invited was former President George H. Bush ("papa Bush"), honorary chairman of the US Olympic team. Seated in the specially prepared room with the two Bushes was Yang Jiechi, an expert on US affairs known in both China and the United States as a diplomat with deep ties to the Bush family.

The ties between Yang Jiechi and the New England patrician family that gave birth to two presidents were nurtured by none other than Deng Xiaoping, who had left behind the legacy of shelving the question of the Senkaku Islands and arguing that the territorial dispute over the islands should be left in the hands of future generations.

Prior to the normalization of US-China relations, the elder Bush had served as director of the US Representative Office in Beijing for an entire year and had grown close to the supreme leader of China, Deng Xiaoping. After his defeat in the presidential election of 1992, Bush retired from public life. It was at this time that Deng Xiaoping extended an invitation to

Bush to visit China and chose as his interpreter a young diplomat who was still in his twenties. This interpreter was Yang Jiechi.

After this visit, Yang Jiechi quickly developed a close relationship with the Bush family. Yang Jiechi was not only born in the year of the tiger but his name also contained the Chinese character for tiger. For this reason, the Bush family referred to him familiarly as "Tiger." Asked about this, the former president is reported to have responded without hesitation, "Tiger is our good friend."

Thus Yang Jiechi, who now stood at the forefront of China's criticism of Japanese actions on the Senkaku issue, was not only the top America hand in China's Ministry of Foreign Affairs but also enjoyed close relations with the Bush family. It is very possible that this close friendship between Yang and the Bush family may have been a contributing factor in the misunderstandings and emotionally charged exchanges between Japan and China following the nationalization of the Senkaku Islands.

"Please consider very carefully what would ensue if the Senkaku Islands were to be acquired by the Tokyo Metropolitan Government." While analyzing the minutia of Chinese words and deeds, Sasae and other Japanese diplomats were making a desperate effort to win over Zhang Zhijun and other elite members of China's diplomatic corps. Ever since Noda had first asked his views on the nationalization of the Senkaku Islands, Sasae had repeated the same advice to Noda, Nagashima, and other members on the political side. "Let us please take a quiet approach."

Several former government officials have outlined what Sasae meant by a "quiet approach." The formula was to eschew all forms of boisterousness on the public stage while carefully observing and weighing until the last possible moment the advisability of nationalization, the actions and reactions of Governor Ishihara, and the actions and reactions of the Chinese side. Parallel to this, Sasae's quiet approach featured a matter-of-fact attitude in steadily moving ahead with preparations for nationalization. On a very basic level, this approach meshed well with Prime Minister Noda's thinking: "The best way forward was to steadily reinforce Japan's effective control by carefully and vigilantly adding to the list of *faits accomplis.*"

Be that as it may, it cannot be denied that Noda, Nagashima, and Sasae were indulging in a bit of wishful thinking of their own at this point. "Nationalization is preferable to acquisition by Governor Ishihara because the Chinese reaction will be muted." But this wishful thinking was not completely groundless. A number of Japanese government officials have all attested that Chinese diplomats had repeatedly given the impression that "ownership by the government is preferable to ownership by Ishihara" in behind-the-scenes meetings that were taking place at the time.

One top government official recounts that Sasae was not the only one who interpreted the Chinese position this way. Assistant Chief Cabinet Secretary Kawai Chikao, who had been seconded by the Foreign Ministry to the Cabinet Secretariat, agreed. "The Chinese side did not vehemently protest the idea of nationalization and seemed willing to accept it." The same government official theorizes that a combination of factors effectively swayed the Japanese diplomats in this direction. Primarily, China's formal and informal pronouncements had fostered a sense among the Japanese diplomats that China would find it easier to accept nationalization than to accept acquisition by the Tokyo Metropolitan Government, leading them to believe that nationalization was the winning strategy.

On the other hand, at this juncture, the Japanese side had no idea whatsoever of the thinking of the Zhongnanhai group that stood at the center of political power in China. In China, the Hu Jintao regime that had continued for a decade was drawing to a close and the transfer of power to a new administration to be led by Vice President Xi Jinping was already in the countdown stage. The two outgoing leaders, Hu Jintao and Wen Jiabao, were reputed to have taken a more "pro-Japan" stance than the previous leadership under Jiang Zemin, and had formulated the principle of "mutually beneficial relations based on common strategic interests" with Japan. For the two, the Senkaku issue had now become the greatest test of their Japan policies.

Taking all of this into consideration, it is highly unlikely that the Chinese side would be satisfied if the Japanese government simply prevented Governor Ishihara from acquiring the Senkaku Islands. Wanting no change in the status quo, which in this instance meant no nationalization, was a close second.

Employing the many channels that were available, the Japanese side continued its efforts to convey its message to the core of China's leadership. Armed with the argument that it was simply seeking to maintain peaceful and stable management, Japan hoped the Chinese leadership could be won over to the advisability of nationalization. Among the channels that were used were the standard diplomatic routes that Japan had with Vice Minister of Foreign Affairs Zhang Zhijun and State Councillor Dai Bingguo. Additionally, there were other channels and personal relationships that had been nurtured over the past 40 years of bilateral diplomatic relations. All were mobilized to send the same message. The crux of the Japan's message was that nationalization did not signify change but would, in fact, contribute to maintaining the status quo, and that nationalization was the only viable path to preserving the implicit understanding that had existed between the two countries since Deng Xiaoping had famously stated, "Let us leave it to future generations to resolve." Japan hoped that China's core political leadership would find this argument convincing.

The Niwa Statement

"If Mr. Ishihara's plans are acted upon, it will result in an extremely grave crisis in relations between Japan and China." This alarming prediction appeared in the June 7, 2012, issue of the *Financial Times* and was attributed to Japan's ambassador to China, Niwa Uichiro. Previously the chairman of Itochu Corporation, a leading general trading company, Niwa had been appointed ambassador by Prime Minister Hatoyama Yukio after the Democratic Party of Japan (DPJ) wrested power from the LDP. Niwa was to be a symbolic figure in the new administration's commitment to ending the bureaucracy's leadership position in the areas of foreign policy and national security.

Niwa was further quoted as clearly opposing Governor Ishihara's initiatives and saying, "We cannot allow decades of past effort to be brought to nothing." The interview with the *Financial Times* had been conducted at the Japanese Embassy in Beijing at the beginning of the month. Needless to say, the Niwa statement instantly raced through Beijing and Tokyo and triggered a tremendous uproar.

"Study your own country's position before opening your mouth. Otherwise, you are not qualified to serve as ambassador." This stinging remark was made by Governor Ishihara at his regular press conference on June 8. He then proceeded to dismiss Niwa in these words. "Whatever his other qualities, this man does not represent Japan in Beijing." On the same day, similar criticisms of Niwa were heard in the LDP's Foreign Affairs Division. "This sends the wrong message to China. For Niwa to be allowed to remain at his post as ambassador would imply that the Japanese government affirms this statement." (Onodera Itsunori, chairman of the Foreign Affairs Division and currently minister of defense) The majority of comments made at this meeting called for Niwa's immediate recall and replacement.

Chief Cabinet Secretary Fujimura tried to explain the situation on June 7 in his afternoon press conference. "This was a statement of the personal views held by Ambassador Niwa, and is by no means a statement of the government's position. It would be a mistake to view Ambassador Niwa's statement as being a government statement, and we have had the Foreign Ministry tell him to be more careful." Foreign Minister Gemba Koichiro warned Niwa in writing on the same day. Efforts to quell the storm continued on the following day with Gemba going out of his way to point out the error in Niwa's statement. "This question of whether or not to transfer ownership of the Senkaku Islands is a purely domestic question and is not an international issue. What the ambassador said clearly differs from the government's position."

Niwa responded to the warning letter from Gemba with a written apology. "I am terribly sorry for having caused trouble. I shall hereafter refrain from making such statements." With this apology in hand, the Noda Cabinet signaled its intention to close the case without taking any disciplinary action against Niwa. Gemba was quoted as saying, "At this point, we have accepted the apology." Noda himself clearly rejected the notion of replacing the ambassador in comments made before the House of Representatives Budget Committee on June 12. Noda started by admitting, "This was an inappropriate statement," but continued to say, "A warning has been issued in the name of the foreign minister, and he has expressed his deep contrition."

Nevertheless, the prevailing sense within government circles was that the Niwa statement had been a serious gaffe. The reason was that, by this time, Noda had already settled on nationalizing the Senkaku Islands and was actively negotiating with both the landowner and the Tokyo Metropolitan Government.

Although now burdened by an uncomfortable internal contradiction created by the totally unexpected Niwa statement, the Noda Cabinet continued to move forward to secretly weigh the possibility of purchasing the Senkaku Islands. Not being one to overlook an opportunity like this, Governor Ishihara went on the offensive.

His chance came on June 11 when he appeared before the House of Representatives Committee on Audit and Oversight of Administration at a time when demands for firing Niwa had not yet abated. His testimony before the committee on the issue of the acquisition the Senkaku Islands developed into a long-winded rant. "So here we are living in our precious homeland and [China] declares that it is going to break into our home and rob us. Where in the world can you find a country that would even fail to lock its door?" Standing on the national political stage for the first time since making his "buy" announcement in April, Ishihara was in his element.

His rapid-fire criticism continued. "Who is going to defend the Senkaku Islands in the present situation? Why have successive administrations totally ignored the will of the people? The root cause is the Ministry of Foreign Affairs. The government and the Diet have failed in their responsibility. I cannot contain my anger any longer." Ishihara then turned his attention to Niwa as a new line of attack against the Noda Cabinet. "There is no need to keep an ambassador who makes statements contradicting the government's position. He should be replaced without delay."

"Tell me, who is going to defend these islands? My choice would be for the government to do this. It does not make sense for Tokyo to take on this responsibility, but we are left with no choice."

Faced with Ishihara's unrelenting attack, Noda was forced into a defensive posture. Two days after Ishihara's testimony, Noda went before the House of Councilors Budget Committee. While rejecting demands that he replace the ambassador, Noda effectively criticized the ambassador's statement and offered an implicit apology. "No territorial issue exists, and therefore the Niwa statement was inappropriate. I am very sorry to have to say that the statement may have been contrary to our national interest." During the Budget Committee session the previous day (June 12), an opposition party member had bitterly criticized Niwa while alluding to his previous career at Itochu Corporation. "It is as though the ambassador is still working for his trading company and has totally ignored the national interest." This obviously had touched a nerve with Noda who seemed unable to control his ire as he got up to respond. "You are free to criticize Ambassador Niwa's statement and our stance. But if you are going to say he is treating this like his business, I demand you present clear proof of your allegation."

A week later on June 19, Noda formulated a formal response on Niwa for presentation in Diet debate and had the Cabinet approve it. The gist of the statement was, "He has expressed deep remorse and we are not at present considering taking such actions as have been suggested, such as recalling the ambassador or taking disciplinary action."

Roughly a month later, Foreign Minister Gemba summoned Ambassador Niwa back to Tokyo and issued this instruction in a meeting that lasted nearly an hour. "You are responsible for accurately conveying the thinking of the Japanese government to the Chinese side." After this meeting, Gemba explained why he had summoned the ambassador back to Japan. "In light of recent developments in Japan-China relations, I wanted to have him report on Chinese policies toward Japan." Gemba indicated that the meeting was held to exchange views on China's actions following the repeated incursions of Chinese fishing patrol vessels into Japan's territorial waters surrounding the Senkaku Islands a few days earlier. Asked about Niwa's posting, Gemba responded, "We did not discuss personnel matters," again rejecting the idea that Niwa should be replaced.

Noda assumed the whole affair had been put to rest by the Cabinet-approved position statement and Gemba's summoning the ambassador to Tokyo. But this did not completely silence the voices both inside and outside the government calling for Niwa to be fired as ambassador. Ultimately, Noda terminated Niwa's posting as part of a regular personnel reshuffling that had been scheduled for the summer of 2012. As his new ambassador to China, Noda turned to Nishimiya Shinichi, a career diplomat who was then serving as senior deputy minister for foreign affairs (economic affairs).

Nishimiya had previously served in the Japanese Embassy in China during the period of serious political tension and large-scale anti-Japanese demonstrations that followed Prime Minister Koizumi's 2005 visit to Yasukuni Shrine and was known as an all-purpose career diplomat who had contributed to improving Japan-China relations. But Nishimiya unexpectedly fell ill and died before assuming his post. Noda was now left with the task of replacing his replacement. After a feverish search, Noda tapped Kidera Masato as Japan's ambassador to China in September 2012. Kidera had just been appointed assistant chief cabinet secretary.

Additionally, Prime Minister Noda became importantly involved in a reshuffling of Foreign Ministry personnel that took place in the fall of 2012. By early September, the decision had been finalized to remove Sasae Kenichiro from his post as vice-minister of foreign affairs and to replace him with Assistant Chief Cabinet Secretary Kawai Chikao. Although Sasae was one of the two main pillars in the Noda team that was secretly moving forward on plans to nationalize the Senkaku Islands, he had always insisted on taking a cautious approach to the idea of nationalization. Thus plans had been made to send Sasae to replace Fujisaki Ichiro as ambassador to the United States, and it was assumed Sasae would be leaving for the United States shortly. Sasae would soon be vacating his seat on the Noda team and Kawai would be relieving him at the Foreign Ministry. Suspicion lingers that the timing of these moves was tied to the brisk pace at which the plan to nationalize the Senkaku Islands was moving toward Cabinet approval.

Plan Exposed

Having received the endorsement of the Ministry of Finance concerning the use of the Cabinet reserve fund, the Noda administration reached a decision on purchasing the Senkaku Islands on June 29, 2012. While the decision was a formal one, it remained unannounced.

"I suppose we have now completed the most difficult part of the process." Nagashima, Nagahama, and the others around Noda who had been conducting behind-the-scenes negotiations with Governor Ishihara and the landowning Kurihara family, let out a sigh of relief. But this proved premature as the Kantei was rocked by a piece of unexpected information. *Asahi Shimbun* had learned of the plan to nationalize the Senkaku Islands and was preparing to run this scoop.

The quiet approach preached so religiously by Vice-Minister of Foreign Affairs Sasae since the start of the project now stood in extreme danger. Stressing the need to avoid needlessly aggravating the Chinese side, Sasae had argued that all initiatives should be pursued in the dark and nothing should be allowed to get out in public. It was hoped that, executed properly, this quiet approach would produce a soft landing. All of the behind-the-scenes maneuvers related to the nationalization plan were now at risk of being exposed. This would undo the weeks of hard work that had gone into setting the stage for nationalization. But that was not the only risk. Exposure of the planning that had gone forward in secret would upset Ishihara and Kurihara, the owner of the Senkaku Islands, in the extreme, and it was impossible to predict what course events would take in the wake of this exposé.

Although the government recognized the threat, there were clear limits to what it could do to influence the *Asahi Shimbun* as a private media organization. Once Noda acquiesced to the realization that the *Asahi Shimbun* article could not be stopped, he acted preemptively and urgently on July 6, ordering Nagashima to contact Ishihara and inform him of the government's decision to nationalize the Senkaku Islands. The *Asahi Shimbun* published its scoop on the front page on July 7.

> The Noda administration has finalized its decision to nationalize the Senkaku Islands (Ishigaki City, Okinawa Prefecture) and informed Tokyo Governor Ishihara Shintaro on July 6 of its intention to purchase the islands. Top administration officials are in touch with the landowner and negotiations are moving forward toward finalizing the purchase. The administration hopes to complete the process

before the end of the year. China and Taiwan, which claim owner-ship of the islands, may step up their opposition.

The Noda administration is considering the purchase of the three islands of Uotsurijima, Minami-kojima, and Kita-kojima. Informal working-level talks have continued with the Tokyo Metropolitan Government. But top administration officials visited the Tokyo Met-ropolitan Government building on July 6 to inform Governor Ishi-hara that the government was considering nationalizing the three islands.

All three islands are uninhabited and are currently owned by a private individual. The islands constitute base points for defining Japan's exclusive economic zone (EEZ), and the Japanese government takes the position that these islands comprise the inherent territory of Japan from the perspective of both history and international law. (Prime Minister Noda Yoshihiko)

Noda responded to the *Asahi Shimbun* article the same day while visiting Iwaki City in Fukushima Prefecture. "From the perspective of peaceful and stable management of the islands, we will continue to comprehensively examine the situation while remaining in contact with the owner [of the islands]." In this way, Noda formally affirmed the nationalization policy. The prime minister also took the opportunity to reiterate the government's basic stance on the Senkaku Islands. "From the perspective of both history and international law, there is no doubt that the Senkaku Islands are an inherent territory of Japan. There exists no issue of territory or territorial sovereignty to be resolved concerning the Senakaku Islands." He then pro-ceeded to explicitly outline the government's position that nationalization was no more than a transfer of title undertaken in accord with the provi-sions of domestic laws.

Noda also touched on the fact that Ishihara had been in occasional con-tact with the landowner and had been moving forward with his own plans to buy the islands. "We need to understand the Tokyo Metropolitan Gov-ernment's plans. The owner probably has his own thoughts on the matter. Therefore, we are currently engaged in consultations on multiple levels." Here again, Noda stepped forward to affirm that the government was talking with both the Tokyo Metropolitan Government and the landowner.

Ishihara was quick to respond the same day. He started by explain-ing that Nagashima and others had visited the Tokyo Metropolitan Government on the 6th and had briefed him on the nationalization plan.

He then continued, "If Tokyo succeeds in purchasing the islands, we will hand them over to the government. They are, after all, a national government responsibility. Therefore I welcome their enthusiasm." Ishihara was now advocating a two-stage approach where the islands would initially be purchased by Tokyo and then transferred to the government at an opportune time.

On the surface, Ishihara continued to signal that he was not going to back off quietly. "This is all a lot of grandstanding for winning votes. The administration must be in real trouble if it is saying something like this now. I have been told by intermediaries that I should rest assured that the owner has no intention of selling to the government."

The government had intended to keep its movements hidden until the end, but all hopes of secrecy were dashed with the exposure of the plan to nationalize the islands. Foreign Minister Gemba Koichiro, who had been charged by the prime minister to head the diplomatic efforts, recalls the situation at the time, stating ruefully that it was "a miscalculation."

In reality, however, even more than Gemba and other government officials, it was Ishihara who was the most surprised by the revelation. On July 6, Nagashima had formally informed Ishihara of the government's plans to nationalize the Senkaku Islands. Ishihara had already been secretly informed of the possibility of nationalization by his close friend, Sonoda Hiroyuki, prior to that. But because he was convinced that "the government has no chance of purchasing the islands," Ishihara refused to take Sonoda's information seriously. Ishihara continued to be in denial to the very end. Yet when the information was formally conveyed to him by Nagashima and the article appeared on the *Asahi Shimbun* front page, Ishihara picked up the telephone to call Sonoda. "You were right all along. I want to thank you."

What Gemba called a miscalculation had totally exposed the secret project for nationalizing the islands. By revealing what had been going on behind the scenes, the *Asahi Shimbun* article had the potential to deal a fatal blow to the Noda Team, which was now in full panic mode. From the very start, both Noda and the foreign policy people led by Sasae had accepted the guiding principle of adopting a quiet approach to maintain peaceful and stable management. What the principle implied was that the status quo as it related to the Senkaku Islands would be preserved as much as possible. It was believed that a short and decisive battle was the key to realizing this objective, and Nagashima, Nagahama, and the other aides to the prime minister were in total agreement on doing everything in their power to avoid a long, drawn-out process.

The *Asahi Shimbun* report forced a fundamental rethinking of these principles and strategies. It was not long before voices began to be heard within the Noda team saying the quiet approach was no longer viable. But what was the alternative? What would happen if the government exercised the powers of state to expropriate the islands in a lightning strike? Considering that Japan had identified nationalization as merely a domestic transfer of title in explaining its position to China, it was highly probable that any such lightning move would invite severe pushback from China.

Ultimately, Sasae and his subordinates at the Foreign Ministry were drawn to a judgment that differed radically from their initial approach. "At this point, a loud and messy nationalization can no longer be avoided." This gradually became the prevailing view, and it was around this time that some foreign policy voices began to quietly suggest a two-stage solution as a real possibility. "Why not just allow the Tokyo government to purchase the islands first and turn them over to the government later? Wouldn't it be better to steer the whole thing in the direction of a two-stage process?"

These voices, however, carried no weight with the prime minister. As the supreme commander of the Senkaku nationalization project, Noda was day by day becoming increasingly convinced that it was "in the best interests of the nation for the government to acquire the Senkaku Islands." By now, the nationalization of the Senkaku Islands had enormous institutional inertia as a national project and was moving inexorably toward a tipping point where it would gain sufficient momentum as to be virtually unstoppable. Once it reached that point, no one would be able to resist it.

CHAPTER

4

The Summit Meeting

Japanese flags on the Uotsurijima lighthouse (August 19, 2012)
Kyodo

A single comment from Ishihara convinced Noda to nationalize the Senkaku Islands. What did Ishihara say and how did Noda respond at their midsummer summit meeting at the Kantei?

Meeting over a Glass of Water

August 2012, and Tokyo was suffering from a stifling heat wave. But the 19th was a rare day of rain that began to fall in the early morning hours. A summit meeting was scheduled for that evening. Prime Minister Noda Yoshihiko had invited Tokyo's Governor Ishihara Shintaro to a secret meeting to be held at the Kantei. It was already past 9 p.m. when the two men sat down to face each other across a large table covered with a plain white cloth. A glass of water had been placed in front of each. For all who had been called to the room, the stark and sterile setting only seemed to amplify the importance of what was about to transpire.

Needless to say, the direct meeting between Noda and Ishihara had been initiated by the Prime Minister's side. Initially, Noda had considered arranging a meeting between Ishihara and his own principal aide, Chief Cabinet Secretary Fujimura Osamu, and had instructed his personal aide, Nagashima Akihisa, to convey the proposal to Ishihara. Nagashima was a natural choice as he had been in close contact with the governor throughout this period. The negotiations with Kurihara Kunioki, who owned three of the five Senkaku Islands, were approaching denouement and Noda felt the situation called for a face-to-face meeting with Ishihara to bring some form of closure to the case.

But Ishihara had not been interested in meeting the Noda administration's second-in-command. The two sides went back and forth on the proposal, but Ishihara showed no sign of budging. Ishihara later described this exchange in a press conference on August 31 at the Tokyo Municipal Government Building. "Again and again they asked me to meet with the chief cabinet secretary. But what's the use of meeting someone like that? The whole affair would have become a game of charades."

Noda grew increasingly impatient with Ishihara's intransigence. Finally, he made up his mind and told Nagashima, "Forget it, I'll meet with him myself." At the same time, efforts were being made on Ishihara's side to convince him to agree to the meeting. Sonoda Hiroyuki, secretary general of the Sunrise Party of Japan, repeatedly contacted Ishihara to press him to show greater flexibility and accept the invitation.

"We have asked him to meet with Mr. Fujimura, but he just won't agree. We want the government to purchase the Senkaku Islands. So please see if you can convince Governor Ishihara to meet with us." Sonoda recalls that he was moved by Noda's fervor that came through clearly over the phone. Sonoda subsequently accepted the task of talking to Ishihara about the meeting. But Ishihara would not relent. Observing the utter confusion that had engulfed the Hatoyama Cabinet, the first Democratic Party of Japan (DPJ) administration, Ishihara had already made up his mind. "Talking with any DPJ administration is out of the question," he said. But Sonoda was not easily deterred. The relation between Sonoda and Noda went back to the days of the New Party Sakigake, and the two had nurtured a sense of mutual understanding. Sonoda pleaded with Ishihara, "You'll never know what they want to say unless you meet them."

Ishihara interrupted Sonoda. "The landowner has sworn that he will never sell to the government. For the sake of argument, let's say the government does acquire the islands. The question is whether the government is prepared to do what I think should be done and build a moorage and a lighthouse." In the end, however, Sonoda clinched the argument with his unconditional guarantee, "Noda knows what he is doing and you can rely on him." Ishihara finally nodded his consent.

The Noda-Ishihara summit meeting remained a secret for several days until Ishihara unexpectedly revealed what had happened during his regular press conference on August 24. "I expect an answer sooner or later, but I should say that I met with the prime minister and we talked for an hour and a half. We went face-to-face. The outcome of our discussions will probably become known today."

At his next regular press conference, on August 31, Ishihara went one step further and gave a detailed account of his exchange with the Noda administration. "Two weeks ago Sunday, I met with Prime Minister Noda. It was a secret meeting held at the Kantei. Before that, Diet member Sonoda Hiroyuki had relayed the prime minister's message to me. 'We are prepared to send Chief Cabinet Minister Fujimura to any place of your choice. So please agree to meet him.' I asked what this was all about, and they replied that it was about the Senkaku Islands. But what's the point of meeting with a useless dimwit like him? So I said I was prepared to meet directly with the prime minister. I asked Sonoda to make the arrangements and I told him that I wanted him to come with me as a witness. The meeting finally took place at the Kantei."

As Ishihara explained it, Sonoda was present at the secret summit meeting as an observer and witness. The two went back a long way. Some time after that fateful meeting, Sonoda would collaborate with Ishihara in establishing the Sunrise Party, which would ultimately merge with the Japan Restoration Party.

Sonoda had been a presence at every critical juncture in Ishihara's Senkaku related initiatives. This began with the autumn 2011 negotiations with the owner of the islands and continued through Ishihara's April 2012 announcement of his plan to purchase the Senkaku Islands. The meeting with Noda was no exception. Sonoda recalls his exchange with Ishihara. "He said he wanted me to be present at the meeting to avoid any misunderstanding [on what was said and what was not said]."

Ishihara's version of his meeting with Noda is as follows. As the two sat down, Ishihara broke the ice with the following statement. "Those islands have to be transferred as soon as possible from the individual who owns them to the Tokyo Metropolitan Government, or to some joint ownership scheme that would include Ishigaki City or Okinawa Prefecture. If possible, I would like to see the national government joining us in owning the islands. Ultimately, I want the government to take the initiative and accept responsibility for effectively administering the islands." Noda understood that Ishihara had come straight to the point without making any detours.

What Ishihara wanted to convey to Noda was that the Tokyo Metropolitan Government was prepared to bow out if the national government was willing to take certain measures to reinforce Japan's effective administration of the Senkaku Islands. One such action would be to construct a port of refuge or moorage. Ishihara went on to pledge his support for nationalization on the condition that Noda accepted this condition, and went as far as to say that the donations that had poured in to the Tokyo Metropolitan Government, amounting to about 1.45 billion yen, would be turned over to the government.

"What else is there to say when the government tells you that they want to purchase the islands? So this is what I said. Let's join forces and get this done. I will even hand over all the donations that we have received. In return, I proposed a single condition. It's the least they could do."

Ishihara made this statement at his August 31 press conference at the Tokyo Metropolitan Government Building. More than a week had passed since the meeting with Noda. Ishihara revealed that he had clearly offered to entrust the government with the donations that had been received.

However, Ishihara later came under pressure from his aides and was eventually forced to retract this offer.

"I am not asking the government to station Self-Defense Forces (SDF) personnel on the islands. What I want is really a bare minimum—something like building a moorage or erecting a radio relay station. If possible, I would really like to see the construction of a lighthouse or a manned meteorological station . . ."

Sitting across the table from the prime minister, Ishihara had gone on the offensive and tried to extract a commitment from Noda on reinforcing Japan's effective control of the Senkaku Islands. But the ploy did not work. According to the explanation that Ishihara gave at the press conference, Noda was not prepared to go any further than to say, "Let me think about it."

Sonoda, who was present at the meeting, has given the following description of what happened. "Ishihara suggested the construction of a number of things, such as a communications relay station, a lighthouse, and a moorage. Noda replied. 'A lighthouse might be possible, but a moorage is out of the question. That would devastate our relations with China.'" Sonoda spoke up in support of Ishihara. "From Ishihara's perspective, what he is putting on the table is a very moderate and reasonable proposal."

But Noda was adamant in his refusal. "We examined a number of options, including the possibility of building a lighthouse and a relay station. The conclusion was that building a moorage was impossible." It should be noted that the policy platform of the Sunrise Party—to which Sonoda belonged and for which Ishihara was an avid cheerleader—included a commitment to stationing SDF personnel on the Senkaku Islands.

"I wasn't asking him to build a harbor. All I was asking for was a moorage for the sake of fishermen. Just dig a hole that would serve as a moorage where someone could take refuge in a storm. The west side of Minami-kojima would be an excellent site. Just pile up some concrete dolosse and use that as a breakwater. I told him that was the least he could do, but all that he was prepared to say was, 'Let me think about it.'"

This was how Ishihara described his exchange with Noda in his regular press conference. According to Sonoda, Ishihara ended the meeting with Noda with this demand. "I will give you a week to think it over and come up with your answer." Sonoda had characterized this a "very moderate and reasonable proposal." Standing before the press, Ishihara provided some additional details on what he had said at the meeting. "Sonoda [who was present to the meeting] was really surprised and said to me. 'I thought you were going to demand SDF personnel be stationed on the islands.' So, I told him, 'I wasn't thinking of saying that. In fact, I never intended to say that.' That's what happened."

About a month before the secret meeting with the prime minister, Ishihara had proposed something quite different at his regular press conference on July 13. Referring to the Senkaku Islands, he said, "Send in the SDF. What we need to do is to permanently station Japanese people there for the purpose of performing some type of work. That is the stance we should take." That is, prior to the meeting with Noda, Ishihara had strongly hinted that he favored permanently stationing the SDF on the islands. Considering this earlier statement, it can be assumed that Ishihara had restrained himself in the meeting with Noda and avoided making radical demands in order to feign moderation. The fact that Ishihara went out of his way in his press conference to describe Sonoda's reaction can be seen as part of a ploy to emphasize his pose of moderation.

But there was something that Ishihara did not mention in any of his many press conferences. This was the "extremely important statement" that had been made during the Noda-Ishihara meeting, a statement that could well impact the fate of the nation or could at least be interpreted as such. The first to expose this extremely important statement was Maehara Seiji, who had enjoyed a close relationship with Sonoda since their days together in the New Party Sakigake. But now Maehara was a member of the ruling party, supporting Prime Minister Noda's DPJ administration, first as chairman of the party's Policy Research Council and later as minister of state for national policy.

"The prime minister [Noda] was astonished by what Ishihara had said and concluded the only way forward was for the national government to take ownership of the islands." Maehara's revelation came during an appearance on TV Asahi on October 12. He had exposed the core of the exchange between Noda and Ishihara, something that until then had remained safely hidden, but then went on to reveal that Ishihara had taken an extremely hardline position and had said something to the effect of, "If this means war with China, so be it." Maehara shared the view that this had so deeply shocked the prime minister that he decided to accelerate the pace of nationalization to preempt any untoward developments.

Maehara explained that his information came from someone who had been present at the meeting. Chief Cabinet Secretary Fujimura Osamu jumped to immediately counter this claim. Facing the press on the same day, Fujimura said this about the meeting between Noda and Ishihara. "No one was there other than the two principals. Therefore no one else can know what they said."

However, this was obviously incorrect and misleading. As already explained, Ishihara came to the meeting with Sonoda as his witness, and there is no doubt that that this witness was privy to all that was said that evening. Moreover, it was well known in political circles that Sonoda and Maehara had not allowed their close friendship to lapse since their days together at the New Party Sakigake.

Oddly enough, though, Maehara had learned of Ishihara's troubling statement from someone other than Sonoda. The source was none other than Noda himself. The prime minister had confided in Maehara, telling him Ishihara's stunning statement and soliciting his agreement and support for the political decision that he had made.

According to Maehara, he was called to the Kantei on the evening of September 4. This was a few days after Ishihara had exposed the details of his secret meeting with Noda. Arriving at the Kantei, Maehara was led to the same room where Noda had met with Ishihara and was treated to a detailed account of what had been said in the secret meeting.

While he had offered Ishihara no more than a glass of water, Noda now treated Maehara to a bento dinner prepared by Rokkatei, a confectionary maker in Obihiro, Hokkaido. As they dined, Noda shared the details of what Ishihara had said, went over the implications of Ishihara's "there is no reason to shy away from war with China," reviewed the attendant security risks, and concluded with an earnest argument for why it was imperative the government buy the Senkaku Islands. For someone who had himself argued in favor of nationalization, the logic that Noda presented sounded natural and easy to accept. Needless to say, Maehara was also taken aback by how Ishihara had described his position.

During his TV Asahi appearance, Maehara severely criticized Ishihara, commenting, "This problem would not exist if the Tokyo governor had not said these things. Tokyo does not command the Self-Defense Forces, so it's easy for him to mouth off and talk tough." But why had Maehara revealed what can be readily characterized as a highly confidential matter of government? Maehara has answered this question by claiming that the interviewer on the television program was convinced that Noda and Ishihara were co-conspirators in pushing for the nationalization of the Senkaku Islands—a theory that was steady gaining currency at the time (October 2012). Maehara explained that he revealed the details of the meeting between Noda and Ishihara because he feared the interviewer was trying to steer the discussion in that direction.

The theory that Noda and Ishihara were co-conspirators seemed plausible in light of the fact that the intermediary between the two sides was Nagashima, a close aide to Noda who was at the same time a long-time Ishihara confidante. Critics claimed that Noda and Ishihara were engaged in a fake and carefully choreographed political kabuki that would ultimately lead to the nationalization of the Senkaku Islands, and the idea that it was all a conspiracy was making the rounds and gaining traction. The Chinese media had lambasted Ishihara's behavior as rightwing political theater and some high-ranking government officials had repeated the banter. At the same time, the conspiracy theory was strangely appealing to some people in Japan. Deeply concerned at this phenomenon, Maehara had used television as his medium for sharing the story that he had heard from Noda.

After the DPJ came to power, Maehara met secretly with Ishihara on two occasions in his capacity as minister of land, infrastructure, transport and tourism (MLIT). These meetings were to discuss the joint military-civilian use of Yokota Air Base—the same subject that Ishihara had broached in his first meeting with Noda. According to Maehara, Ishihara had invited him to the Tokyo Metropolitan Government offices in the Prefectural Assembly Hall (where all 47 prefectures have liaison offices) just a few minutes from Liberal Democratic Party (LDP) headquarters. During the meeting, Ishihara had presented his case for joint military-civilian use of Yokota Air Base in great detail and sought Maehara's understanding and support.

"There was an older gentleman present who looked like an advisor to the governor, and this person showed me a map. Then, I was given a presentation on joint military-civilian use of the base. At the time, I was working on increasing the number of landings at Haneda [Tokyo International Airport], so I was not very interested in the topic and did not pay much attention."

This is how Maehara recalls the meeting. But there was something that lodged itself even more deeply in his memory, and that was the unrelenting criticism that Ishihara had heaped on the Ministry of Foreign Affairs. Ishihara expressed a deep-seated distrust of the Foreign Ministry and went so far as to name a high-ranking official in the North American Affairs Bureau to emphasize that he was "totally hopeless." This was the same sort of thing that Ishihara had said in his two meetings with Noda.

Ishihara's View of the United States

Returning to the conversation between Noda and Ishihara that took place at the Kantei, the question remains as to what words Ishihara actually used in conveying his message to Noda, a message that Maehara has paraphrased as "there is no reason to shy away from war with China." Drawing on the memories and testimonies of a number of people who were either at the meeting or privy to its details, the gist of what Ishihara conveyed to Noda can be recreated as follows.

"If building a moorage [to reinforce Japan's effective control of the Senkaku Islands] leads to war with China, so be it. As long as the war is fought with conventional weapons, Japan will win." At that moment, Noda heard his own voice mentally yelling. "You must be kidding! The governor of Tokyo is not the commander-in-chief of the Self-Defense Forces. You are encroaching on my responsibility and prerogative as prime minister."

In numerous press conferences held in the past, Ishihara had reiterated, "What is important is that you show that you are prepared to shed blood to defend your homeland." Perhaps the words he chose in his meeting with Noda were not significantly different. Whatever the exact words, there is little doubt that Ishihara managed to deeply shock Noda. As the person responsible for Japan's national security, the prime minister found that he could not overlook or forget the words that he had heard from Ishihara. The words had pierced his heart and continued to echo in his mind.

Nagashima has testified concerning this exchange between Noda and Ishihara. "In private meetings with his inner circle, Ishihara had been saying, 'If it means war with China, so be it. Territory comes before business or economic relations.' His thinking was that, 'Japan will win a war fought with conventional weapons.' He repeatedly referred to a scenario run by US experts that concluded that the SDF capabilities far exceeded those of the People's Liberation Army in terms of both naval and air power."

Deputy Chief Cabinet Secretary Nagahama Hiroyuki provides similar testimony from his one meeting with Ishihara at the Tokyo Metropolitan Government Building when he accompanied Nagashima. "When we went together. I heard him say the same kind of thing. At the time, I wondered if he was serious, but the situation was certainly not one where you would expect him to be joking."

Why was Ishihara constantly making these hardline statements in both public and private settings? One possibility is that he was channeling a concept that was being discussed by some national security experts based on simulations of dispatching an SDF mission to regain control of the Senkaku Islands. The simulation exercise that was being bandied about during this period had its origins in the following hypothetical scenario. How should Japan respond, experts were asking, if People's Liberation Army special forces disguised as fishermen were to land on the Senkaku Islands and stay put to claim territorial sovereignty? The basic concept of the SDF mission was that Japan would dispatch a force to regain control of the islands. The Japanese force would be organized around a core of Ground SDF personnel and would execute a surprise landing to quash the Chinese military presence and regain control of the islands.

On October 24, 2012, *Record China*, Japan's largest website dedicated to China-related information, quoted a report appearing in the *Peoples' Daily Online*, a website created by the *Peoples' Daily*, the official newspaper of the Chinese Communist Party. *Record China* prefaced its article saying, "Officials at China's Defense Department have commented on a simulation exercise that indicates that Japan would easily emerge the victor in a naval conflict with China over the Senkaku Islands." This was followed by the Chinese report.

Japan's Maritime SDF has been running simulations on the possible outcome of a military conflict with China over Diaoyutai [Senkaku Islands]. The studies predict that Japan will be able to repel two Chinese naval fleets with minimal losses to itself. Rightwing forces in Japan are jumping for joy. Chinese military experts have laughed this off, saying this is a Japanese pipe dream and a modern version of practicing swimming on dry land. Anyone with a modicum of common sense knows there is a huge difference between mock battles and real war. If China and Japan were to engage in a naval battle, could Japan really ignore the thought of Chinese missiles?

What did Japanese experts have to say about this? Former Lieutenant General Oriki Ryoichi, who rose to be the top uniformed officer as chairman of the Joint Chiefs of Staff at the Ministry of Defense and who later served as special advisor to Defense Minister Morimoto Satoshi, has said "The war games run by military professionals have nothing to do with winning or losing. There is a totally different dimension to these exercises." Having dispatched the report with a single stroke, Oriki fumes that this kind of thinking is "dangerous in the extreme."

According to Oriki, it simply would not be enough to regain control of the uninhabited Senkaku Islands. "It would be totally meaningless for the nation if it cannot ultimately win the war." Such an armed conflict would not end as a localized guerilla fight or a lightning war. Both sides would gather all their forces and closely examine how far to take the fight. In other words, the exercise of military force without first determining how far to take the fight and mustering the necessary national will is pure and simple an act of suicide. As a military professional, Oriki believed that the final arbiter of victory in war is the power of mass or material that a nation can mobilize. If the Chinese Navy and Japan's Maritime SDF were to confront each other over the Senkaku Islands and the East China Sea, the two sides would not be exempt from all the principles and forces that have governed warfare since the beginning of human history.

Mao Zedong, the founder of the Chinese Communist Party, has said this about the land battles that he engaged in with the Japanese Imperial Army.

Japan is today a leading power in the world, and its military might far exceeds ours. But there is something that China possesses and Japan lacks. That is the capacity to endure a long war, which is possible because of our country's vast size, our immense population, and the fact that right is on our side. Therefore, this war will go through three stages. In the first stage, Japan will advance deep into the Chinese heartland. But as a result, it will become bogged down economically. In the second stage, Japan will try to resist by establishing a puppet government. But it will become exhausted by our guerilla warfare. Finally, in the third stage, our side will have accumulated enough power to expel the Japanese, at which time the war will come to an end.

If the People's Liberation Army (PLA) were to fight a twenty-first century naval version of Mao's war of attrition, that would be a nightmare for Japan, Oriki says. He concludes his analysis by warning that it is absolutely imperative Japan not discuss the use of force and the question of winning or losing focusing on the Senkaku Islands as a localized issue and failing to fully examine the wider ramifications of armed conflict. This view is shared by every military professional associated with the SDF.

In addition to these common-sense issues of national security and the use of military force, there are other matters to consider. The logic of Ishihara's flagrantly irresponsible statement that Japan would win a war with China over the Senkaku Islands cannot escape a fatal internal contradiction. Under the Japan-US Security Treaty, Japan is the beneficiary of "extended deterrence," a seldom heard term that is commonly referred to as the nuclear umbrella that the United States holds over Japan. In arguing his position, Ishihara displays extreme distrust of the reliability and efficacy of this nuclear umbrella. Herein lies the obvious internal contradiction. Ishihara's book, *Shin darakuron* [New theory of decadence] (1991,

Shincho Shinsho), contains a chapter titled "The Choice of Nuclear Arma-
ment" which includes the following passage.

China, Russia, and North Korea are located in close proximity to
Japan. These are undemocratic, militaristic nations that are by no
means friendly toward Japan. Suppose the countries of Europe and
America were to be placed in the same political situation that Japan
finds itself in today. There is no doubt that they would opt for deterrence by creating and maintaining the capacity for nuclear retaliation.
    While we find ourselves in this setting, the United States has main-
tained its hegemonic interests by using the lie of an absolute guarantee of nuclear deterrence to force Japan to remain subservient to it.
Now, the United States is experiencing relative decline. However, we
have no intention whatsoever of looking to China for protection.
On the contrary, in order for us to be able to face China on an equal
footing, it is in Japan's best interests to clearly indicate an intent to
establish a defensive deterrent including nuclear arms.

It is well known that Ishihara has long argued that Japan must have its
own nuclear arsenal if it is to achieve true autonomy and independence.
The gist of his argument can be summarized as follows. The US nuclear
umbrella is unreliable. Therefore, Japan should have its own nuclear
umbrella and should open it wide for other countries to see. This will allow
the nation to shuck off its dependence on the United States and to build a
foundation on which it can stand independently on its own two feet.
    Shortly after this, the Japan Restoration Party was hurriedly established
with Ishihara as its co-representative in preparation for the general election
slated for the end of the year. During the election campaign, Ishihara presented his case in a speech at the Foreign Correspondent's Club of Japan.
"Japan should at least run some simulations on nuclear arms. That itself
would serve as a form of deterrence. The question of whether or not to
possess nuclear arms is a question that will come up after that."
    Having first qualified it as merely his "personal opinion," Ishihara went
on to outline his position. "In today's world, any country that does not
have nuclear weapons is very weak in terms of diplomacy. Without nuclear
weapons, you don't have anything more than a very feeble voice in the
world. It is because North Korea has a nuclear program that the United
States is on edge." Then he turned his attention to other neighbors. "Russia
stole our territory, but it has nuclear weapons. The Chinamen next door

have nuclear weapons and want to grab our territory. You can say Japan suffers a form of peace dementia." Concluding his remarks, Ishihara said, "On the issue of the Senkaku Islands, Japan has to be willing to shed its own blood. Without that level of commitment and determination, the United States won't come to our aid."

Ishihara had always argued that the United States offers its nuclear umbrella for the purpose of achieving hegemony, and that Japan could thus not depend on it. He also argued that Japan could beat China in a conventional war. But this obviously assumed that the US nuclear deterrence would deter China from resorting to the use of nuclear weapons in an armed confrontation with Japan. In other words, Ishihara's position on national security manifests a serious and extremely dangerous self-contradiction. As Ishihara tells it, the United States is "both a country that I love and a country that I hate." This love-hate relationship may be said to have nurtured in him a view of the United States that contains elements of an Oedipal complex, a motif that is perhaps evidenced in such words as, "Japan would win a conventional war."

It seems that Noda, the son of an SDF officer, reacted to this statement on a visceral level. As Noda sat across the table from Ishihara in the Kantei, these words seemed to wash over him in recurrent waves. Noda recalls the unspeakable sense of urgency that gripped him at that moment. "I thought the islands would have to be nationalized. Granted there were negatives to nationalization, I concluded that the changes that the Tokyo Metropolitan Government could make and his easy acceptance of the inevitability of war were detrimental to the nation's best interests."

Chief Cabinet Secretary Fujimura Osamu, the principal aide to the prime minister, was not present in the meeting with Ishihara. However, in strategy sessions convened before the meeting with Ishihara, the Kantei staff had formulated an extensive menu of proposals for convincing Ishihara not to move forward with his plan to acquire the islands. Fujimura recalls, "We were quite sure Ishihara would not take the bait if the bait were small."

According to Fujimura, several options were studied. These included some of the proposals that Ishihara had mentioned, such as the construction of a moorage or some other form of harbor facility, the construction of a new lighthouse, and the installation of improved communication relay stations. Among the various options considered, Fujimura felt the most realistic one would be the installation of LED lamps in the existing lighthouse and the addition of solar panels to power them.

Fujimura had good reason to think so. Once a year, the Japan Coast Guard was landing personnel on the islands to adjust and repair the lighthouse that had been erected by a rightwing organization. Needless to say, the Chinese side monitored these movements. Fujimura was worried that, at some point, the Chinese side would use these activities as an excuse for taking action.

Noda had Fujimura's extensive menu of proposals firmly in mind when he met with Ishihara. Once the meeting started, Noda proceeded to very cautiously explore what Ishihara had in mind. In the end, however, not only Noda but the entire Kantei staff were appalled by what Ishihara said that night.

Thinking back to his conversations with the prime minister, Fujimura has given the following explanation. "After the meeting with Ishihara, Prime Minister Noda told us what Ishihara had said. When I heard it, I thought to myself, 'This is pretty outrageous stuff.'" Ishihara himself revealed the gist of his exchange with Noda in his speech at the Foreign Correspondent's Club of Japan in downtown Tokyo on November 20, 2012. As previously mentioned, he was speaking as the co-representative of the newly formed Japan Restoration Party. Referring to what Maehara had reported, one of the correspondents asked, "Is it true that you said in your meeting with Prime Minister Noda that Japan should not shy away from war?"

Ishihara answered. "I was afraid that bad rumors like the one you have mentioned would come out of my conversation with Noda. So, what I did was to take a witness with me. This was Sonoda, an outstanding politician who also happens to be close to Noda. This is what Sonoda told me after the meeting. 'I was afraid you were going to say something like soldiers should be stationed on the islands.' All that I said was, 'Why not, as a bare minimum, build a moorage or lighthouses for small-scale fishermen? That isn't asking too much. Noda, you should be able to do that.' At no time did I mention anything about being prepared to go to war or stationing SDF personnel there. You can ask Mr. Sonoda if you like."

Sonoda, the witness that Ishihara brought along and who had firsthand knowledge of what was said, concurs with Ishihara's description. According to Sonoda, Ishihara did not say a word about not shying away from war or how Japan would win a conventional war in the meeting with Noda. "Noda said that if a moorage were to be built at Senkaku Islands, that would destroy our relations with China. Ishihara's thinking was that building something as minor as a moorage would not destroy our bilateral relations. With that thought in mind, he may have said something along the lines of 'If the relationship is going to collapse, so be it.' But I don't think that can be taken to mean anything like we should be prepared to go to war with China or Japan would win a conventional war."

Sonoda continues to unequivocally deny the affirmation of war that even today is frequently attributed to Ishihara. At the same time, however, Sonoda has admitted that Ishihara is given to routinely saying things like Japan could out-punch China in conventional war.

Sonoda has added to his description of the meeting with the prime minister. "I was in agreement with Ishihara. That is, I was also thinking that building something as inconsequential as a moorage would not lead to a clash between Japan and China. It was based on this thinking that Ishihara said something along the lines of 'If that's what happens, so be it.'"

Having first qualified his statement with, "I want to say this for Ishihara's sake," Sonoda continues with his testimony. "There are those who claim that Ishihara is to blame for causing turmoil in our relations with China. But don't forget that this whole affair started on the Chinese side and that fishing vessel collision." Sonoda made sure to vociferously reject the notion that Ishihara was responsible for the turmoil.

How did Nagahama, the person the prime minister selected to lead the secret negotiations with the owner of the Senkaku Islands, view the exchange? Nagahama starts by pointing to the undeniable difference in rank and weight between the prime minister of Japan and the governor of Tokyo, who is no more than a local government head. He then argues that, as the person solely responsible for ensuring national security, Noda had not misinterpreted the intent of Ishihara's language and was correct in arriving at the final decision that he made based on that interpretation.

"I had been appointed by the prime minister to negotiate with the land-owner. That was my role, and I was committed to excluding my personal views and feelings from the negotiations. However, my personal judgment as a politician who shares responsibility for ensuring Japan's peace and prosperity was that it would be better for Prime Minister Noda to national-ize the islands than to allow Governor Ishihara to purchase them."

Noda himself has remained mum on the details of Ishihara's problem-atic statement. Reflecting his sense of responsibility as a former prime min-ister, Noda has not gone beyond commenting, "I probably shouldn't be saying anything about this." On the other hand, Noda has strongly hinted that Ishihara's statements played a critical role in his decision to national-ize the Senkaku Islands. "There is no question but that part of our discus-sion was central to my decision."

While what actually happened in the meeting boils down to a he-said-he-said argument, there is little doubt that the meeting that lasted for about 90 minutes, most of which was given to discussion of the Senkaku Islands, ended in stalemate with both Noda and Ishihara refusing to budge an inch on the question of whether or not to construct a moorage and other facilities. At least, this is how Noda, the top leader of the Japanese government, assessed the outcome.

Seeing the direction the meeting was taking, Noda consciously switched to small talk mode during the last 30 minutes, and the three exchanged stories about Prime Minister Hosokawa Morihiro, who had gallantly came into office in the early 1990s heading a coalition that excluded the LDP, and his cabinet.

More than ten days after the summit meeting, Ishihara described what had happened in the days following the meeting in a press conference on August 31. "He said he would give me an answer within a week. But I received no word. Then they said they need a one-week extension. They are supposed to answer before the end of the day today. But I don't expect to hear anything. Can you believe this? The government can't even get something like this done. What are they afraid of? Here we have a government that can't even build a little moorage on Minami-kojima—the easiest place to build one—to protect the lives and interests of small-scale fishermen. This government is no longer worthy of the name of government. This is not a government of the Japanese people."

Ishihara reserved his most barbed sarcasm and scorn for Noda and his government after they apparently opted to remain silent. At the same time, Ishihara had not given up completely on receiving some sort of answer from Noda. "I am waiting with bated breath. I am hoping to receive a positive answer."

"I went in thinking he was a good-for-nothing. But contrary to my expectations, I found that he is quite a solid fellow." According to Sonoda who was present at the direct meeting between the two, this is how Ishihara assessed Noda Yoshihiko the politician after the 90 minutes they spent together. The assessment was to an extent positive. It would not be surprising if this change in attitude toward Noda had influenced Ishihara's words and kept him wavering between bitter criticism and high expectation.

It is ironic that, true to Ishihara's assessment of his character, Noda had already made his final decision by the end of the August 19 meeting, i.e., he had made up his mind to nationalize the Senkaku Islands. "During my conversation [with Ishihara], I realized that something like [building a moorage] could very well happen. That really heightened my sense of urgency. We have to act quickly, I concluded."

Noda has provided a very candid recounting of the tension and sense of crisis that prevailed. Noda had set the ball rolling in late April when he instructed Nagashima to meet with Ishihara. In private conversations with Nagashima that followed the first contact with Ishihara, Noda had admitted that nationalization by the central government was the logical thing to do. Then, throughout May, June, and July, Noda had instructed his staff to negotiate with the landowner and to sound out China and the United States. Throughout this entire period, Noda had continued to tell himself to be patient and to "monitor the situation until the last possible moment." But finally it was decision time, and Noda made the decision that the government would purchase the Senkaku Islands.

In the same press conference where he revealed his secret meeting with the prime minister, Ishihara boasted that he had proposed the central government and the Tokyo Municipal Government sign a not-so-secret agreement. "If the government's going to do it, let's do it. Let's do it together. I'll throw in all the money I've collected for this, and all I ask is that you meet my minimum request. It's the least you can do. Let's exchange written vows on this. I'll sign it with my own blood, and all you have to do is your thumbprint. A ceremonial memorandum of understanding, out in public for all the people to see."

However, Noda had no intention of accepting Ishihara's proposal. The two differed on whether or not to build a moorage or some type of harbor facility. But that was not the only difference that became apparent in the meeting. It would be no exaggeration to say that the meeting with Ishihara made it clear to Noda that there was a dramatic difference of opinion and an unbridgeable gap between them on how Japan as a nation should navigate the stormy seas of the twenty-first century. The difference in opinion underscored a serious divergence in their fundamental political philosophies, thinking, and positions.

Responsible for the nation's fate, Noda feared the collapse of Japan-China relations. Whatever Ishihara's true intentions might have been, it was this anxiety that drew Noda to interpret his words as saying "If this means war with China, so be it."

Ishihara revealed the details of the secret meeting with Noda in his August 31 press conference. Meeting the press on the same day, Chief Cabinet Secretary Fujimura responded to Ishihara's claim that the ball was now in the government's court. Fujimura took this opportunity to emphasize that the government was not going to respond to Ishihara's demands. "We have not received any formal proposal [from the Tokyo Metropolitan Government]."

Speech on Territorial Sovereignty

"It is extremely regrettable that there has been a series of incidents since the beginning of this month that pertain to territorial sovereignty. Such acts cannot be ignored. We shall approach the situation with calm determination, presence of mind, and indomitable resolve."

Thus declared Prime Minister Noda on August 24, 2012, five days after his meeting with Ishihara. The place was the Kantei press conference hall. This was a highly unusual press conference in that the nation's territorial sovereignty and territorial waters were the main subjects. Noda continued, "To protect our national interests, we shall assert whatever needs to be asserted and we shall steadfastly move forward on whatever needs to be moved forward on." Noda closed with defiant bravado. "I myself shall stand on the front lines in defending our territories and territorial waters by conveying our position to all, both in Japan and overseas."

The press conference was particularly notable for the hardline stance that Noda took on territorial issues related to Shimane Prefecture's island of Takeshima (Korean name: Dokdo). Noda pointed out, "South Korea claims that its effective control of Takeshima predates Japan's. However, their logic is very vague and there is no concrete evidence to back their claim." He then proceeded to state unequivocally that South Korea's effective control of Takeshima constituted "illegal occupation" of the island and adamantly declared in public that Takeshima was the inherent territory of Japan.

"There can be no constructive discussion if one side cannot move beyond unilaterally proclaiming its own justness. The right way to deal with this is to refer the matter to the International Court of Justice." Noda very clearly expressed a willingness to resolve the Takeshima problem by submitting it to the international community's judgment. Throughout the postwar period, Japan had given a degree of special consideration to South Korea. As part of this basic policy, Japan had maintained what has been called "compassionate diplomacy" in its interactions with South Korea. Noda's proposal for referring the Takeshima problem to the International Court of Justice for resolution was interpreted as signifying a fundamental change in this traditional stance.

What had pushed Noda to adopt this hardline position? Needless to say, the answer was the sudden and unexpected visit and landing of South Korean President Lee Myung-bak on Takeshima two weeks earlier. President Lee had flown to the island on August 10, flying by fixed-wing aircraft for the first leg of the trip and taking a helicopter for the remainder of the distance. This was the first time that any South Korean president had landed on Takeshima. Once on the island, Lee spoke forcefully before the police authorities stationed there. "There is absolutely no question that Dokdo belongs to us. It is so valuable that we must protect it with our lives. We must rigorously patrol the area to protect this environment." These words seemed to indicate that South Korea was prepared to implement additional measures to reinforce its effective control.

The Japanese government registered its protest the same day as Lee Myung-bak landed on Takeshima by temporarily recalling the Japanese ambassador to South Korea, Muto Masatoshi. As a further measure, Noda sent a personal letter to the government of South Korea expressing regret at the sudden landing. However, the South Korean side returned the letter to Japan unopened in what Foreign Minister Gemba Koichiro referred to as an "outrageous act." The content of the letter had appeared in the media on August 23, and the South Korean government reacted very strongly to the fact that the letter identified the island as "Shimane Prefecture's Takeshima." South Korea's Ministry of Foreign Affairs commented that this showed that "Japan wanted to use this occasion to identify Dokdo as a disputed territory."

South Korea attempted to return Noda's letter by having a staff member in its embassy in Tokyo deliver it to the Japanese Foreign Ministry. But the Foreign Ministry refused to make an appointment on the grounds that the "purpose of the visit was unclear" and did not allow the car from the South Korean embassy to enter the premises. Through this tit for tat, Japan ultimately refused to take the letter back.

Three days before Noda faced the press, Nagashima met with the prime minister to advise him to hold a press conference. As the prime minister's assistant in charge of foreign affairs and national security, Nagashima had long wanted to set the stage for Noda to deliver a foreign relations speech. He saw this as an opportunity for the prime minister to expound upon the basic principles of Japan's foreign relations and security policies in the twenty-first century. Nagashima had cherished this wish ever since Noda had taken office.

Contrary to Nagashima's hopes, the Noda Cabinet had become completely preoccupied with pressing domestic matters. The most important among these were raising the consumption tax rate, coping with the aftermath of the Great East Japan Earthquake, and the question of abandoning nuclear power generation following the accident at Tokyo Electric Power's Fukushima Dai-Ichi nuclear power plant. This left little time for an in-depth treatment of diplomatic and security issues. Moreover, public interest had inevitably become fixated on these urgent domestic problems.

Ironically, what changed the atmosphere was Ishihara's surprise announcement in Washington, DC, that the Tokyo Metropolitan Government intended to purchase the Senkaku Islands. Following Ishihara's announcement, Chinese naval ships suddenly became more active in the waters around the Senkaku Islands. The resulting sharp increase in bilateral tensions had the effect of drawing public attention to questions of territory and territorial waters.

"Let's hold a press conference." Noda and Nagashima wanted to deliver a broad-based appeal that highlighted the importance of defending the nation's territory and territorial waters from the dual perspective of both national security and economic policy. The two agreed that this should be done in the context of "Japan: a maritime nation," a concept that Noda had long advocated. Nagashima explains what he was thinking: "What I wanted to do was to go public with a well-balanced presentation that covered the Takeshima problem with South Korea, the Senkaku problem with China, and the Northern Territories problem with Russia."

Noda and Nagashima were also in agreement on another point. Both felt that in explaining what Nagashima has called the maritime nation vision, it would not be enough to call for maintaining the status quo in the Senkaku Islands as previous prime ministers had done. That kind of passive stance, they thought, would be unconvincing and insufficiently compelling. With this in mind, Nagashima was looking for a way to include the key message that nationalizing the Senkaku Islands is an unavoidable step that must be taken for the sake of Japan's national strategy in Noda's foreign relations speech

To Nagashima's suggestion that he hold a press conference, Noda responded, "Alright, we'll do it," and immediately instructed the foreign policy establishment to draft a speech that he would read at the beginning of the press conference. However, the draft that came back to him was focused almost exclusively on South Korea and Takeshima—an issue that had engaged the government in a war of nerves right up to that point.

One glance at the draft and Nagashima concluded, "This will never do!"

According to his rough estimate, nearly 80 percent of the first draft was given over to South Korea and Takeshima, less than 20 percent to China and the Senkaku Islands, and less than 10 percent to Russia and the Northern Territories. Nagashima immediately began to rewrite the speech to correct the weighting to 60 percent South Korea, 30 percent China, and 10 percent Russia.

Why did the foreign policy establishment allocate the bulk of the speech to South Korea, and why was the draft so sparse in its treatment of China? It seems this was rooted in what amounted to a form of "Korea fatigue" that was spreading throughout the Foreign Ministry, a phenomenon that had been stoked by one demand after another from South Korea. There were, for example, repeated loud demands for an apology for the comfort women history involving the Japanese Imperial Army, then President Lee Myung-bak's landing on Takeshima, and finally the reference to a visit to South Korea by the Emperor. Equally important was the quiet approach that had been advocated by Japan's top diplomat, Vice-Minister of Foreign Affairs Sasae Kenichiro. This quiet approach had fostered an unspoken understanding that it was best not to irritate China on the Senkaku problem.

According to media reports, there was a sense among top Foreign Ministry officials that "At least with China, we are still able to engage in calm diplomacy." This was borne out by the behind-the-scenes exchanges that were still going on between Japanese and Chinese diplomats at this time. On the Japanese side, the general consensus emerging from these exchanges was that China realized that nationalization by the Noda administration was preferable to the islands' acquisition by Ishihara and the Tokyo Metropolitan Government. "As reluctant as China may be, the groundwork is in place for them to accept nationalization." This wishful thinking had come to prevail on the Japanese side. With all these factors in play, it should come as no surprise that the draft delivered to the Kantei was primarily focused on South Korea.

Noda and Nagashima, however, had been developing a completely different perspective. Both were convinced that the Senkaku Islands could no longer be glossed over in discussing the nation's territorial issues. "There is no doubt that the Senkaku Islands are clearly an inherent territory of Japan, in light of historical facts and based upon international law. Indeed, the Senkaku Islands are now under the effective control of Japan."

Noda chose these words to express himself in the press conference on territorial sovereignty. He also announced that monitoring and information-gathering would be stepped up in the waters around the Senkaku

Islands, indicating that Japan would continue to respond calmly to the situation. But Noda says that in his heart he was thinking different thoughts and was already convinced that, "Given the current situation, it is imperative we nationalize the Senkaku Islands."

Noda explains that two factors had pushed him to arrive at this conclusion. The first, of course, was the meeting that he had had with Governor Ishihara. The second factor or set of factors related to the events that had occurred on the anniversary of the end of war (August 15) immediately before Noda's press conference. On this day, for the first time since the days of the Koizumi administration (March 2004), a group of Hong Kong activists forced their way onto the Senkaku Islands. The August 15, 2012, landing began to unfold at around 5:00 p.m. as a group of Hong Kong activists from the Action Committee for Defending the Diaoyu Islands, a Hong Kong based organization claiming territorial rights to the Senkaku Islands, approached Uotsurijima Island. When their protest vessel, the *No. 2 Qi Feng,* reached the shore, seven activists scampered up the rocks and landed on the island.

The Okinawa Prefectural Police and the 11th Regional Coast Guard arrested a total of 14 individuals on the spot, including the seven who had actually landed on the island. Immediately after their arrest for violating the Immigration Control and Refugee Recognition Act, the 14 activists were transferred to the Okinawa mainland.

"This is extremely regrettable in light of the fact that they were given repeated warnings." As stated by Chief Cabinet Secretary Fujimura in his press conference the same day, the landing by this opposition group on the 67th anniversary of the end of the war deeply shocked Noda and many other Japanese government people.

The Japanese side had made detailed plans to prevent such landings by activist groups, and the ministries and agencies concerned had been consulted on formulating effective measures. In addition to these preventive measures, 20 minutes before the protest vessel arrived, nearly 30 people from the Japan Coast Guard, Okinawa Prefectural Police, and Immigration Office landed on Uotsurijima as a second line of defense. This reflected the many lessons that had been learned from the 2010 collision involving a Chinese fishing vessel. Notwithstanding these measures, the Japanese side was ultimately unable to keep the activists from landing.

The Coast Guard had been preparing for the protest vessel's arrival since confirming its departure from Hong Kong. As the *No. 2 Qi Feng* approached the waters near the Senkaku Islands, the Coast Guard warned it not to enter Japan's territorial waters. Next, Coast Guard patrol boats blocked the protest vessel and used water cannons to deter it. However, the protest vessel broke through these obstructions and entered Japan's territorial waters.

But the activists had another surprise for the Japanese government officials. As they neared the island, the activists did not deploy a rubber dinghy as they had done before. This time, they resorted to the highly risky maneuver of simply crashing their vessel on the rocks that marked the shoreline. At the time of landing, the waves were some two meters high, leading the Coast Guard to think that landing would be very difficult. But contrary to expectations, the activists accepted the risk of running aground or sinking by ramming their vessel against the rocks. The Japanese side could not hide its astonishment.

"The Senkaku Islands are the territory of Japan. These culprits should be arrested and put on trial." Thus spoke Ishihara to a group of journalists who had congregated in front of his home that night. After demanding that the activists be punished to the full extent of the law, Ishihara started sarcastically criticizing the clumsiness of the Noda administration. "The prime minister himself should go to the Senkaku Islands. He put his life on the line to raise the consumption tax rate. Why not put his life on the line for the Senkaku Islands as well?"

At about the same time, Noda was sitting alone in the Kantei overcome with a sense of crisis and extreme frustration. How was it possible that the activists had landed on the island despite the multiple lines of defense that had been put in place? "I thought we had learned our lessons and made every necessary preparation. On the other hand, the Chinese side was not able to control the activists, either. This is probably not the last time this sort of thing is going to happen." Recalling his state of mind on that lonely evening, Noda has made the following confession. "As hard as they may try, there are obvious limits to what the Coast Guard can do—especially if China puts its mind to it."

Immediately after the incident became news, Noda was asked how the government planned to handle the case, to which he answered on the evening of August 15, "We will deal with the case rigorously and in accordance with laws and regulations." Some of the arrested activists had initially denied the charges, arguing that the arrests were groundless because the island is the sovereign territory of China. The legal process had been put in the hands of the Okinawa Prefectural Police, which quickly transferred the 14 arrestees to the Naha District Immigration Office of the Fukuoka Regional Immigration Bureau. Once there, the Immigration Office made a determination of illegal landing and illegal entry and issued deportation orders. It is notable that none of the arrestees protested when presented with their deportation orders.

Noda had learned the lessons of the 2010 collision incident that had occurred under the Kan administration and followed the same procedures that had been taken by the Koizumi administration in 2004. The activists were arrested on the spot for violating the Immigration Control Act and forcibly deported to Hong Kong two days later, thus achieving a quick resolution.

Ahead of this action, the decision to deport all 14 activists was confirmed in a meeting of the cabinet ministers concerned. Noda was feeling increasingly certain that the war of nerves with China over the Senkaku Islands would continue and that its gradual escalation was virtually unavoidable. By this time, Noda was sensing that one false move on the Senkaku Islands could quickly develop into a major incident that would overturn the very foundation of Japan-China relations. For Noda, this grim prospect was rapidly mutating from a premonition to a firm conviction.

"Governor Ishihara says that he wants a moorage. But consider what would happen in a typhoon. On humanitarian grounds, we would have to accept Chinese, Taiwanese, and Hong Kong fishermen as well as Japanese fishermen. So it could actually have the perverse effect of inviting such people to the islands."

As prime minister, Noda was ultimately responsible for the nation's crisis management, and it was from this bird's-eye perspective that he had come to this conclusion. That said, the problem still remained of how to deal with the oft-repeated request by Kurihara that Ishihara not be made to lose face. Indeed, Kurihara had seemed to imply that construction of a moorage was a precondition for the sale of the islands to the government. However, Nagahama, who had been charged by Noda to negotiate with Kurihara, concurred with Noda's final judgment. "The waters around the Senkaku Islands are teaming with Chinese and Taiwanese fishing vessels. During a typhoon, they would have to be allowed to use any moorage we might build there. This is a basic question of respect for human life and equal and humanitarian treatment. But suppose there is ulterior intent on the other side. What would happen if these ships refused to leave after taking refuge? This possibility cannot be ignored."

The government was busily engaged in negotiating and exchanging views with the Tokyo Metropolitan Government, the landowner, and the Chinese government. However, there was nothing to be gained and much to be lost from prolonging this process. Once he realized the risks of pro-longing the negotiations, it did not take long for Noda to come to a simple conclusion. "It is better for the government to place the islands under its own effective control. The situation has to be stabilized. The sooner the better."

Between a Rock and a Hard Place

"We are seriously concerned with the issue of the Senkaku Islands as it impacts Japan-China relations. I would like to have your thoughts on how you expect this to play out." High-ranking US government officials visiting Japan frequently stay at the Hotel Okura located near the US Embassy and the ambassador's residence. One such visitor staying at the hotel on July 8, 2012, was Kurt Campbell, assistant secretary of state for East Asian and Pacific affairs. In his position, Campbell was responsible for the Obama administration's Japan and Asian policies. On this day, Campbell sat in the living room area of his hotel suite, flanked by a number of secretaries and note takers.

By this time, the Senkaku Islands and the build-up of tension in Japan-China relations were well known worldwide. The situation had drawn the attention of the international media, national leaders, and policy mak-ers everywhere. The country exhibiting the most serious concern was the United States, Japan's principal ally. In the State Department, Campbell was responsible for US Japan policy, and now he was in Tokyo asking Nagashima, his old friend and an assistant to Prime Minister Noda, for a detailed exposition of the Japanese position.

Sitting in Campbell's hotel suite and speaking as the prime minister's special advisor, Nagashima outlined the plan to nationalize the Senkaku Islands. This was the first time that the Japanese government was present-ing its position and plans to the United States. Nagashima explained that Ishihara would move to construct various facilities, such as a moorage and lighthouses if the Tokyo Municipal Government were allowed to acquire the islands, and that this could draw a very strong reaction from China for having "effected a change in the status quo." Then he argued that, to prevent this outcome, it was deemed best for the government to purchase the islands with public funds and to work to maintain peaceful and stable administration of the islands.

Nagashima's explanation had more or less become the official line by now. However, as Nagashima elucidated the Japanese position, Campbell interrupted him again and again with the question, "Is this really necessary?" According to what Nagashima recalls from the meeting, Campbell expressed understanding but repeatedly emphasized that the Chinese reaction to nationalization is sure to be extraordinary and unpredictable. To this, Campbell added an ominous request. "We very much hope the Japanese government will exercise extreme prudence in this matter."

As previously mentioned, the Chinese side was wedded to the idea that Noda and Ishihara were working hand-in-glove in a secret arrangement aimed at unilaterally altering the status quo in the Senkaku Islands. China was now actively spreading rumors of this "national conspiracy" in the international community. It was clear that Campbell did not believe the rumors coming out of China. However, the conversations that Nagashima and other Japanese officials had with Campbell on the Senkaku Islands always seemed to be marred by a "basso continuo." Although it was never explicitly acknowledged, there was no doubt in anyone's mind that the source of this "basso continuo" was the American distrust of and dissatisfaction with Japan.

"I believe he understood and accepted that Japan had no intention of acting to alter the status quo. But he appeared to be very anxious about the prospect that the US could be drawn into the Senkaku turmoil." Nagashima let out a long sigh as he described his conversation with Campbell. The testimony of Fujisaki Ichiro, the Japanese ambassador to the United States, who was in regular contact with Campbell during this time, substantiates Nagashima's telling. "During the early stages, in certain areas [the Obama administration] seemed to exhibit a degree of understanding and sympathy for the arguments made by China."

Fujisaki recalls how he explained the Japanese position in the series of meetings that he had with Campbell and others. "The whole problem started in 2010 when the Chinese fishing boat rammed the Japanese Coast Guard patrol ship. By no means did Japan throw the first punch."

While expressing a certain level of understanding for the explanations provided by Nagashima and Fujisaki, Campbell used back channels to contact American affairs experts in Japan to convey his deep-seated concerns. At times, Campbell conveyed his concerns very directly, and at other times he chose to be more indirect.

One expert whom Campbell contacted describes the concerns that Campbell expressed to him. "I sensed he was trying to say he appreciated the logic behind nationalizing the Senkaku Islands, but Japan needed to realize that China has no intention of abiding by the rules of the international order. He was warning that Japan should be aware of what kind of country it is dealing with."

Campbell himself has confessed that, within the Obama administration, the overall attitude toward nationalizing the Senkaku Island was initially "negative." Still, he added, "Of course we stood with Japan as our ally and never sided with what China was saying."

Campbell explains the Obama administration position. "It is true we made some suggestions to Japan and asked if there was some way Japan could avoid giving China the impression of a change in the status quo. What we were saying is, "Why don't you consider some alternatives?" According to Campbell, the Japanese Embassy in Washington and the Ministry of Foreign Affairs were regularly briefing the American side on developments in the Noda administration during this period. These exchanges took place behind the scenes and on an informal basis.

"What we were hearing [about the nationalization of the Senkaku Islands] was that nationalization was a possibility or that Japan might nationalize the islands. Later it became very clear to us that this was indeed the direction Japan was going to take." Campbell had joined the State Department reporting directly to Secretary of State Hillary Clinton. According to Campbell, he was advising Clinton almost daily on Asian affairs and policies. This naturally included the question of the nationalization of the Senkaku Islands.

Campbell says the Obama administration was trying to convey to both Japan and China a clear message that consisted of three distinct points. First, the United States would not take sides on matters of sovereignty and occupation of territories. Second, it was the position of the United States that during the transitional period of 1972, when the United States and China moved rapidly toward reconciliation and normalization of their relations, the right of administration [of the Senkaku Islands] had been assigned to Japan [through the tacit understanding proposed by Deng Xiaoping and others to leave the matter to future generations]. Third, the United States recognized that the Senkaku Islands continued to be under Japanese administration.

During June and July, Campbell took time to explain the complex historical background of the Senkaku Islands to Clinton and carefully outline the diametrically opposing positions of the two countries that brought them into direct conflict. At the same time, Campbell was gradually expanding the circle of people with whom he was sharing this information. He started with people at the State Department, such as Jake Sullivan, Clinton's deputy chief of staff, and Denis McDonough, deputy national security advisor to the president. From there, he further expanded the circle to include Tom

Donilon, national security advisor to the president, and other members of the Obama team in the White House. Campbell led the discussions in the US government on how China might react to the nationalization of the Senkaku Islands and describes the atmosphere that prevailed in these discussions as follows. "Everyone, including those at the top levels of the Obama administration, expressed concern."

Though Campbell's responsibilities as assistant secretary of state covered both Japan and China, he had considerably more policy experience with Japan. Nevertheless, Campbell had time and again encountered the uncompromising and inflexible positions taken by China on matters related to such "core interests" as Taiwan and Tibet. After taking part in extensive negotiations with China on such matters as the visit of the Dalai Lama, the Tibetan religious leader, to the United States, and arms sales to Taiwan, Campbell had concluded that considerable time would be needed to complete China's transformation into a responsible stakeholder. These experiences also affected how Campbell interacted with Japanese American affairs experts he had known for years, and he made no attempt to hide the irritation and frustration that he felt regarding Japan's position on the nationalization of the Senkaku Islands.

There was one more factor that may have pushed Campbell in this direction. A pall of perennial tension had descended upon Japan-US relations after 2009 when the reins of political power in Japan were placed in the hands of the DPJ and its three consecutive administrations. The trouble began with Prime Minister Hatoyama Yukio and issues related to US forces in Okinawa and the relocation of the Futenma Air Base and continued with Prime Minister Kan Naoto and the turmoil associated with the Great East Japan Earthquake and the accident at Tokyo Electric Power's Fukushima Dai-Ichi Nuclear Power Plant. Now under Japan's third DPJ administration, headed by Noda, Japan's relations with China were deteriorating due to the pending nationalization of the Senkaku Islands, and relations with South Korea were also suffering. As the Obama administration's leading expert on Japan, it would be no surprise if Campbell had found these developments personally embarrassing and deeply frustrating.

In the 2008 presidential election, Campbell had joined Senator Clinton's campaign at a very early stage. Consequently, there was initially a tendency in the Obama administration, to treat Campbell as somewhat of an outsider. Upon taking office, President Obama had brought together an Asian policy "iron triangle" which included Campbell as the Japan expert. The other two members of the triangle were former career diplomat Jeffrey

Bader (senior director for Asian affairs on the National Security Council), an expert on Chinese affairs, and Jim Steinberg (deputy secretary of state) who had honed his skills as a strategist in the Rand Corporation. These other two were arguably closer to Obama than Campbell was.

To overcome this handicap and to raise his standing in the administration and within the Democratic Party, Campbell had to leverage his strength as a Japan expert. But events in Japan conspired against him. Shortly after the inauguration of the Obama administration, the Hatoyama Cabinet came into office as the first administration led by the DPJ. Almost immediately, an awkward atmosphere set in between the two new administrations. Far from letting this slow him down. Campbell worked full-out to strengthen the Japan-US alliance.

"We are all old friends going back a decade or more. This is the best team imaginable." On July 18, 2009, Campbell was in Tokyo for the Japan-US Security Sub-Committee (SSC) meeting, the first to be held in Tokyo in nine years. As the participants seated themselves, Campbell found himself surrounded by "old friends," an expression that seemed to reflect his confidence that the two sides would be able to make smooth progress on strengthening the bilateral alliance. Present at the meeting from the Japanese side were Umemoto Kazuyoshi, director of the Ministry of Foreign Affairs North American Affairs Bureau, and Takamizawa Nobushige, director general of the Bureau of Defense Policy. On the US side sat Wallace Gregson, assistant secretary of defense. Campbell had worked with Umemoto and Takamizawa since the mid-1990s, and the group had met on multiple occasions during the Clinton administration to discuss US forces in Okinawa and the relocation of the Futenma Air Base. This gathering of old friends presumably had all of the bases covered, or so Campbell thought. In the pre-Obama days, the Japan-US alliance had been bolstered by the personal relationship between Prime Minister Koizumi and President Bush. Campbell had called this an "inverted V-shaped" alliance. Prior to this and particularly during the Cold War, the Japan-US alliance was "V-shaped," a reference to the fact that the alliance rested primarily on the shoulders of sub-cabinet officers from the two sides—the Department of Defense for the United States and the Ministry of Foreign Affairs for Japan. Comparing the two patterns, Campbell had concluded that the advantage of the "inverted V" lay in its faster decision-making made possible by its top-down design and emphasis on political leadership.

However, an "inverted V" alliance contains a fatal flaw. Its success requires both leaders to have a strong political base at home and demands that they get along well on a personal level. In the absence of these pre-requisites, an "inverted V" alliance can instantly fall dysfunctional. When Hatoyama came to power as the first prime minister from the DPJ, he assumed the reins of government with all the excitement of having wrested it away from those who had monopolized it for decades. Perhaps this excitement was partly to blame, but Hatoyama wasted no time in publicly stating in China that, "In the past, Japan was too dependent on the United States," and then proceeding to promote the idea of an East Asian Community that did not include the United States. Naturally, there was absolutely no positive chemistry between Hatoyama and Obama. As Campbell had feared and predicted, in the blink of an eye, the Japan-US alliance began to sink to its lowest level in the postwar period.

Campbell acted to forestall the collapse and reinforce the alliance. First, he worked to revitalize the SSC process under the Hatoyama Cabinet. Next, he launched a new sub-cabinet level meeting designed to discuss the US nuclear umbrella, whose reliability was being called into question by Japan as North Korea continued to push its nuclear development program forward.

But Campbell's hopes for an alliance shouldered on the sub-cabinet level were dashed by the Hatoyama Cabinet's commitment to disempow-ering the bureaucracy, a key feature of the political platform that had car-ried Hatoyama and his party to power. It is not difficult to see how these developments might have further diminished Campbell's standing in the Obama administration.

"I am sure there were people in the US Navy, the Pacific Command, and the Pentagon who were paying attention to the military implications of the Senkaku situation. On the other hand, I didn't see anyone except Kurt Campbell doing anything to speak of on the political side."

Thus did Michael Green describe how the Obama administration was handling the Senkaku issue. Green was a trusted confidante on Japan-re-lated policies who worked well with Campbell even though they came from the opposite side of the political aisle. According to Campbell him-self, a number of high-ranking officials in the Obama administration had expressed concern over the Senkaku Islands. However, Campbell was the only high-ranking official in the Obama administration engaged in com-prehensively examining the Senkakus' ramifications for the Japan-US alli-ance and the various problems that could arise.

Resigned to the prospect of a lone struggle, Campbell did everything in his power to stem the deterioration in the alliance, in some instances with the support and assistance of the Republican doyen of Japan experts,

Richard Armitage. A good example of this can be found in the developments that followed the summer of 2010 collision involving a Chinese fishing vessel and a Japan Coast Guard patrol ship. As discussed in a previous
chapter, Armitage had warned Chief Cabinet Secretary Sengoku Yoshito
that, "China is testing Japan." The Obama administration had formulated
specific policies for assuring Japan that the "Senkaku Islands fall within the
scope of the US-Japan Treaty" by picking up on the thinking that Armitage
had expressed.

The United States Playbook
"The Senkaku Islands clearly fall within the scope of the US-Japan Treaty."
These words of assurance were spoken by Secretary of State Hillary Clinton
in September 2010. The occasion was her meeting in New York with Maehara Seiji, the newly appointed foreign minister in the Kan Cabinet. This
marked the first time that a senior official in the Obama administration
had unequivocally conveyed to the Japanese side that the Senkaku Islands
came within the scope of the defense of Japan. Standing behind this statement was Campbell, Clinton's trusted advisor on Asian policies. By this
time, China was fully engaged in various forms of diplomatic harassment
related to territorial rights over the Senkaku Islands. With this in mind,
Maehara jumped to the occasion and immediately responded, "We are
in total agreement." He appeared to exude confidence in the future of
Japan-US cooperation.

Thus the US government had stated that the Senkaku Islands "fall
within the scope" of Article V of the US-Japan Security Treaty. This position harked back to the Clinton administration in the 1990s and a statement that had been made by former Vice President Walter Mondale, who
was then serving as US ambassador to Japan: "The United States will not
defend the Senkaku Islands if it comes under attack from a foreign country." To put the Mondale statement in context, then-Deputy Assistant Secretary of Defense Campbell had formulated a document that now provided
the basis for Secretary Clinton's assurances.

With the wording of Article V in mind, Campbell crafted the following
interpretation. In case of an "armed attack against either Party in the territories under the administration of Japan [e.g., the Senkaku Islands], each
Party . . . declares that it would act to meet the common danger." What
Clinton had done in her meeting with Maehara was to restate this interpretation in simple terms, which was to say that the "Senkaku Islands fall
within the scope of Japan-US Security Treaty."

Taking this at face value, the statement can be interpreted to mean that the United States would automatically come to Japan's assistance in case of a conflict between Japan and China over the Senkaku Islands. On the other hand, as reflected in a statement attributed to Michael Green, former special assistant to the president, the mental landscape that prevails on the American side is not necessarily that simple. "In principle, the United States will remain neutral and will not intervene in a territorial dispute, even if this involves an ally."

As previously noted, Campbell's interpretation that "Senkaku Islands fall within the scope of Article V of the Security Treaty" traces back to the Mondale statement, which in turn traces back to Green's principle of non-intervention in territorial disputes. Perhaps overly eager to emphasis this principle of non-intervention, Mondale had put a highly ambiguous and questionable statement on record, which prompted Campbell to step in with an interpretation that would close the critical gaps in the ambassador's wording. It should be noted that Ishihara Shintaro, who would later become governor of Tokyo, was a vociferous critic of Mondale's ill-advised statement.

According to Green and other Japan experts, the question of whether or not the United States would actually invoke the provisions of the Security Treaty in the Senkaku Islands depends on which side throws the first punch. In other words, if the United States judges that Japan was the first to fire, it would weigh its alliance with Japan against the importance of its relations with China as relations between superpowers. In this case, the United States would not necessarily throw its full approval and support to Japan. This is why Ambassador Fujisaki had emphasized in his conversations with Campbell that, "Japan absolutely was not the first to place its finger on the trigger."

As the "listener" in these exchanges, Campbell was not totally convinced by the arguments presented by the Japanese side. But as can be surmised from his following interpretation, Campbell was somewhat understanding of Japan's claim that "China is also responsible." "The problem lies in the growing number of [aggressive] actions that China has taken over the past several years. The truth is that China is stepping up its aggressive actions, and this is causing friction with Japan and other neighboring countries."

Recalling his involvement in the Japan-China dispute over the Senkaku Islands, Campbell says, "This problem was especially difficult because of the extremely complex Japanese and Chinese positions." An example of this was the issue of referring the matter to international arbitration. With regard to the territorial disputes between China and Vietnam and China and the Philippines in the South China Sea and the Spratly Islands, Japan was saying that it "strongly supported referring these matters to international courts in compliance with international norms and practices." On the other hand, Japan was claiming no dispute exists in the Senkaku Islands and insisting that it would not accept referring the matter to international courts because the islands are ours. The dilemma of how to justify and support this double standard in the Japanese position weighed heavily on Campbell and other members of the Obama administration who emphasized the importance of the Japan-US alliance.

"As a rule, every nation trys to maximize its own position. Japan is no exception." Campbell repeated this mantra to himself as he continued to ponder the situation alone. There was no comfort in being caught between the Japanese side and its arguments and the American commitment not to be drawn into the dispute. This state of mind manifested itself in the dry and matter-of-fact attitude he exhibited in his meeting with Maehara Seiji when Maehara visited the United States as chairman of the DPJ Policy Research Council. This meeting took place in mid-September 2012—the day the Noda Cabinet formally approved the nationalization of the Senkaku Islands.

During the meeting, Maehara had proffered the following explanation. "The government had concluded a lease agreement with the landowner and all was quiet in the Senkaku Islands. This situation was perfectly acceptable until the Tokyo Metropolitan Government came along and proposed acquiring the islands. So here we had a prospective buyer that was no more than a local government entity totally incapable of taking responsibility in the foreign relations and national security areas." Maehara went on to ask for the Obama administration's understanding and cooperation. "A decision was made to nationalize the islands and we have reached an agreement with the landowner. The objective of this decision is to continue effective control in a stable and resolute manner in a calm environment as in the past." Campbell went no further than to respond in a studiedly perfunctory manner, "We understand what the Japanese government did."

Maehara took this occasion to bring up the statement that had been made earlier by Campbell's superior, Secretary of State Hillary Clinton. The Senkaku Islands "fall within the scope of the Japan-US Security Treaty," she had assured the Japanese side. Referring to the Clinton statement, Maehara went out of his way to express his thanks, saying, "Once again, I would like to say that this statement is highly appreciated." Here again, Campbell responded in an almost nonchalant tone, "There has been no change whatsoever in our position." Throughout the entire exchange, Campbell took pains not to comment in any way on the Japanese government's decision.

A glimpse of the atmosphere that prevailed at this time in the Obama administration can be gained from a book written by Jeffrey Bader, the former assistant to the president, who remained in the White House until recently to direct US policy on China and Japan. Bader wielded considerable influence in determining the White House's Asian policies, and his book *Obama and China's Rise: An Insider's Account of America's Asian Strategy* (Brookings Institution Press) was written shortly after he left his post. "The United States did not take a position on the respective territorial claims of Japan and China over the Senkakus. Although Washington wanted to show solidarity with its ally Japan in the face of bullying, Japan's handling of the incident seemed maladroit. Above all, it was absurd to think that China and Japan could have an armed conflict over these rocky islets or that the United States would be drawn in."

Bader, who had come to be trusted by State Councillor Dai Bingguo as the Obama administration's leading China expert, made some interesting comments toward the end of 2012. Referring to the Noda administration's desire to avoid a new disturbance in Japan-China relations such as would have resulted from the acquisition of the Senkaku Islands by the Tokyo Metropolitan Government, Bader expressed the view that "the Chinese side actually probably understands this logic." Bader also commented that the "United States would have no special reaction" to the nationalization of the Senkaku Islands, indicating that he expected the Obama administration to watch over the situation quietly.

China did not fail to pick up on the signals coming from the United States. While on the one hand affirming that the Senkaku Islands come under the Japan-US Security Treaty, the United States was on the other hand urging both sides to find a peaceful resolution because it was wedded to the principle of non-intervention in territorial disputes. Having confirmed the parameters of the actions that the United States was willing to take, China began to engage in provocative behavior on a daily basis in the waters around the Senkaku Islands.

Observing these developments, Campbell, who had managed to have Secretary Clinton aver that the Japan-US Security Treaty applied to the Senkaku Islands, came up with the next move. By this time, the Noda Cabinet had formally approved the nationalization of the islands and, as Bader had predicted, China was sending navy vessels to the vicinity of the Senkaku Islands and Japanese territorial waters on a daily basis and engaging in a campaign of diplomatic and military harassment.

"When it became clear that China was not going to let this matter go, we began to feel that we needed to do something. That is why Secretary Clinton expressed her dissatisfaction and very clearly stated, 'We are concerned with the projections of [military] power and hostile behavior' in the vicinity of the Senkaku Islands."

In this way, Clinton, known to be the strongest voice in the Obama administration, issued China a warning. But Campbell now came up with and implemented a unique diplomatic maneuver designed to cool the situation.

On October 24, 2012, four former high-ranking US diplomats paid a courtesy visit on Noda at the Kantei. The ranking member of the bipartisan group was former Deputy Secretary of State Richard Armitage (Republican and Campbell trusted confidante). The other three were Harvard Professor Joseph Nye (Democrat and former assistant secretary of defense), Jim Steinberg (Democrat and former deputy secretary of state), and Steve Hadley (Republican and former assistant to the president for national security affairs).

"The tension has been building because both sides [Japan and China] have taken inflexible positions, and there is a risk that this may move toward armed conflict. We want to examine what can be done to get back to a stable situation." This is how Steinberg explained the purpose of the bipartisan four-man mission of former officials that had been hastily put together. Steinberg's explanation appeared in a *New York Times* article.

After their meeting with the prime minister, Hadley said, "There is no difference between Democrats and Republicans when it comes to our understanding of the importance of Japan-US relations. This will not be affected by the outcome of the presidential election." With election day fast approaching, Hadley was trying to give the impression that the mission had come to reassure Noda that there would be no major change in the Japan-US alliance whatever the election's outcome. However, there is little doubt that the main subject of the meeting was the ongoing war of nerves between Japan and China over the Senkaku Islands.

Armitage and his group later met with LDP Secretary-General Ishiba Shigeru. It is notable that Ishiba has offered a very straightforward description of the discussions. "We talked about means to prevent further escalation in the tension between Japan and China."

The next day, October 25, the group left Tokyo for Beijing where they met with State Councillor Dai Bingguo, China's top diplomat. This was followed by a meeting with Vice Premier Li Keqiang, who was widely expected to become the number two man (premier) in the next leadership group that would be headed by Xi Jinping. Then Armitage and Nye flew back to Tokyo to once again meet with Noda at the Kantei. The two Americans also separately met with Deputy Prime Minister Okada Katsuya. In the course of these meetings, the two sides exchanged information on Chinese reactions to the Senkaku issue.

According to Armitage, during their meetings in Beijing, the American side strongly called for a halt to Chinese harassment related to the Senkaku issue. More specifically, they very clearly stated that if China were to resort to threatening behavior backed up by military might, the United States would support Japan in accordance with the provisions of the Japan-US Security Treaty. Li Keqiang and others responded that the nationalization of the Senkaku Islands was a manifestation of Japan's militarization, and demanded that the United States stand neutral. Armitage later recounted that "We rejected these suggestions."

Drawing on his close relations with Armitage, Nye, and Steinberg, it was Campbell who had worked behind the scenes to put together this foursome and their "shuttle diplomacy" linking Japan and China. Campbell had also arranged for Armitage and Nye to attend a symposium in Tokyo co-hosted by the Center for Strategic and International Studies (CSIS) where he previously worked. Campbell had coordinated all of these arrangements while repeatedly touching base not only with Secretary Clinton but also with Tom Donilon, President Obama's national security advisor. Ultimately, President Obama personally signed off on the diplomatic mediation mission by Armitage and his colleagues.

In September 2012, National Security Advisor Tom Donilon, National Security Council Senior Director for Asian Affairs Daniel Russel, and others travelled to China where they met with Vice Premier Xi Jinping who was soon to assume the top leadership position. According to White House sources, the two sides discussed the resumption of the bilateral comprehensive strategic dialogue that had been temporarily suspended during the presidential election. A tentative agreement was reached when the American side stated they would like to resume the talks by early the next summer.

It is true that the United States had come to understand the strategic importance of Chinese cooperation in resolving various thorny problems, such as the Iranian and North Korean nuclear programs and the need to address global warming. It would thus not be surprising if China's refusal to back down from its hardline positions on the Senkaku Islands and other issues in the Asia-Pacific region was at least in part due to the hand that the Obama administration was extending to China behind the scenes.

While needing to avoid undermining the cooperative mood with China, Campbell also needed to convey to both Japan and China that the Japan-US Security Treaty system stood on solid ground. Instead of going through regular diplomatic channels, Campbell chose for this task to dispatch a bipartisan mission of "big guns" who had retired from active service. This method had an obvious advantage. Compared to an official exchange between governments, this approach made it easier to convey both the naked truth about the American position as well as some more nuanced messages. What Campbell wanted to do was to give fair warning to both Japan and China that they should not trigger contingencies over the Senkaku Islands.

Around the same time, the Congressional Research Service (CRS) published its revised and updated report on US military obligations in the Senkaku Islands under the Japan-US Security Treaty. Entitled *The Senkakus (Diaoyu/Diaoyutai) Dispute: US Treaty Obligations* (January 22, 2013 revised edition), the report concluded that the Security Treaty has been applicable to the islands since the reversion of Okinawa.

In this report, which has been used as an important reference material in Congressional budget and policy deliberations, a CRS specialist on Asian affairs points out that the "US-Japan Security Treaty covers the islands because Article V stipulates that the United States is bound to protect the territories under the administration of Japan and Japan administers the Senkakus," and goes on to conclude that there are firm legal grounds for applying the provisions of the Security Treaty to the Senkaku Islands.

However, contrary to Campbell's hopes, China dismissed Armitage's overtures and focused on justifying its own actions. As it continued to argue its unyielding position on the Senkaku Islands, the Chinese side argued that the nationalization of the Senkaku Islands was "an act that would destroy the postwar international order." Throughout these meetings, the Chinese side consistently refused to accept the Japanese government's ownership of the three Senkaku Islands as the status quo.

Noda recalls the various exchanges that he had with the American side during this period. "The initial sense was that the United States felt the whole affair was 'a major nuisance.' This feeling was very strong." As to the shuttle diplomacy by Armitage and Nye, Noda says, "It attracted attention from the Japanese public, who were counting highly on the Japan-US Security Treaty, and also from the South China Sea countries [Vietnam and the Philippines]. But the feeling that I got from my conversations with Armitage and Nye was that the American side was probing to find out where we stood."

"We would like to see calm and prudent communication on a sustained basis." Having joined Armitage in Tokyo after his return from Beijing, Campbell delivered the keynote address at the Nikkei-CSIS Forum held on October 26, 2012, in which he urged both sides to exercise restraint. While avoiding specific references to Japan's territorial issues, such as the Senkaku Islands and Takeshima, Campbell took the opportunity to sound a warning to China on its hardline maritime expansion, stating, "The United States is committed to [promoting] the principles of freedom of navigation, peaceful dispute resolution, and use of international judicial mechanisms. Disputes should be resolved through mature and prudent methods."

Describing his conversations with Li Keqiang in Beijing, Armitage related what he had said in his normal candid and straightforward manner. "The United States will not remain neutral if the Senkaku Islands are attacked or threatened. We will respond."

Joseph Nye, who had accompanied Armitage to Beijing, explains that he also clearly conveyed to the Chinese side that the Senkaku Islands fall within the scope of the Japan-US Security Treaty and followed this up with an unequivocal warning. "Any attack on Japan, where US forces are stationed, will be deemed to be an attack on the United States."

Given his somewhat ambiguous position in the Obama administration, Campbell had sought the support of Armitage and Nye in his lonely battle on the issue of the Senkaku Islands. Therefore, the words spoken by these two heavyweight Japan experts were taken by the Japanese side to represent Campbell's reply to their all-out effort to convince him on the nationalization of the Senkaku Islands.

Voices from Beidaihe

Beginning around June, Japanese diplomatic efforts to seek China's understanding on the nationalization of the Senkaku Islands were revved up on Prime Minister Noda's instructions. As behind-the-scenes exchanges with Chinese diplomats were accelerated, the Japanese side was sensing what seemed to be a promising message from their Chinese counterparts—a message that hinted that China might be willing to live with the nationalization of the islands. Though always stated informally, the message could be heard in the words of both Vice Minister of Foreign Affairs Zhang Zhijun and his superior, State Councillor Dai Bingguo. "It's better than letting [Governor] Ishihara to do as he wishes."

"The purchase of the islands by the Tokyo Metropolitan Government and nationalization were both unacceptable to China. But if pressed to say which they disliked more, it is very obvious what their answer would have been." This is how Nagashima analyzed the Chinese response based on the contacts he had had with the Chinese Embassy in Tokyo as instructed by the prime minister. Nagashima was certainly not alone in coming away with that impression. A number of Japanese diplomats also testify that this definitely was the impression they received from their Chinese counterparts during this period.

On July 11, 2012, Foreign Minister Gemba Koichiro met with Chinese Foreign Minister Yang Jiechi in the Cambodian capital of Phnom Penh, where he explained Japan's policy decision to nationalize the islands. After the meeting, Gemba explained, "I emphasized the importance of handling this matter calmly from a broad perspective. I believe a degree of understanding was achieved." Gemba has explained that during the meeting, the Japanese side conveyed the importance of maintaining peaceful and stable administration in the Senkaku Islands. This statement was meant to effectively announce Japan's policy to nationalize the islands.

This meeting took place four days after Noda's first public statement about nationalizing the islands. However, in Phnom Penh, Foreign Minister Gemba and the Japanese diplomats who accompanied him had revealed the government's intent to nationalize the islands without once using the word "nationalization." The reason for this was that the Japanese side wanted to clearly set forth the Japanese position in the formal setting of a ministerial meeting that the Senkaku Islands were the "inherent territory of Japan," that the forthcoming measure was being carried out in accordance with domestic laws, and that it constituted a transfer of title with no foreign policy significance. Having set out its position, Japan was asking China to understand its position and to react calmly.

"It is important we treat this issue calmly so that it does not affect the overall picture of Japan-China relations." Gemba called on his Chinese counterpart in these words, urging China to take a flexible stance on the issue of nationalization. According to the Foreign Ministry, the Chinese side only repeated its standard claim that "Diaoyutai is the inherent territory of China." This was followed by a statement that turned Gemba's words back on him. "We urge Japan to maintain the overall situation in Japan-China relations through dialogue and cooperation, and through its actions." However, the Chinese side did not say anything about the nationalization of the islands. Nor did the Chinese side give any expression to a position that could be construed to be a statement of "opposition" to nationalization.

The Japanese side was building up hopes that China would opt for a tolerant and accepting stance on nationalization. But the climate underwent a sudden and dramatic change in August. What could have been behind this sharp shift? Kawashima Shin, associate professor at the University of Tokyo and a young China researcher with numerous connections in the Chinese government, speculates, "There is a possibility that something happened at Beidaihe in August that turned everything upside down."

Located in Hebei province, Beidaihe is widely known as a summer resort where top Chinese Communist Party officials congregate to engage in informal discussions on various matters. This mid-summer event takes on special importance in years when once-in-a-decade changes are to be made in the leadership ranks. In such years, elder statesmen, conservatives and the old guard, reformists, internationalists, and members of other cliques descend on the resort town to engage in heated debates and complex political maneuvering on personnel matters. As a rule, the discussions gradually begin to converge and a consensus emerges by the end of the summer on who should stand where in the lineup of new leaders. This is then finalized in the plenary session of the Central Committee, which meets immediately before the National Congress of the Communist Party in the fall.

However, the summer of 2012 was an exception to the rule. Agreement was reached on the appointment of Xi Jinping as the paramount leader and general secretary of the Communist Party. But every other appointment remained up in the air. This led to the highly unusual step of postponing the National Congress that was originally scheduled for mid-October. According to Kawashima and others, the source of the trouble was that the roster of appointees that had been put together under the leadership of Hu Jintao drew loud protests from Jang Zemin, the former general secretary, as well as the full range of elder statesmen, old guard members, and reformists.

The following picture emerges when the analyses of Kawashima and various other China experts in Japan are pieced together. When high-ranking party officials gathered in Beidaihe that year, Hu Jintao initially took the upper hand in the discussions. Consequently, the initial leadership roster included numerous people from the Communist Youth League that Hu Jintao himself led. At one point, it looked as if agreement would be reached on this line-up. However, this is when opposition began to brew in earnest. Members of the old guard, including the PLA and party members close to Jang Zemin, suddenly came together to form a united front against Hu Jintao. The pushback mounted by the old guard exceeded anything that Hu Jintao and Wen Jiabao had anticipated.

This dramatic reversal was foreshadowed in the bitter debate over the question of how to discipline Bo Xilai, the former Communist Party secretary of Chongqing who had fallen from power after his top lieutenant sought asylum at the American consulate. While Jang Zemin and other conservatives who backed Bo Xilai called for "moderation in disciplinary action," Hu Jintao and his group argued for stern punishment as a necessary means to reinforce party discipline. The latter group ultimately prevailed. Bo Xilai was stripped of his party membership and criminal charges were brought against him.

Bo Xilai was an unusual politician. The son of a high-ranking party official, he captured the public's imagination by returning to the Mao Zedong ideology of promoting egalitarian values and eliminating disparities. Hu Jintao and his group had justified Bo Xilai's removal as a means to clean up the party, but this had earned the ire of the elder statesmen and old guard who remained faithful to Mao's ideologies and had always been suspicious of opening-up policies. The opposition had united around their common distaste for Hu Jintao's policies. This is how Kawashima and Japan's other China watchers interpret what happened.

Even as the center of Chinese political power was embroiled in a heated tug-of-war over the Bo Xilai case, tumult was emerging around Ling Jihua, one of Hu Jintao's closest of advisors. In his position as director of the General Office of the Communist Party, Ling Jihua had worked faithfully to support the leadership, and it was initially rumored that he would be elevated to membership on the Politburo. However, this failed to materialize. Next, China watchers in Hong Kong were abuzz with rumors that Ling Jihua would be demoted and reassigned to the post of director of the United Front Work Department while retaining his former status as member of the Central Committee of the Communist Party.

Hu Jintao and Ling Jihua went back to the days when Hu Jintao held the top post in the Communist Youth League, which constituted his political base. After serving Hu in various capacities, Ling Jihua was appointed director of the General Office during Hu Jintao's second term (fall of 2007). No one doubted that Ling Jihua would eventually be elevated from the Central Committee to the Politburo if Hu Jintao were to remain in power. At the same time, given his position in the hierarchy, Ling Jihua out-ranked Dai Bingguo, China's top diplomat and someone who was watched very closely in Japan.

It would be no exaggeration to say that the virtual demotion of Ling Jihua was an ominous sign that the sun was beginning to set on Hu Jintao and his group. The faction that appeared in the early stages of the Beidaihe conference to have the elder statesmen and the old guard squarely in check was beginning to lose ground.

The Ling Jihua situation continued to deteriorate when it became known that his son had been killed in an automobile accident in March 2012 while driving with two women in an expensive Ferrari. Hong Kong's *South China Morning Star* reported that Ling Jihua had been forced to take responsibility for the accident and had been demoted, ruining his prospects for elevation to the Politburo Standing Committee.

In early August, just as the power struggle within the Chinese leadership was reaching its peak, two of China's vice-ministers of foreign affairs appeared before the Politburo Standing Committee of the Communist Party—China's supreme decision-making body. The two senior diplomats came to report on the Japanese government plans to nationalize the Senkaku Islands. The report was based on explanations received from the Japanese side and was delivered by Zhang Zhijun and Fu Ying, considered by Japan's diplomatic establishment to be their main line to Chinese diplomatic channels.

"It probably would be advantageous to aim for peaceful and stable administration through nationalization. This would be better than acquisition by Ishihara and the Tokyo Metropolitan Government." Hoping to sound out the thinking of the Zhongnanhai where China's highest political powers congregate, Zhang Zhijun and Fu Ying repeated the explanation that Japan had given the Chinese side on numerous occasions. One of the top leaders angrily interrupted their presentation: "Shut up with this report! I can't take anymore of this."

According to Kawashima and various other Chinese experts, as well as officials in Japan's foreign policy and defense ministries, Zhang Zhijun and Fu Ying had delivered their report to someone thought to have a pro-Japanese outlook—Vice Premier Li Keqiang, the leading candidate for appointment to the number two position in the next leadership group. As a supporter of the policies of reform and openness, Li Keqiang was an internationalist with close ties to Wen Jiabao. But this relation was now beginning to work against him as he found himself retreating into an increasingly difficult political position. In the informal discussions at Beidaihe, the conservative wing had openly criticized the Hu Jintao reform and openness policies. However, these attacks soon engulfed the mutually beneficial relations based on common strategic interests, the diplomatic strategy in relations with Japan that had been hammered out between Wen Jiabao and Prime Minister Abe Shinzo, the representative of the conservative wing of the LDP.

Criticism of Wen Jiabao—Li Keqiang's long-time backer—was mounting. After the *New York Times* reported that members of Wen's family had accumulated questionable funds and massive investments amounting to at least $2.7 billion, Wen Jiabao was forced to play defense. Commenting on these developments inside China, Kawashima speculates, "It is very likely that Li Keqiang was being put to a loyalty test of the highest order." Kawashima explains that, in order to protect Wen Jiabao, the leader of his faction, Li Keqiang found it necessary to erase all traces of what could be interpreted as a pro-Japanese stance.

"I understand what you are trying to say, but can you tell me where the center of power is in Japan?"

According to Tomisaka Satoshi, one of Japan's leading China watchers, Li Keqiang cut short their explanations and immediately dismissed Zhang Zhijun and Fu Ying. Tomisaka explains, "The situation probably no longer allowed Li Keqiang to say, 'Yes, that's fine.' It was no longer that simple." Kawashima basically agrees with this interpretation. "This was a critical turning point. After this incident, Chinese Foreign Ministry officials were no longer granted opportunities to address the top leadership on issues related to Japan and the Senkakus."

Kurt Campbell, assistant secretary of state for East Asian and Pacific affairs, was anxiously monitoring the contacts between Japan and China and was secretly counseling his Japanese counterparts on the importance of "keeping the lines of communication open with China on the [Senkaku] problem." Looking back on this period, Campbell agrees with Tomisaka and Kawashima.

"I had come to believe that the Japanese were doing their best to convince the Chinese side, but I didn't think they were as successful at this as they themselves thought. The Japanese side had thought long and hard about this and had concluded that they had gained China's understanding. But that was clearly not the case."

Tomisaka shares what Li Keqiang is rumored to have said after he furiously rejected Zhang Zhijun and Fu Ying's attempt to explain the Japanese government's logic on nationalizing the Senkaku Islands. "How do you propose we explain this to the people?" Since normalizing relations with Japan in the 1970s, the Chinese leadership had adopted the position that a limited group of Japanese rightists and radical elements were the cause of everything that happened in wartime Japan-China relations. Standing behind this interpretation, the leadership had been able to pull the public along notwithstanding the enormous hostility toward Japan that prevailed among the people. Central to this position is the argument that all responsibility rests with the Class-A war criminals enshrined in Yasukuni Shrine. Indeed, this is why China reacts so harshly whenever the prime minister or other cabinet ministers visit Yasukuni.

From the Chinese perspective, Governor Ishihara of Tokyo, who announced plans to purchase the Senkaku Islands, is part of this limited group of Japanese rightists. For the Chinese side, there is thus nothing contradictory in denouncing what Ishihara says and does while maintaining good relations with the government. But the situation gets complicated when the Japanese government itself steps forward to assume direct ownership of the Senkaku Islands because this completely undercuts the logic that was used in promoting the bilateral relations between Japan and China. "The postwar Japanese government and Japanese people should not be blamed for what happened during the war. All blame rests with the war criminals and the band of rightists that have succeeded to their evil legacy."

Li Keqiang had asked Zhang Zhijun and Fu Ying, "How do you propose we explain this to the people?" Tomisaka reasons that these words were rooted in the distortions that had accumulated over the years in China's policies toward Japan. It goes without saying that, caught in the grips of a power struggle that would determine the course of China for the next ten years or more, Li Keqiang and Xi Jinping simply did not have room for correcting these distortions or altering the foundations of a Japan policy that had been in place since the normalization of relations. It is very likely that these developments derailed all the diplomatic efforts Vice-Minister of Foreign Affairs Sasae and others made to convince the Chinese side to accept the Senkakus' nationalization.

Nagashima recalls it was about this time that Sasae began to repeat the suggestion that he had previously made to Noda in the secret meeting held at the Kantei. "Maybe it would be better to allow the Tokyo Metropolitan

Government to own the islands temporarily before transferring them to the government." Sasae may well have been driven to utter these words by the sense of irony that he had nurtured over the years as Japan's top diplomat. However, people who were familiar with what was happening at this time have testified that, in fact, there is no evidence that the Japanese side had an accurate understanding of what was taking place in the halls of power in China, nor did it have any inkling that their carefully presented suggestion had been quietly but conclusively rejected.

After a formal decision had been made to nationalize the islands, Maehara Seiji and some other top officials from the DPJ had taken it upon themselves to arrange a top secret meeting with Cheng Yonghua, the Chinese ambassador to Japan, to explain the nationalization plan. It is reported that Maehara and his colleagues later speculated that the Senkaku problem was conveniently used in the Chinese power struggle, but perhaps "used" does not correctly portray what had happened. Actually, it would be more accurate to say that the Chinese leadership, caught in the middle of a vicious internal power struggle and political conflict, simply did not have the time or energy to properly assess the Noda administration's true intent in pushing for the nationalization of the Senkaku Islands.

Not long after this, China's new leadership emerged with Xi Jinping at the pinnacle of power, flanked by six other members of the Politburo Standing Committee of the Communist Party. There is evidence that the Japanese side later received information indicating that five of these seven top leaders had rejected the idea of nationalization.

According to concurrent media reports, criticism of Japan started immediately following the Noda Cabinet's September 10 formal decision to nationalize the islands. The first to denounce the move was Wen Jiabao who stated, "We will not retreat even half a step." Others quickly followed his lead, including Wu Bangguo, Li Keqiang, He Guoqiang, and Jia Qinglin. Shortly thereafter, Xi Jinping and Zhou Yongkang added their voices to the chorus of criticism. It is reported that, at this point, only two members of the nine-man Politburo Standing Committee (the former leadership structure) refrained from criticizing Japan: Li Changchun and Hu Jintao.

Noda described his state of mind at this time as: "I am sure there was a lot going on inside China. And I am aware there are many opinions on the timing of our announcement. But my idea was that this nationalization of the Senkaku Islands should take place at the end of the Hu Jintao administration. The thinking was that this would allow us to engage in normal dialogue with the incoming Xi Jinping administration."

On matters related to China, President Obama's trusted advisor was Jeffrey Bader, the former presidential assistant (senior director for Asian affairs on the National Security Council) who continues to influence White House policymaking. On the issue of Japan's nationalization of the Senkaku Islands, Bader's interpretation of the situation remained unchanged throughout this period. "The Chinese side may understand the Japanese logic, but they will never formally accept it."

Extrapolating from this position, Bader went on to predict that China might lump its disputes with Vietnam over the Spratly Islands and the Philippines over the Scarborough Shoal (Huangyan Dao in Chinese) together with the Senkaku problem and take an even more militant stance in its policies toward Japan.

As Bader had hinted, the territorial dispute with the Philippines over the Scarborough Shoal had become China's hottest territorial issue by the spring of 2012. The Scarborough Shoal is a small coral reef in the South China Sea located 230 kilometers from the Philippine capital of Manila. China began claiming this reef when rich deposits of natural gas and other resources were discovered in the surrounding seabed. This has ignited a heated dispute between China and the Philippines.

This dispute then escalated with the military standoff between China and the Philippines that started on April 8, 2012. On this day, Filipino authorities sighted a number of Chinese fishing vessels in the waters around the Scarborough Shoal and called for the dispatch of naval ships to the scene. China protested this move and criticized the Philippines for "suddenly calling naval ships into an issue involving fishing vessels." Two days later, China backed up its protests by rashly sending a fleet of patrol boats from its State Oceanic Administration to the scene. This began a regular pattern of maritime military harassment in which Chinese patrol boats closed within a couple hundred meters of Philippine Coast Guard vessels, dangerously heightening tensions in the Scarborough Shoal area.

China then began to ratchet up its pressure on the Philippines by dispatching patrol boats and other government ships from the Fisheries Law Enforcement Command. According to reports appearing in the Hong Kong media and elsewhere, the combined Chinese fleet of government ships and fishing vessels reached a peak of 97 vessels at one time. This in turn invited some dramatic commentary that appeared in the Hong Kong media. "This is reminiscent of the Nazi wolf pack tactics when Germany deployed its fleet of submarines to interdict American ships delivering wartime supplies to Great Britain."

The tension continued to mount with China reinforcing its claims of effective control by drilling for oil and carrying out naval exercises in adjoining waters. On the other hand, on April 30, the Philippines held its first two-plus-two talks with the United States, a ministerial meeting bringing together the top diplomatic and defense officials from both countries. At this meeting, the Philippines formally requested US cooperation in breaking the Scarborough impasse.

Even as tensions between China and the Philippines were mounting, the Fourth Round of the China-US Strategic and Economic Dialogue was convened in Beijing on May 3, 2012. Addressing the opening session of the meeting, Hu Jintao delivered a strong appeal emphasizing the importance of strategic stability between China and the United States. "Throughout history," he said, "major countries have repeatedly confronted and clashed with each other. However, the major countries of this age of economic globalization must find a new path."

In the course of his address, Hu Jintao introduced a new key phrase to the dialogue: "a new type of great power relationship." He explained the goal as the pursuit of a new path to developing the relations between great powers that breaks free from the history of conflict. The key phrase was further elucidated by Dai Bingguo, Hu Jintao's top foreign affairs advisor, who emphasized the importance of maintaining and nurturing friendly relations between the two countries. "China and the United States are not seeking to be the G2. China and the United States can build a C2 to strengthen our communication, coordination, and cooperation."

Two years earlier, in December 2010, Dai Bingguo had published a paper entitled "Adhere to the Path of Peaceful Development." In it, he referenced a phrase that is said to be from the teachings of Deng Xiaoping, "keep a low profile and make due contributions," and argued that Deng's intent in using the phrase had been misunderstood. "There are some people in the international community who have misinterpreted these words. The meaning of keeping a low profile is that China should be modest and prudent, not serve as leader or standard bearer for others, and not seek expansion or hegemony."

The paper went on to comment on remarks attributed to Deng. "As Comrade Deng Xiaoping once said, if one day China tries to seek hegemony in the world, the people of the world should expose, oppose, and overthrow it." As an alternative, Dai Bingguo provided this outline of Chinese intentions. "What we pursue is a policy of friendship, security, and prosperity with our neighbors."

An interesting critique of this paper is found in Bader's book *Obama and China's Rise: An Insider's Account of America's Asia Strategy*:

This change in course became public in early December, when State Councilor Dai Bingguo published a lengthy article on the Foreign Ministry's website (subsequently reprinted in the *People's Daily*) offering a resounding defense of Deng Xiaoping's traditional policy of prudence, modesty, and caution (*tao guang yang hui*) in foreign policy. China's interests had been well served by this policy, said Dai, as it had laid the basis for China's spectacular economic growth and emergence on the international stage.

It would be counter to China's interests, he added, to abandon this approach in favor of seeking to become a superpower, a hegemonic power, or a peer competitor of the United States.

Dai's article obviously was intended to be an authoritative rebuttal of the public narrative dominated by hard-liners. Dai had the support of Hu Jintao for this strong public position. It amounted to a rebuke of those who had been arguing for a more assertive policy toward the United States, and it emboldened others to call for a more moderate regional diplomacy. It simultaneously provided official justification for a more accommodating approach to the United States.

The Chinese phrase "Keep a low profile and make due contributions," usually interpreted in Japan as the Chinese equivalent of Japan's own "The skilled hawk hides its talons and does what it has to do," was adopted by Deng Xiaoping as the guiding principle in the formulation of China's foreign policy shortly after the end of the Cold War and the collapse of the Soviet Union in 1991. This had been preceded two years earlier by the Tiananmen Square incident of 1989 and the sanctions implemented against China by the United States and other countries.

The US-China strategic rapprochement had been pushed forward by the overarching confrontation between the US and the USSR. But suddenly, strategic rapprochement was on shaky ground with the disappearance of its primary catalyst. The end of the Cold War had defused the confrontation and, as a result, China's international position was becoming increasingly uncertain. It was in this political environment that Deng Xiaoping formulated China's national strategy of minimizing friction with foreign countries while concentrating on internal economic development and building national strength.

As Bader has pointed out, Dai Bingguo's article had the effect of quieting the hardline criticism of Deng's policy line. However, there is a growing sense today among Japan's China experts and within Japan's defense establishment that this criticism is once again gaining momentum. In the words of one China expert, this revisionist criticism advocates that China's "keep a low profile and make due contributions" policy should be limited to its relations with the United States, and that this policy does not and should not apply to Japan. According to one Foreign Ministry official, this creeping suspicion has been taken a step further within Japan's Foreign Ministry, the Defense Ministry, and the Self-Defense Forces where there is a growing sense that, "China has clearly shifted its sights from the Scarborough Shoal to the Senkaku Islands."

Hu Jintao had come out with the concept of a new type of great power relationship to reinforce strategic stability in China's relations with the United States. This was done just as the Philippines was turning to the United States for help in coping with its territorial dispute with China over the Scarborough Shoal. It is impossible to determine whether Hu Jintao was acting on diplomatic foresight in making this pronouncement or whether it was mere coincidence.

"In order to find the path to a new type of great power relationship, both countries must stay on the right course. They must respect each other, deepen mutual cooperation, control and overcome contradictions and differences in opinion, pay attention to the people's will that constitutes the foundation of amicable exchange, and pursue the sustained advancement of friendly and stable relations."

It was with these words that Vice Premier Li Keqiang greeted his American visitors six months later on October 23, 2012. The meeting with the four former US government officials—Armitage, Nye, Hadley, and Steinberg—was held at the Violet Light Tower (Ziguangge) in Beijing's Zhongnanhai. Li Keqiang's greeting was intended to emphasize that the new leadership under Xi Jinping intended to faithfully follow the path that had been laid out by Hu Jintao and Dai Bingguo.

According to reports carried by the Xinhua News Agency, Li Keqiang took this opportunity to once again explain the Chinese position on the Senkaku Islands and made a point of implicitly warning the United States against siding with Japan by stating, "The international community must protect and preserve the fruits of victory in the Second World War and the international order that was created after the war."

Armitage found it strange that Li Keqiang, who was primarily responsible for economic matters, was meeting with him and his colleagues, who were in the national security field. "Why is someone from the economic side sticking his nose into national security matters," Armitage thought to himself. However, it should be recalled that it was Li Keqiang who had stood up to directly and loudly reject the efforts made by both Japanese and Chinese diplomats to convey the Noda administration's justification for nationalizing the Senkaku Islands. When this is taken into account, a degree of consistency can be seen in Li Keqiang's meeting with the unofficial mission of the diplomatic intermediaries headed by Armitage and Nye. Moreover, this meeting can be understood as signaling that the new Chinese leadership had by this time come to a decision to launch a strategic anti-Japanese campaign centered on the Senkaku problem.

The validity of this interpretation is borne out by events that occurred six months later in Potsdam, Germany. On May 26, 2013, Li Keqiang—now the number two man (premier) in China's new leadership—was in Potsdam, home to the Potsdam Declaration in which the Allied Powers had called for Japan's unconditional surrender in the closing days of the Second World War.

Standing in Potsdam, Li Keqiang strongly criticized Japan's nationalization of the Senkaku Islands by repeating the claim that the Potsdam Declaration had upheld the implementation of the Cairo Declaration, which he said had demanded that "all the territories Japan has stolen from the Chinese" be returned to the People's Republic of China. He then went on to emphasize that "the peace and the postwar order that was obtained in exchange for millions of lives lost must be preserved." Li Keqiang was broadcasting to the world China's unique interpretation that the nationalization of the Senkaku Islands by Japan was "destroying the postwar order." In so doing, Li Keqiang was implicitly claiming that the Senkaku Islands were part of China's sovereign territory.

Li Keqiang's persistent criticism of Japan went back to late 2011 and was foreshadowed by the arguments he presented to Armitage and his group in their Beijing meeting. Exasperated by the self-righteous pronouncements of Li Keqiang, Armitage spoke up toward the end of the meeting to check his host. Speaking as if to vent the frustration that had been slowly building up in him, Armitage inserted in his remarks a key comment that was sure to rile the Chinese side. The willful insertion was designed to convey that the United States was not about to join the Chinese campaign and to act as China wanted it to act.

"What would happen," Armitage asked, "if we responded to the Spratly and Paracel issues the same way as we will respond [based on the Security Treaty] in the Senkaku Islands?" According to Armitage, Li Keqiang changed color at this and screamed, "That is completely out of the question!" But he did manage to rein in the belligerent tone that had characterized his previous comments.

CHAPTER

5

The Final Decision

Prime Minister Noda meets Secretary of State Clinton (APEC)
Kyodo

The "150 day war" in 2012 between Noda and Ishihara ended when the Cabinet approved the purchase of the Senkaku Islands. Shortly afterward, Ishihara resigned the Tokyo governorship and launched a new political party.

Hallway Chat that Turned into a Summit Meeting

Located in the Russian Far East is Vladivostok, whose name means "to rule the East" in Russian. As the only warm-water port in the region, Vladivostok served as a base for the Soviet Union's Pacific Fleet during the Cold War. On the morning of September 9, 2012, Prime Minister Noda Yoshihiko was in Vladivostok to attend the Asia-Pacific Economic Cooperation (APEC) Conference. Moments before the start of the plenary session, Noda spotted Chinese President Hu Jintao standing at the entrance to the hall. Noda turned to the person he was conversing with, politely excused himself, and casually walked up to Hu Jintao. "That was a terrible earthquake that hit your country."

Noda was referring to the earthquake that had occurred two days earlier in the Chinese province of Yunnan. Aware of the extensive damage caused by the quake, Noda felt that, "Failure to express my sympathies would run counter to the principles of humanism." Prodded by that thought, Noda had taken the initiative to break the ice.

Hu Jintao mumbled some diplomatic niceties but quickly shifted gear. "It is all unlawful and therefore null and void! We resolutely oppose this action. Japan must fully realize the gravity of the situation and must avoid mistaken decisions. Japan must contribute to maintaining the general direction of developing our relations." Hu Jintao did not even stop to catch his breath as the words came flooding out his mouth.

Recalling Hu Jintao's reaction to his words spoken in sympathy, Noda recounts, "It was all very sudden and unexpected." As described by Noda, Hu Jintao was livid as he decried the nationalization of the Senkaku Islands. Still fuming, Hu Jintao had gone on to add, "Relations between China and Japan have become extremely strained," as he urged Noda to reconsider the decision. Noda responded with words that skirted the controversy. "China's development provides Japan and other countries of the region positive opportunities. As this is the 40th year of our diplomatic relations, we wish to further deepen the mutually beneficial strategic relations." Noda ended by saying, "We hope to address the current situation in Japan-China relations from a broader perspective." Although the words were spoken with the Senkaku Islands in mind, it was obvious that the two leaders were simply talking past each other.

This unofficial meeting between Prime Minister Noda and President Hu Jintao continued for no more than 15 minutes. Each accompanied by no one but an English-speaking interpreter, the two leaders had remained standing during the entire exchange.

The Japanese side had come to Vladivostok with no plans to seek a meeting with Hu Jintao. Noda himself had echoed this decision in a press conference held shortly before the APEC Conference on September 7. Mindful of the deteriorating relations with China and South Korea, Noda had formally announced that he would not hold summit meetings with Hu Jintao or South Korea's President Lee Myung-bak in Vladivostok. But during the same press conference Noda had stated, "If an opportunity presents itself for a hallway chat, I may use that chance to once again convey Japan's position." The implication was that opportunities might arise for informal contact during the banquet or elsewhere during the conference.

Noda recounts what was going on before the APEC Conference. "No meetings had been scheduled, so we didn't spend any time preparing for one. Nevertheless, I did mention to my aides that maybe something informal could come up. If there is a chance to have an informal chat, it would be only right to express our sympathies. That possibility was certainly discussed."

This is borne out by a high-ranking Japanese government official who states that Noda met with a number of aides before the plenary session to make sure everyone was thinking along the same lines and to make detailed preparations for the possibility of a close encounter with Hu Jintao. In addition to the prime minister's advisor, Nagashima Akihisa, these aides included Deputy Vice-Minister for Foreign Affairs Nishimiya Shinichi and Director-General of the Foreign Ministry Asian and Oceanian Affairs Bureau Sugiyama Shinsuke. Administrative aides had gone so far as to prepare a questions and answers scenario for such a chance meeting.

The press had also asked the Chinese side about the possibility of meeting with the Japanese leader at the APEC Conference. At a press conference on September 8, a member of the Chinese delegation responded to the query. The respondent was Qin Gang, chief spokesman for the Foreign Ministry. Qin Gang said that Japan "must squarely face the determination and commitment of the Chinese government and the people to defend the nation's sovereignty and territory" and took the position that it was up to Japan to "take real action." At the time, the Japanese side interpreted this to be conveying a specific message from the Chinese side, which was that "Japan would have to be the first to make a concession." As described above, it is true that the hallway summit meeting happened when Noda took the first step. In hindsight, this complied with the Chinese demand. Japan had taken the initiative to get this informal meeting in the hope that it would help narrow the gap between the two countries. However, contrary to Japan's expectations, the meeting only resulted in a widening of the chasm.

The next day, the cabinet ministers concerned met at the Kantei to discuss the Senkaku problem. In the course of the meeting, the ministers formally confirmed the policy of nationalizing the islands. The key elements of the decision were to purchase the three islands of Uotsurijima, Kita-kojima, and Minami-kojima from Kurihara Kunioki. Whereas the government had been leasing the islands from Kurihara since fiscal 2002 for 24.5 million yen per year, the government was now proposing to purchase the three islands for a total of 2,050 million yen. At one point, Governor Ishihara had announced that he intended to also purchase the fourth island, Kuba-jima, in a single comprehensive purchase. The government had considered this but given up on it because the person who owned Kubajima, Kurihara Kunioki's younger sister, had refused to sell. Consequently, the decision on Kubajima was to continue having the Ministry of Defense lease it.

Among those present at this meeting were Chief Cabinet Secretary Fujimura Osamu, Minister of Finance Azumi Jun, Minister of Foreign Affairs Gemba Koichiro, and Minister of Land, Infrastructure, Transport and Tourism Hata Yuichiro. Strangely enough, Noda himself was not present. It is very probable that this absence was meant to underscore Japan's assertion that "nationalization constitutes no more than a transfer of ownership and is unrelated to territorial rights," an explanation that China continued to reject.

In fact, the cabinet ministers had earlier agreed that the purchase of the three islands would thereafter be officially referred to as the "acquisition and ownership of the Senkaku Islands." Kawashima Shin, an associate professor at the University of Tokyo who has ties with various Chinese government officials, explains the pitfall that the ministers were trying to avoid. Kawashima explains that the nuance of the term "nationalization" as used in Japan—a democratic market economy—"simply cannot be conveyed" to the Chinese people living in a totalitarian system ruled by the Communist

Party and aspiring to state capitalism. In the Chinese usage, "nationaliza-tion" carries the sense of the "Japanese government coercively annexing the territory of our nation." Thus the "nationalization" of the Senkaku Islands had already spawned a mindset of virulent protest opposition in China.

"The acquisition and ownership of the Senkaku Islands represents the transfer of ownership of a property that is the territory of Japan from its former owner to the Japanese government. As such, there is nothing in this transfer that can raise an issue in Japan's relations with other countries."

This statement was released by Chief Cabinet Secretary Fujimura on September 11 and came on the heels of the cabinet decision to approve the nationalization of the Senkaku Islands and the formal signing of a pur-chase contract with the owner of the three islands. Fujimura took the occa-sion to once again emphasize that nationalization was adopted as a means to ensure the "maintenance of peaceful and stable administration" of the Senkaku Islands. Fujimura time and again repeated the official position, which was that the government had "merely purchased what it previously held as a leased property." It was as if Fujimura was hoping the repetition would leave no room for misunderstanding.

During the same press conference, Fujimura provided a detailed expla-nation of the developments culminating in the cabinet decision and called for the public's understanding and support. The key points of his expla-nation were: the landowner had agreed to sell the islands on September 7; the purchase would be paid for by drawing on the general reserve fund in the government's fiscal 2012 budget; the purchase price of 2,050 mil-lion yen was based on a special formula known as the "replacement cost method;" this amount represented the ceiling price set by the government in advance of the negotiations; and the three newly purchased islands would be formally held and placed under the administration of the Japan Coast Guard.

As the spokesman for the Noda Cabinet, Fujimura wanted to emphasize that the government had rejected Governor Ishihara's requests that it con-struct harbor facilities and lighthouses. Fujimura made it abundantly clear that the government would take no action that would further underscore the fact that the islands were under Japan's effective control. "We do not want the situation in the Senkaku Islands to affect the general picture of our relations with China. It is important to avoid all forms of misunder-standing and unintended consequences."

After emphasizing this point, Fujimura revealed that Sugiyama Shin-suke, director general of the Foreign Ministry Asian and Oceanian Affairs

Bureau, was being immediately dispatched to Beijing to explain the nationalization of the islands to the Chinese side.

On September 10, the Democratic Party of Japan (DPJ) had announced the forthcoming election for its party leadership. Running for re-election as president of his party, Noda had released a number of campaign pledges, including nationalizing the Senkaku Islands. He had followed this up with the "ironclad pledge to defend Japan's territories and territorial waters." Exactly two months had passed since early July when Noda himself had said, "We will contact the owner and comprehensively review the situation." There was little doubt in anyone's mind that the matter had been brought to a speedy conclusion. Recalling the thoughts that were going through his mind at the time, Noda's voice betrays a sense of excitement. "The owner was wavering [on whether or not to sell to the government]. So, I thought to myself, we just have to push through and wrap the matter up. That was my thinking."

Following the Cabinet decision, a statement attributed to Premier Wen Jiabao appeared on the front pages of all major Chinese newspapers: "We will not retreat even half a step." The headlines screamed that China was going to stand up as a nation united in opposition to Japan's nationalization of the Senkaku Islands. In writing on China's deep distrust of Japan that provided the backdrop for Wen Jinbao's words, the September 11 edition of the Chinese newspaper *Beijing Times* carried the comments of Wang Xiaopeng, a maritime problems researcher at the Chinese Academy of Social Sciences. "The purchase of the islands by the Japanese government is no more than a critical first step. Inhabitation and mainland treatment will soon follow."

Noda had been in Vladivostok immediately before the Cabinet decision on nationalization where he met with Hu Jintao and with Secretary of State Hillary Clinton, who was participating in the APEC Conference on behalf of President Obama. While there was no doubt Noda and Clinton discussed the Senkaku Islands, the Japanese government took the unusual step of postponing any statement on the content of the meeting. This was done in consideration of the Cabinet decision that was scheduled for a few days later.

On September 8, Noda met with Clinton, and on the next day Clinton met President Lee Myung-bak of South Korea. Following this meeting, Clinton held a press conference where she revealed that she had discussed the Japan-South Korea dispute over Shimane Prefecture's Takeshima in her meetings with the leaders of both Japan and South Korea.

"The United States hopes that the growing tension between Japan and South Korea over this problem can be eased through bilateral talks. I urged both sides to lower the temperature and work together in a concerted way. I believe the two leaders understood our expectations," Clinton said at the press conference.

Clinton's statement reflected the Obama administration's growing concern that the Japan-South Korea dispute could undermine US foreign policy toward North Korea and China. She had taken the occasion to emphasize that the United States viewed the Japan-South Korea dispute as an urgent issue in its Asia diplomacy. In his meeting with Clinton, Noda had said, "It is important we solve this problem calmly, fairly, and peacefully according to international laws." To this, Clinton had indirectly called for greater restraint on both sides. "Cooperation between the United States and Japan, and trilateral cooperation among the United States, Japan, and South Korea, continue to be critically important."

Immediately before she went to Vladivostok on September 5, Clinton had visited Beijing for a flurry of meetings that began with Hu Jintao, followed by meetings with Vice Premier Xi Jinping, who was slated to assume the top leadership position in the next administration, and State Councillor Dai Bingguo. On the previous day (September 4), Clinton had met with Foreign Minister Yang Jiechi and said, "Over the past three and a half years, [the Obama administration] has been deeply engaged in consultation with China. But what is important is real cooperation." With this circumspect statement, Clinton had prodded China to approach the Senkaku issue calmly.

China, however, responded by publicizing its position via state-owned Xinhua News Agency. "It is clear the United States supports Japan's provocative stance against China. This is part of the pivot-to-Asia strategy that is designed to suppress the rise of China." Clearly, China had not forgotten, nor was it shy about voicing, its strong criticism of the Japanese and US stance on the Senkaku Islands.

These developments were in Clinton's mind when she held a press conference in Vladivostok. Qualifying her statements as being strictly about Japan-South Korea relations, Clinton nonetheless explained the Obama administration's concerns and fundamental stance on Japan-China relations and the issue of the Senkaku Islands.

"This region of the world is the economic engine in what is still a very fragile global economy. We can't let anything go wrong. It's not in the interest of any of the Asian countries, certainly not in the interest of the

United States or the rest of the world, to raise doubts and uncertainties about the stability and peace in the region. The United States will do what it can to try to ensure that these longstanding disputes don't become significant problems for our friends or for the broader region."

The Prime Minister's Special Envoy

"It was only yesterday that you met Hu Jintao in Vladivostok and engaged in a hallway summit meeting. How can you turn around and finalize a cabinet decision tomorrow? Won't you let me keep talking with China for a while longer? It's not that I am opposed to nationalization—only that I believe tomorrow's cabinet decision should be postponed. For procedural reasons, the Tokyo Metropolitan Government will not be able to purchase the islands any time before the end of the year. That gives you another two or three months you could wait."

This candid advice came from Vice Minister of Foreign Affairs Yamaguchi Tsuyoshi, who had been elevated to this post in the Noda administration in light of his previous career as a diplomat. It was September 10 when Yamaguchi had come to the Kantei to offer his advice. Yamaguchi later released the text of his advice on his personal website (uploaded on February 21, 2013) and went on to describe the prime minister's reaction, expressing his deep dissatisfaction with the government's nationalization of the Senkaku Islands. "I pleaded for patience, but he wouldn't change his mind. Thus the cabinet decision went through on September 11. You are well aware of the developments that followed, which I find to be most regrettable. "Although the details have not been finalized, the APEC Conference will be held on October 8, which gives us a chance to hold a summit meeting. We (my Chinese contacts and I) had been discussing the need for Japan and China to take every available opportunity to engage in talks at all levels."

Approximately one month before the Vladivostok summit meeting between Noda and Hu Jintao, Yamaguchi was in Beijing on August 31, 2012, as the prime minister's special envoy as sanctioned by both Noda and Foreign Minister Gemba Koichiro. Notwithstanding his status as the Foreign Ministry's number two man, Yamaguchi had used his own personal contacts and channels to get a meeting with Dai Bingguo (State Councillor with vice-premier status), the principal player in China's foreign policy establishment.

During the meeting with Dai Bingguo, Yamaguchi handed him a personal letter from Noda addressed to Hu Jintao. The letter was written in the context of the upcoming 40th anniversary of the normalization of Japan-China relations and was described by Chief Cabinet Secretary Fujimura Osamu in the following manner. "The letter focuses on the broader picture and touches on the need to promote the steady development of Japan-China relations." More specifically, Fujimura noted that the letter called for a "deepening of mutually beneficial relations based on common strategic interests."

The remarks Yamaguchi made in his meeting with Dai Bingguo closely mirrored Noda's letter to Hu Jintao. He emphasized the importance of high-level talks between Japan and China and argued that bilateral summit meetings should be held frequently and at every available opportunity, such as at the upcoming APEC Conference. This was the explanation that Yamaguchi repeated to the press after the meeting, but when asked for the details of the meeting, Yamaguchi demurred saying, "Our discussion extended to all areas of concern."

Yamaguchi had pressed Dai Bingguo, a member of the government with very close ties to Hu Jintao, with his argument that, "It is extremely important to maintain mutual understanding through high-level talks and other government-level exchanges." But this hastily arranged meeting had gone through many twists and turns before materializing.

Yamaguchi had met with Vice-Minister of Foreign Affairs Fu Ying the previous day. In light of the anti-Japanese demonstrations that had taken place in a number of Chinese cities and the attack on an embassy vehicle transporting Ambassador Niwa Uichiro, the two had concurred that both sides needed to approach the situation with calm and reserve. Following the meeting, the two were joined by Foreign Ministry officials from both sides in an informal dinner where the discussion continued in a more candid tone.

Even before this meeting, Yamaguchi had used his personal connections to ask for a direct meeting with Dai Bingguo and was confident his request would be approved. Thus he had kept Noda's personal letter to Hu Jintao and delayed delivering it to the Chinese side. Contrary to expectations, however, Yamaguchi was suddenly informed by his Chinese counterparts that, "No further meetings have been scheduled," implying that his request to meet with Dai Bingguo had been rejected. Taken by surprise, Yamaguchi had returned to his personal network and lobbied vigorously for the meeting, which ultimately took place.

"I have come to see you after meeting with President Hu Jintao today. Let us discuss Japan-China relations from a broad perspective." Dai Bingguo opened the meeting with these words. From his past experience on the staff of the Japanese embassy in Beijing, Yamaguchi immediately sensed that Dai Bingguo had come to the meeting with full knowledge of everything that had been said in the meeting with Fu Ying the previous evening. As the discussions moved forward, Dai Bingguo conveyed a very clear message to Yamaguchi on the nationalization of the Senkaku Islands. Dai Bingguo's blunt message was that China would not accept any change in the status quo, regardless of whether that change was brought about by the Tokyo Metropolitan Government or by the national government. No change would be acceptable.

Yamaguchi interpreted this as coming from China's supreme leader, Hu Jintao. Yamaguchi says Dai Bingguo also entrusted him with a message to be conveyed to the Japanese government. Ten days after this, Noda and Hu Jintao met in Vladivostok. One day after that (September 10), the state-owned Xinhua New Agency reported on the message that Hu Jintao had conveyed to Noda in their short hallway-chat summit meeting.

China-Japan relations have come to a serious juncture due to the Diaoyutai issue. The Chinese position on the Diaoyutai issue has been consistent and clear. Any means the Japanese government may use to acquire the islands is illegal and void, and China will resolutely oppose all such moves. The position of the Chinese government on the protection of territorial sovereignty is absolutely immovable. The Japanese side must understand the magnitude and gravity of the situation. It must not make mistaken decisions and must work with China to further China-Japan relations from a broad viewpoint.

What was the message that Dai Bingguo had entrusted to Yamaguchi? Yamaguchi was reluctant to give a clear description of the message he was tasked with. Judging from all that had preceded, it is highly likely that Dai Bingguo had directly and absolutely opposed nationalization, and in so doing had urged the Japanese government to forego a Cabinet decision as an approximate extension of the implicit agreement that remained in place since the days of Prime Minister Tanaka Kakuei and Zhou Enlai to shelve the question. The problem, however, was that Noda, to whom such a message would have been addressed, and everyone at the Foreign Ministry who would have been privy to this message had the same comment. "We don't recall receiving a special message of that sort."

Noda reminisces about the discussions that were going on at the time. "It was the same line that we had heard in the past. In other words, they did not accept the nationalization [of the Senkaku Islands]. That was it, and nothing more. On this matter, we had already received reports [of the meeting between Yamaguchi and Dai Bingguo by diplomatic cable]."

"Some response should have been made to the proposal received from State Councillor Dai Bingguo, even if the proposal were unacceptable. Notwithstanding [my urgent pleas], the proposal went unanswered." Yamaguchi uploaded this explanation on his personal website and continued in an angry tone, "The government of Japan failed to respond to the message from Dai Bingguo." Contrary to Yamaguchi's protestations, Noda insists that he had not received any message requiring a response. It is highly likely that this "misunderstanding" served as one of the sources of Chinese arguments that "Japan was at fault." We will return to this question later.

Yamaguchi's request for a meeting with Dai Bingguo had been once rebuffed, but Yamaguchi had persisted with the assistance of what he called his personal network. Who was it that had sufficient standing to intervene successfully on his behalf? The personal contact that Yamaguchi had called on was Li Xiaolin, a childhood friend of the supreme leader in waiting, Xi Jinping.

Li Xiaolin, widely known as the daughter of the former President Li Xiannian, was appointed chairperson of the Chinese People's Association for Friendship with Foreign Countries in September 2011. Since then, she regularly appeared at important junctures in China's relations with Japan and the United States. She had thus become a person of interest among China experts in Japan. The Chinese People's Association for Friendship with Foreign Countries was established in May 1954 for the purpose of promoting private-sector exchanges and diplomatic relations with countries around the world. According to the Japanese Foreign Ministry, this association is deemed an organization for supporting "overseas exchange programs with an emphasis on culture and the arts." In other words, this is an organization dedicated to playing a part in China's smile diplomacy and the projection of its soft power.

Born in Hubei Province in October 1953, Li Xiaolin was 59, the same age as China's new supreme leader, Xi Jinping. As her curriculum vitae amply testifies, Li Xiaolin is one of the Party's "Crown Princes," a label attached to the children of the first generation of China's prominent and influential revolutionaries. As such, she is reputed to be politically close to Xi Jinping, the group's chief representative.

It is worth reviewing Li Xiaolin's activities over the past several years. For example, on May 3, 2012, Xi Jinping met with a Japan-China Friendship Parliamentarian's Union mission headed by former Foreign Minister

Komura Masahiko (currently, vice president of the Liberal Democratic Party [LDP]) at the Great Hall of the People. Li Xiaolin was on hand as the chairperson of the Chinese People's Association for Friendship with Foreign Countries. A month later on June 3, Xi Jinping met with a US-China Peoples Friendship Association of Iowa mission headed by Governor Terry Branstad at the Diaoyutai State Guesthouse. Li Xiaolin was present together with Zhang Qingli, secretary of the Communist Party of Hubei Province.

Some observers have noted that Li Xiaolin is also close to the Bush family. When Xi Jinping visited the United States as vice president to make his debut in China-US diplomacy, according to a person involved in Japan-China diplomatic relations, it was Li Xiaolin who was in charge of working behind the scenes to make the necessary arrangements. As previously noted, another Chinese high official who was extremely close to the Bush family was Foreign Minister Yang Jiechi. In light of the fact that Yang Jiechi had stridently opposed the nationalization of the Senkaku Islands throughout the whole process, it would not be surprising if Li Xiaolin had used her relationship with Yamaguchi to endeavor to at least delay Japan's decision on nationalization.

Visiting Japan in April 2012 on the 40th anniversary of the normalization of relations, Li Xiaolin had said, "Normalization of diplomatic relations was achieved by Chairman Mao Zedong and Prime Minister Tanaka Kakuei when they opened their hearts and rose to transcendent heights to pledge themselves to peace and to renounce war between the two countries. If we fight, both will be hurt. If we stand on the heights, problems can be resolved through negotiation."

These words were spoken at a press conference held for the Kyodo News member newspapers on April 18. During the press conference, Li Xiaolin also commented on the proposed purchase of the Senkaku Islands by Tokyo's Governor Ishihara. "The territorial sovereignty of China is unquestionable, and Japanese actions have done injury and damage to the sentiments of the government and people of China." Having thus expressed her strong disapproval, Li Xiaolin went on to urge the Noda administration to make a political decision to rethink its position on nationalization with this warning. "The government of China will not accept whatever unilateral action Japan might take with regard to the Diaoyutai Islands, and the Chinese people will never give their consent to such an action."

On November 24, 2011, even as Governor Ishihara was secretly negotiating for the purchase of the islands with Kurihara Kunioki, the owner of the islands, Li Xiaolin had gone to the Kantei to pay a courtesy call on

Noda. Touching on the long history of friendship between the two countries, she said, "The 40th anniversary of the normalization of relations will be celebrated next year. The Chinese People's Association for Friendship with Foreign Countries intends to take this occasion to make the greatest possible effort to further expand exchanges between China and Japan."

A Ministry of Foreign Affairs release on the meeting lists the people present at the meeting. From the Japanese side, a number of the prime minister's aides were present, including Deputy Chief Cabinet Secretary Saito Tsuyoshi and Nagashima Akihisa. Strangely enough, the list also includes Yamaguchi Tsuyoshi, the second in command at the Foreign Ministry.

The Senkaku nationalization project was being carried forward by a very small group within the Kantei, and Yamaguchi was still completely out of the loop at this time. When he saw the words "nationalization of the Senkaku Islands" reported in the July 7 *Asahi Shimbun*, Yamaguchi turned to Sugiyama Shinsuke, director general of the Foreign Ministry Asian and Oceanian Affairs Bureau, and sought an explanation of what was going on. "Isn't it about time that you gave me the whole story?" Yamaguchi had said. "What am I supposed to do when you suddenly spring something like this on me?"

Relations between Yamaguchi and Foreign Minister Gemba had always been warm and close, but Yamaguchi was now registering a strong protest. For Gemba, this was a decisive moment. "The prime minister and I have been discussing this matter over the past several months." From that moment on, or perhaps even before this exchange, there was a marked chill between them, as confirmed by numerous DPJ members and Foreign Ministry officials.

This was the situation when Yamaguchi was ordered to go to Beijing, but now that he had the chance, he decided to steer clear of the usual diplomatic channels and to use the Li Xiaolin channel to secure a meeting with Dai Bingguo. Regarding his decision to go through his personal back-channels, Yamaguchi has sought to justify his decision by saying, "I gave Vice Minister of Foreign Affairs Sasae prior notice and secured his consent before taking any action." Yamaguchi takes on a defensive tone when explaining that this was not dual-level diplomacy.

Contrary to his hopes, however, what awaited Yamaguchi in Beijing was the disappointing news that the anticipated meeting with Dai Bingguo would not take place. In a panic, Yamaguchi called on Li Xiaolin to tell her what had happened. It is reported that Li Xiaolin in turn contacted Xi Jinping directly to make the case for Yamaguchi.

"Dai Bingguo has to meet Yamaguchi," she had argued. "Furthermore, it has to be a long meeting, not a perfunctory one." As Yamaguchi tells it, things started to move immediately after Li Xiaolin presented her case to Xi Jinping, and a meeting was arranged with Dai Bingguo on short notice—a meeting that clearly contravened diplomatic protocol given Yamaguchi's lower status in the government. Having absorbed the thinking of Li Xiaolin, Dai Bingguo, and Hu Jintao in the course of these exchanges, Yamaguchi, once back in Tokyo, rushed to meet Noda at the Kantei to convey the message from the Chinese side.

"I spoke up several times to make my recommendation known. China deserves a proper response," Yamaguchi recalls telling Prime Minister Noda after his return from Beijing. Yamaguchi's main argument was that, at the very least, the Cabinet decision on nationalization should be delayed, particularly in light of the meeting that had just been held between Noda and Hu Jintao in Vladivostok. But Noda had already made up his mind, and no amount of advice or protestation was going to sway him.

The consensus within the Kantei was that even if Yamaguchi's recommendation were to be adopted and the Cabinet decision delayed, there was no guarantee that the Chinese side would then relax its uncompromising position. In the absence of a clear exit strategy, it would not be surprising if Noda and his closest advisors had calculated that any postponement in Cabinet approval of nationalization would only give Japan and the rest of the world the erroneous impression of weak resolve and lack of focus.

There was no room to waver. The risk of another landing by Chinese activists loomed, while the deal with Kurihara Kunioki had to be sealed before he changed his mind about selling. Then there was the psychological battle that continued with Governor Ishihara and the worst-case scenario that could very well materialize if the Tokyo Metropolitan Government were to acquire the islands.

As the nation's top decision-maker, Noda had to keep a close eye on all these factors as he finalized his decision. As he approached his decision, in a sense, Noda resembled an aircraft carrier plying the waters at full speed. With the tremendous energy that this aircraft carrier (Noda) had stored up within it, there was no possibility for bringing it to a stop or even causing it to veer off course. It simply sped forward on its own self-determined course. The immense momentum it had gained was such that no tugboat (Yamaguchi)—no matter how capable or maneuverable—would be able to redirect it.

"The foreign minister or the prime minister should have explained the situation to China in advance. This is what I had hoped for." Yamaguchi chose these words to express his regret in a press conference on September 13, two days after the Cabinet decision. His disappointment with the Noda administration's failure to exhaust all available means to explain itself to the Chinese side was palpable.

The Noda-Ishihara Conspiracy Theory
Yamaguchi's meeting with Dai Bingguo in Beijing caused a stir back in Japan and quickly gave rise to all manner of speculation. One strain of speculation said that, coming immediately after the summit meeting in Vladivostok, the Noda Cabinet's decision on nationalizing the Senkaku Islands had caused Hu Jintao to lose face. It had been a slap in the face for the Chinese leader.

It was soon being argued that Japan's failure to pay due attention to diplomatic niceties had pushed China to adopt an even more intractable position on an issue of great sensitivity for China, and that this had triggered China's inflexible stance on the nationalization of the islands. Gradually, this argument would emerge as a central pillar in the "anti-Japanese information war" that China would wage internationally over the Senkaku Islands.

Addressing a mission of Japanese politicians in Beijing on September 27, 2012, Tang Jiaxuan, a former member of the State Council (with vice premier status) and widely reputed to be China's leading Japan hand, said "China has been slapped in the face!" The mission was intended to commemorate the 40th anniversary of the normalization of Japan-China relations and included a bevy of Diet members known as friends of China, including Kono Yohei, former speaker of the House of Representatives (chairman of the Japan Association for the Promotion of International Trade), Kato Koichi, former secretary general of the LDP (chairman of the Japan-China Friendship Association), and Komura Masahiko, former minister of foreign affairs (currently, vice president of the LDP and chairman of the Japan-China Friendship Parliamentarian's Union).

Tang Jiaxuan was a former foreign minister and chairman of the China-Japan Friendship Association, an organization dedicated to promoting China's exchanges with Japan. With the Japanese leaders of various Japan-China friendship and amity organizations arrayed in front of him, Tang Jiaxuan took the Noda administration to task for its rash actions. Tang explained that President Hu Jintao had directly told Noda of his very strong opposition to the nationalization of the Senkaku Islands. Notwithstanding this direct expression of opposition, the Noda administration had immediately moved to finalize its decision on nationalization. Tang Jiaxuan then proceeded to emphasize that this was one of the principal causes of China's angry response and opposition. "We wish to postpone all commemorative ceremonies on account of recent developments."

On September 23, four days before this meeting, China had informed Japan of its decision to cancel all ceremonies feting the 40th anniversary of the normalization of Japan-China relations that had been scheduled to be held in Beijing. Their reasons for the cancellation were outlined in an article appearing in *Xinhua News*. "The Japanese government ignored China's resolute opposition and insisted on purchasing the islands. This action has completely ruined the atmosphere for celebrating the 40th anniversary of the normalization of diplomatic relations. All quarters of Chinese society are now extremely angry." At the same time, the Chinese government had not forgotten to invite a group of prominent Japanese politicians to Beijing in an effort to maintain a semblance of continued dialogue with Japan. In addition to Kono and the leaders of seven Japan-China friendship associations, the invitees included a dozen or so individuals with close historical ties with China. One such person was Tanaka Makiko, a former minister of foreign affairs and daughter of Prime Minister Tanaka Kakuei, who was in office when diplomatic relations between the two countries were normalized. Among the other invitees were several former Japanese ambassadors to China.

This was a remarkable departure from the celebratory tone set ten years earlier at the 30th anniversary of normalization when a grand ceremony was held at the Great Hall of the People. President Jiang Zemin was on hand to greet the Japanese guests, as was Vice President Hu Jintao, who was already recognized as the leader-in-waiting. The 40th anniversary celebrations had been cancelled outright. What is more, the new leader-in-waiting, Vice President Xi Jinping, made no appearance before the Japanese delegation. The person who showed up instead of Xi Jinping to host the Japanese delegation was Jia Qinglin, chairman of the National Committee of the People's Political Consultative Conference, who stood fourth in line in the hierarchy of the Chinese Communist Party. Addressing the gathering at the Great Hall of the People, Jia Qinglin said, "There is no change in our wish to promote friendship. I call on you all to use your influence to bring the current situation to an end."

Kono responded on behalf of the Japanese delegation. "Our hope is that [China's reaction to the nationalization of the Senkaku Islands] does not spill over to affect other areas of our relations. It is our hope that such an outcome can be avoided." According to reports, the meeting lasted slightly less than an hour and remained focused on the Senkaku Islands. The Chinese side went so far as to say, "Japan must immediately correct its error." Kono addressed the press after the meeting and summarized the session calling it a "tension filled meeting." His choice of words aptly conveyed that China had been extremely upset by Japan's decision on nationalization.

China had been similarly upset when Prime Minister Koizumi Junichiro visited Yasukuni Shrine in 2006. But even then, the delegation of seven Japan-China friendship associations had been able to meet with President Hu Jintao. Although official summit meetings had already been suspended at this time, Hu Jintao had at least been willing to give some consideration to the seven friendship associations, and China had used this meeting to signal its interest in avoiding a complete collapse in bilateral relations.

But the situation in 2012 was fundamentally different. Hu Jintao refused to meet the Japanese delegation. The same applied to his successor, Xi Jinping, as well as to Xi's right-hand man, Li Keqiang. Moreover, Jia Qinglin, the substitute who was sent to meet the Japanese, was already past the age of 72 and was slated to retire from the frontlines of politics at the upcoming National Congress of the Communist Party. There is no question that this alone was enough to impress upon Kono and the members of the Japanese delegation the grave impact nationalization had on Japan-China relations and the depth of China's anti-Japanese sentiments. But as if to say that this was not enough, Tang Jiaxuan had raised his voice in anger. "China has been slapped in the face!"

Given its shared Confucian tradition, the argument that "China has been slapped in the face" as presented by Tang Jiaxuan to Kono and the other members of the Japanese delegation would prove to be very easy to understand in Japan. As a result, this argument almost instantaneously spread to all corners of Japan. To make matters worse, it was followed by a rumor that spread like a contagion throughout the Japanese political community. The rumor was that Yamaguchi, who had strongly advised Prime Minister Noda and Foreign Minister Gemba to hold off on the Cabinet decision and had continued to run around until the last possible moment arguing for postponement, had misled the Chinese side or engaged in double talk in his meeting with Dai Bingguo. Epitomizing these rumors, Yamaguchi was accused of having told the Chinese side it might be possible to delay the cabinet decision on nationalizing the Senkaku Islands if China issued high-level protests.

Rumors of the Yamaguchi concession were rife not only in the LDP but also within the ruling DPJ and the foreign policy establishment. In the following article written for his website and uploaded on February 21, 2013,

Yamaguchi pleaded his own innocence and rebutted the reports appearing in magazines.

When I met with State Councillor Dai Bingguo on August 31, what I did was to very accurately convey the Japanese position on the islands. I would like to very clearly state and establish that I did not say anything that could be construed to be a concession. Records of the meeting are available. It was a one-on-one meeting that continued for about three hours, from 11:00 a.m. to 2:00 p.m. We covered a broad spectrum of topics that we discussed in depth, including the future of Japan-China relations and the geopolitical situation in various parts of the world. We were so caught up in the discussion that we both lost track of the time. State Councillor Dai Bingguo insisted on a one-on-one format and did not allow anyone other than interpreters to be present. As a result, a quick decision was made to bring [Foreign Ministry Asian and Oceanian Affairs Bureau Second China and Mongolia Division Section Chief] Ishikawa in as an interpreter.

On the subject of the Senkaku Islands, various developments have occurred since April last year when Governor Ishihara announced his intent to purchase the islands. From the very start, what I proposed to Foreign Minister Gemba and Prime Minister Noda was that we wait and see how the whole situation would unfold. I had two reasons for this. (1) If he were serious about acquiring the islands, Governor Ishihara would have laid the groundwork in advance with the Tokyo Metropolitan Assembly. But he hadn't done this. (2) If he were serious about acquiring the islands, he would have contacted the Ishigaki City municipal government in advance. But he hadn't done this. And if he had been serious about the whole thing, he would have made the announcement in Japan, not in Washington. Sure enough, Ishihara quit his governorship in the middle of the term and completely forgot about the Senkaku issue.

Every statement that I made in meetings with the Chinese side had been fully vetted in advance. As the first step, I went over every word and phrase with Ishikawa. This was then reviewed in turn by the bureau chief, the vice minister, and finally Foreign Minister Gemba. Everything was thoroughly reviewed and duly approved before I embarked on my mission. I did not veer a hair's breadth from the approved line when I met with the Chinese side. All of this is fully recorded and conveyed in the Foreign Ministry's diplomatic cables.

In my meeting with Deputy Chief Fu Ying, I gave a detailed explanation concerning nationalization and received detailed questions, to which I responded. This process continued for approximately five hours. I made an earnest effort to speak sincerely, and I believe the Chinese side appreciated that I was being truthful. However, this did not mean that the Chinese side was convinced. What it came to was that I spoke, and they took note of what I said.

When I met with State Councillor Dai Bingguo, he said that the issue of the islands had already been discussed in detail with Deputy Chief Fu Ying on the previous day and that he wanted to have a one-on-one dialogue on deep philosophical subjects. Therefore, we discussed such topics as the future of Japan-China relations. Both of us lost track of the passage of time as we heatedly traded our views and opinions. Toward the end of the meeting, State Councillor Dai Bingguo tabled a proposal concerning the Senkaku Islands, and I responded that I would take his proposal back and we would consider it.

As an advisor to the prime minister, Nagashima Akihisa was fully apprised of the details of the dialogue between Yamaguchi and Dai Bingguo. Based on this knowledge, Nagashima affirms the veracity of Yamaguchi's explanation posted on his website. As emphasized by Yamaguchi himself, Nagashima agrees that Yamaguchi did not stray from the approved text in making his comments. Nagashima further affirms that Yamaguchi pleaded with China to understand that the procedures taken by the Noda administration for nationalization were solely intended to facilitate maintaining peaceful and stable administration of the islands.

On the other hand, it should be remembered that Yamaguchi was a late arrival to the confidential discussions on nationalization that had been going on secretly within a very small group. The fact of the matter was that Yamaguchi had not been initiated into the secret proceedings until the very last possible moment. Consequently, Yamaguchi had no inkling of how Kurihara Kunioki had constantly vacillated during the negotiations that pitted him simultaneously against Governor Ishihara of Tokyo and against the central government, nor did he have any knowledge of the gloves-off exchange that Noda and Nagashima had had with Ishihara when he combined bursts of bluster with subdued moments of pessimism. Not knowing this background meant that Yamaguchi had no way of appreciating the extreme sense of urgency that permeated the Senkaku team beginning at the very top with Noda, Gemba, and Nagashima.

Yamaguchi had not been given a bird's eye view or a comprehensive picture of the situation on hand. What is more, he had never been briefed on the details of the affair. Led by his instincts as a former diplomat, Yamaguchi departed on his mission with a simple commitment "to not repeat the mistakes of Pearl Harbor." He was now preparing to act on that commitment. No less important was the fact that, as Yamaguchi notes in his website postings, he remained fundamentally skeptical of the Senkaku nationalization project.

"I sensed that the spirits of those who had gone before me at the Foreign Ministry were descending upon me. Tears began to flow from my eyes. I felt they were begging me saying, 'Remove from us the stain and bitter regret of failing to stop Pearl Harbor.' I heard myself responding, 'Oh, if only I had the power to do that . . .' This is what was going on in my heart then."

Even today, Yamaguchi is overwhelmed with a sense of shame and regret as he recounts his mental state as he prepared to leave on his mission. While being barred from expressing his deepest feelings in words, is it possible that Yamaguchi unconsciously projected this same sense of shame and regret as he conversed with such Chinese foreign policy leaders as Fu Ying and Dai Bingguo? This possibility cannot be discounted. Nor can the possibility that the Chinese side over-estimated and over-reacted to what they had sensed in Yamaguchi's words.

Carrying this hypothesis a step further, what would have happened if Dai Bingguo had relayed to Hu Jintao the sense that he had picked up from Yamaguchi? If this is indeed what happened on the Chinese side, this could go a long way toward explaining the extreme fury with which Hu Jintao expressed his opposition to the nationalization of the Senkaku Islands at the Vladivostok meeting with Noda.

A Japanese government official with detailed knowledge of what was going on at the time agreed that this was possible. "Of course, I don't know what Hu Jintao was thinking at that time. But it is quite possible that [based on reports received from Dai Bingguo] he was thinking, 'Maybe this approach is going to work.' This possibility simply cannot be denied." Another government official drops his voice to say, "The story from China is that Dai Bingguo was very upset with the whole episode with Mr Yamaguchi, and that he is calling the whole thing a terrible nuisance."

Yamaguchi once again took to his website to summarize and analyze the rumors and unsubstantiated stories that made the rounds after the nationalization of the Senkaku Islands.

First and foremost, the whole problem started with Ishihara's plan to purchase the islands. Next, a very small group of people in the Kantei and the Foreign Ministry acted furtively to advance the nationalization plan (without waiting to see if Ishihara would actually follow through with the purchase). Even the chief of the Foreign Ministry's Asia Bureau and China Division was left out of the discussions. As a result, it became utterly impossible to mount an organized institutional response to what was unfolding. Furthermore, when I carried the prime minister's personal letter to State Council member Dai Bingguo, I received a proposal from Dai Bingguo. Although his message was duly conveyed to Japan by means of diplomatic cable, it was totally ignored. Finally, the Cabinet decision on nationalization was finalized on September 9, which immediately followed the unscheduled meeting between Prime Minister Noda and President Hu Jintao in Vladivostok.

Why had Noda sent a personal letter to China at a time when the nationalization process was already approaching its denouement? And why had Yamaguchi been chosen to deliver the letter to China when he had only very recently been inducted into the inner circle? Noda provides this explanation. "My thinking was that we needed to present a careful, thorough explanation to China." As to the assignment of this critically important task to Yamaguchi, Noda offers. "The idea was to convey our position strictly through established channels. It was my belief that the optimal choice was to assign this mission to a vice-minister of foreign affairs."

It is also true that Noda was feeling somewhat guilty about have left Yamaguchi out of the loop on the Senkaku issue. In the interest of protecting the secret, no information whatsoever had been shared with Yamaguchi, a fact that had fostered Yamaguchi's a deep sense of powerlessness. In picking his foreign minister, Noda had given the nod to Gemba—a choice that overlooked Gemba's limited experience in foreign affairs. On the other hand, well aware of Yamaguchi's background as a career diplomat, Noda had chosen Yamaguchi as Gemba's second-in-command, hoping the two would complement each other to form an effective duo. Perhaps it was this initial hope that left Noda with an awkward and uncomfortable sense of guilt that drove him to immediately accept when Yamaguchi volunteered for the mission of carrying the prime minister's letter to China. "Please let me do this," Yamaguchi had pleaded.

When he met Noda in Vladivostok, Hu Jintao had no way of knowing of the forces at play in Noda's mind that had led to Yamaguchi's appointment as special envoy. "Japan must fully realize the gravity of the situation and must avoid a mistaken decision. Japan must contribute to maintaining the general direction of developing our relations," Hu Jintao had said this in Vladivostok as if to confirm the rapid hardening of China's stance toward Japan after the emergence of the Senkaku problem. The fury with which Hu Jintao had spoken was such that even Campbell (who was monitoring the war of nerves between China and Japan from the sidelines) was made aware of it. "We sensed the atmosphere was extremely tense during the APEC summit. China's reaction to Japan was extreme. I had never seen this level of intensity before."

Shortly after Japan's Cabinet decision, Wen Jiabao had delivered a speech at the China Foreign Affairs University in Beijing to a group of young diplomats in the making. Wen Jiabao took the opportunity to declare, "On matters of sovereignty and territorial integrity, the government and the people will never compromise or retreat even half a step," making it clear that China was determined to confront Japan on the issue of the Senkaku Islands. As a further step, Yang Jiechi and the other Senkaku hardliners at China's Ministry of Foreign Affairs summoned Ambassador Niwa Uichiro to deliver a scathing protest. Simultaneously, China released a lengthy statement entitled "Determined Opposition and Fierce Protest by the Government and People of China." The statement closed with these disturbing words: "Japan will be made to pay the debt that it has incurred in this affair."

As the Chinese reaction intensified, voices began to be heard within the Japanese government saying, "China is reacting far more harshly than expected." There was even the sense in some quarters that the extreme reaction followed on the false hope that Yamaguchi had inadvertently given Dai Bingguo and Li Xiaolin. Some stubbornly clung to the argument that the Chinese side had picked up on the hope that Yamaguchi harbored and that this had encouraged China to redouble the fury of its protests. But there was no evidence to support these views. Moreover, the possibility remains that the furious Chinese cries of " We were duped! We were lied to!" were actually being orchestrated by other quarters.

One story that supports this theory comes from several people close to the Japanese government. According to these sources, China's Vice-Minister of Foreign Affairs Zhang Zhijun visited Tokyo secretly in early September. This was immediately before the Noda administration's Cabinet decision on nationalization. It is reported that Vice-Minister of Foreign Affairs Sasae Kenichiro and others at the Foreign Ministry duly informed Zhang Zhijun during his visit that a Cabinet decision was in the offing.

According to Japanese government sources, Zhang Zhijun went to the Chinese Embassy in Tokyo during his stay on the pretext of "inspecting China's overseas missions." Suppose Zhang Zhijun had told the embassy that, "A Cabinet decision will be made soon, and there is no prospect for delaying this decision." If this is in fact what happened, that would completely overturn the argument made by Tang Jiaxuan and others that, "Hu Jintao had been led to believe that some progress would be possible at the summit meeting. But ultimately, Hu Jintao was made to lose face." This would also undermine the argument that Yamaguchi had misled Dai Bingguo and the others he met in Beijing.

Observing the extreme allergic reaction that China exhibited following the nationalization of the islands, some began to argue a different possibility. "Perhaps the true purpose of nationalization had not been properly and fully conveyed to the Chinese leadership and to Zhongnanhai." Even this argument began to gain traction. Thus the view gained currency that China had not been accurately informed that Japan was not prepared to budge on this matter. Proponents of this view theorized that, because China had not been properly informed, it mistakenly assumed that Japan was amenable to compromise, which ultimately led to China's ferocious wrath at the imagined slight and slap in the face. In a sense, this view reinforces the position taken by Tang Jiaxuan.

There is no shortage of sources within the Japanese government to refute this theory. According to these sources, the message that the "Senkaku Islands will be nationalized for the purpose of maintaining peaceful and stable administration of the islands" was fully and unequivocally conveyed to officials with direct access to Hu Jintao. These included Chinese Foreign Ministry Asia Bureau Chief Luo Zhaohui, Vice-Minister of Foreign Affairs Zhang Zhijun, and State Councillor Dai Bingguo. Nor did the Japanese efforts end there. Other channels were also used to convey the same message to Zhongnanhai. Taking these explanations into consideration, one member of the Japanese government whispers his theory. "That whole story [rumors and unsubstantiated information] about Mr Yamaguchi was used as an alibi [to add credibility to Tang Jiaxuan's position by suggesting that messages were either improperly or mistakenly conveyed to Zhongnanhai]."

Writing in his book *Minshu no teki* [Enemy of democracy] (Shinchosha Publishing), Noda recounts his 2004 visit to China as a middle-echelon Diet member with roots in the Matsushita Institute of Government and Management. In the relevant passage, Noda states that he met Tang Jiaxuan during this trip and "engaged in a debate with him." According to Noda, Tang Jiaxuan addressed him in an overbearing manner saying, "Don't you know that Deng Xiaoping said that the question of the Senkaku Islands should be postponed for 20 to 30 years and left to the wisdom of future generations to solve?" Noda rose to the challenge and responded, "From a historical perspective, it is clear the islands constitute the sovereign territory of Japan. There is no room for argument here. It is true that Deng Xiaoping proposed that the issue be shelved for the future. But then why did China proclaim the islands belonged to it when it enacted its Law on the Territorial Sea and the Contiguous Zone in 1992?"

Eight years later, on April 26, 2012, Tang Jiaxuan paid a courtesy call on Prime Minister Noda. By this time, Tang Jiaxuan had retired from the frontlines of politics and was serving as chairman of the China-Japan Friendship Association. On this occasion, Noda told his visitor. "Deepening our mutually beneficial relations based on common strategic interests will lead to the strengthening of Japan-China relations." After the meeting, Tang Jiaxuan appeared before the press to share this comment. "We are hoping that bilateral relations will not be eroded by certain problems." The statement seemed to imply that China was expecting the Noda administration to take some action to counter Governor Ishihara's plan to purchase the Senkaku Islands.

Two months later, on June 23, 2012, Tang Jiaxuan was in Shanghai to deliver the keynote address at a Japan-China scholarly symposium held to fete the 40th anniversary of the normalization of bilateral relations. At one point in his speech, he stated with considerable irritation, "Certain politicians created the problem of island purchase for the purpose of political and personal aggrandizement. They have plotted conflict and are guided by ulterior motives."

At this point in June 2012, the Noda administration's plans for nationalization still remained a closely guarded secret. On the other hand, donations were pouring in to facilitate the purchase by the Tokyo Metropolitan Government, giving the impression that the plans were well on the way to being realized. There is little doubt that Tang Jiaxuan observed the progress being made in the Ishihara plan with growing anxiety. At the same time, it is highly probable that his words were intended to send a critical message of warning to Noda on his failure to block the Ishihara plan.

During his keynote address, Tang Jiaxuan gave vent to his frustration while avoiding mentioning names. "There are those who attempt to gain personal profit by manipulating the views of the people of both countries." He then went on to use a phrase that would later stand as an important theme in arguments surrounding the nationalization of the islands: "This can be called a conspiracy."

When Prime Minister Koizumi Junichiro's 2001 visit to Yasukuni Shrine emerged as a diplomatic issue between the two countries, Tang Jiaxuan had met with Foreign Minister Tanaka Makiko. In the press conference that followed that meeting, Tang delivered his message in Japanese. "What I voiced was that this [visits to Yasukuni Shrine] must stop." His gentle appearance and reputation as a career diplomat with long ties to Japan belied his identity as a "tough customer" with close ties to Chinese leaders who espoused a hardline stance on Japan, including former President Jang Zemin. Shortly after the meeting with Tanaka Makiko, a huge argument famously erupted in Japan over the interpretation of Tang's choice of the word *genmei* (translated here as "voiced"). Did he use this word to mean, "clearly said," or did he intend to convey the homonymous "strictly ordered"? The vagaries of the spoken word in Japanese did not allow a definite conclusion to be drawn on what Tang Jiaxuan had really meant.

Mention has already been made of the conspiracy theories that would soon gain credence. One claimed that Nagashima was acting as an intermediary between Noda and Ishihara to promote the nationalization of the Senkaku Islands. Another held that Noda and Ishihara were directly working hand-in-glove to promote nationalization. It is easy to imagine how these conspiracy theories may have been spawned by the relentless anti-Japanese campaign Tang Jiaxuan orchestrated.

With his prior experience in arguing with Tang Jiaxuan, Noda laughed off and categorically refuted the Noda-Ishihara conspiracy theories as well as the Japanese national conspiracy theory. Instead, Noda offered this interpretation. "I met with Ishihara [on the subject of the Senkaku Islands] only once, and this meeting took place on August 19. Surprisingly, he did not come forth with any specific criticism after the Cabinet decision on nationalization. This may have fueled the Noda-Ishihara conspiracy theories and given the Chinese claims an aura of reality."

The Cabinet approved nationalization on September 11, 2012. Three days later, on the morning of September 14, the Japan Coast Guard confirmed that six vessels from China's Maritime Surveillance Agency had entered Japan's territorial waters around the Senkaku Islands. While this was not the first infringement, it certainly was the first time that six ships had entered these waters together. The scale of infringement was clearly unprecedented. Coast Guard patrol boats radioed the Chinese vessels to leave the waters, to which one responded in Japanese. "The islands are the sovereign territory of China. We are engaged in lawful operations, and you must immediately leave these waters." The two fleets were thus caught in a standoff.

By the next day, September 15, anti-Japanese demonstrations protesting the nationalization of the Senkaku Islands had spread to all over China. Particularly noteworthy were the events in Beijing, where 20,000 demonstrators surrounded the Japanese Embassy, some of whom clashed violently with the police. Demonstrators held up Chinese flags and placards that read, "Diaoyu Islands [Chinese name for Senkaku Islands] belong to China!" "Little Japan [derogatory name for the Japanese] go home!" and "Down with Japan! This means war!" The mob threw plastic bottles, rocks, and eggs at the Japanese flag that stood in the embassy grounds. When these riotous scenes appeared on Japanese television accompanied by the voices of frightened Japanese residents in China, they quickly fired up anti-Chinese sentiments in Japan.

Rumors were rife that some 1,000 Chinese fishing vessels would enter the waters around the Senkaku Islands on September 18, the anniversary of the Liutiaohu Incident that marked the start of the Manchurian Incident in 1931. Although it later became known that this was no more than a groundless rumor, the Japanese government responded to the rising tension by increasing the number of Coast Guard patrol ships in the Senkaku waters. The government also considered deploying Okinawa Prefectural Police to counter landings on the Senkaku Islands by Chinese activists.

The Ministry of Defense and the Self-Defense Forces (SDF) were also caught up in the rising tension. To prepare for unintended consequences, the possibility of issuing an order for maritime security operations involving the deployment of SDF personnel was considered. As an extremely tense atmosphere enveloped Japan, the nation appeared to be going on full alert.

The Rikidozan Generation

"Unlike the prewar, wartime, and early postwar generations, those of us who belong to the Ron-Yasu generation can discuss the Japan-US alliance from the perspective of an equal footing." Nagashima liked to say that he was a "member of the Ron-Yasu generation." Within the DPJ, Nagashima was, along with Maehara Seiji, recognized as one of the party's leading experts on American affairs. "Ron-Yasu" of course refers to President Ronald Reagan and Prime Minister Nakasone Yasuhiro, who led the two countries in the 1980s. Their legendary friendship and personal ties provided the basis for strengthening the Japan-US alliance during the 1980s.

What was Nagashima trying to convey with his "Ron-Yasu generation"?

His point was that a new generation had emerged which, unlike the pre-war, wartime, and early postwar generations, did not approach Japan-US relations from the perspective of victor and vanquished. This generation was far more aware of the strong trust and mutual respect that had come to bind the two countries together in the course of the Cold War and in developing a united front against the Soviet Union. This generation believed that Japan-US relations should be accepted as relations between two allies that trusted, respected, and cooperated with each other.

In the history of Japan-US relations, the personal bonds that were developed between Ronald Reagan and Nakasone Yasuhiro, and later between George W. Bush and Koizumi Junichiro, stand out as the closest and most robust personal relations between the leaders of the two countries. As a close witness to these two relationships during his term as President Reagan's chief of staff and later as US Ambassador to Japan, former Senate Majority Leader Howard Baker has described these relations in his book *Chotoha no seishin* (The spirit of bipartisanship, Nikkei Publishing, 2009):

> Reagan and Nakasone, and Bush and Koizumi. The two relations had many points in common. In both instances, the leaders were recognized domestically as remarkable politicians, and in both instances, the leaders treated each other as equals and with deference. In addition to mutual respect, most importantly, the leaders shared an awareness of the extreme importance of the other country as an ally.
>
> Reagan felt he got along well with Prime Minister Nakasone on a personal level. Bush also had positive feelings about Prime Minister Koizumi. If I had to point to differences, I would say the Bush-Koizumi relationship was more personal in nature, while the Reagan-Nakasone relationship was more of an institutional relationship. This is because the two shared a common philosophy of a new conservatism that was then becoming mainstream throughout the world.

As opposed to Nagashima's concept of the Ron-Yasu generation, Noda—who is five years older—presents his own unique perspective of what the United States stands for in his mind. To make his point, Noda uses the symbolism of Rikidozan, the extremely popular professional wrestler during Japan's postwar reconstruction years.

Born in 1957, Noda calls himself a member of the "last generation that watched Rikidozan live." When television sets began appearing in ramen shops and private homes in the mid-1950s, wrestling matches featuring the immensely popular Rikidozan drew enormous crowds. Basically the script was always the same. A match would start with a white wrestler using every conceivable dirty trick to attack Rikidozan, who would bear his attacker's onslaught with superhuman endurance and patience. Pushed to the point of breaking, Rikidozan would suddenly go on the offensive with his karate chops. The white wrestler would then be beaten down to the point of begging miserably for pity. Alternatively, the white wrestler would continue to take a severe beating through to the end of the match. Notwithstanding this all too transparent fiction that was repeated time and again in the wrestling ring, the Japanese people loved the contrived script and wildly applauded Rikidozan's exploits.

In the postwar reconstruction years, Rikidozan was one of the few "shining stars of hope" that the Japanese public could look up to. Rikidozan stood invincible in the wrestling ring, frequently covered in blood, but always rising at the end to discipline and punish his white opponents who resorted to every form of injustice. And he would drop his opponents to the mat with the force of his bare hands—the deadly force that he mustered with his right-handed karate chop. The scene was enough to make the prewar and wartime generations forget for a moment the deep-seated inferiority complex toward America and Americans that festered in their hearts. After all, this was the opponent that they had fought in the Pacific War, an opponent that had come to the battlefield armed with an overwhelming material advantage and scientifically formulated tactics and strategies. The Japanese people, on the other hand, had been taught, "We will not ask for anything until the day of victory." They were sent into battle armed with the sheer force of spirit and ultimately committed to death in suicide charges. The outcome of the battle was near annihilation. For those who had lived the trauma of this experience, Rikidozan proffered a rare and precious shot in the arm that reinvigorated his fans with the hope and energy to face yet another day.

Noda was still a small child in those days, but he eagerly looked forward to watching Rikidozan's heroics on the family's black-and-white television. As Noda recalls, the wrestling matches were shown every other Friday, and on Fridays when there was no wrestling, he watched the *Wonderful World of Disney*.

Thus Noda alternated between watching "Rikidozan covered in blood" (Noda's description) and Walt Disney's "world of dreams" (again Noda's words). The former rose up as a fierce god of destruction to beat down even the United States, while the latter portrayed the affluence of the American

Dream. Looking back on this period of his life, Noda says about himself. "I belong to the generation that understood the language and the philosophy of the prewar, wartime, and postwar generations."

From this vantage point, Noda felt he understood what was going through the mind of Ishihara who, at age 80, represented the generation that grew up during the war years. Admiration for the United States was interwoven with raw anger, giving rise to a deep sense of ambivalence toward the United States. Similarly, Noda had no problem understanding Nagashima and the postwar generation that he represented. He was equally at ease with the Ron-Yasu generation and the Cold War generation.

Noda's book, *Minshu no teki* [Enemy of democracy], contains the following passage. "Knee-jerk anti-Americanism is a position taken by those who have not examined history critically." Noda categorically states that, "An examination of postwar Japanese foreign policy shows that the Japan-US alliance stands unquestionably as the cornerstone." He then continues with an analysis of the Anglo-Japanese alliance that was concluded in 1902 and dissolved in 1921. The dissolution of this alliance, he states, "Led to the unmooring of Japanese foreign policy and acted as one of the causes for Japan's march toward the Pacific War."

Referring to the April 2012 Japan-US summit meeting in Washington, Noda had said, "What I really wanted to do in Washington was to announce a Pacific Charter patterned after the Atlantic Charter." Given this mindset, the value and significance of the Japan-US alliance was self-evident and beyond questioning for Noda. His position clearly differentiated him from Ishihara, who had caused a stir with his book that bore the provocative title *The Japan That Can Say No*. Noda's position was also at odds with the late socio-political commentator Matsumoto Kenichi, who was an advisor to the Cabinet under Prime Minister Kan Naoto and who has publicly questioned the justification for hosting US military bases in Japan.

Matsumoto was a student of the political philosophy of Kita Ikki, the prominent prewar idea man who was known for his doctrine of right-wing socialism. In his book entitled *Naze Nihon ni Amerika gun no kichi ga arunoka* [Why there are American military bases in Japan] (Makino Shuppan, 2010), Matsumoto expressed his very strong suspicions concerning Japan-US security arrangements. "The current Japan-US security agreement stipulates that US forces can remain in Japan near-indefinitely. However, if Japan is truly an independent nation, or if it aspires to be a truly independent nation, I believe this should be understood to be no more than an emergency stationing of forces."

It is interesting to note that Matsumoto was a classmate of Chief Cabinet Secretary Sengoku Yoshito, Prime Minister Kan's principal supporter and aide. On a very deep level, Matsumoto's thinking was closely tied to the position taken by Hatoyama Yukio, the first prime minister from the DPJ, who had run the ship of state aground with his position on the relocation of US military's Futenma Air Station in Okinawa. "The minimum condition is the removal of this base from Okinawa. Relocation abroad would be best if possible," Hatoyama had boldly announced. To amplify this further, Matsumoto's position that postwar Japan is a "vassal state of the United States" can also be linked to Ishihara's thinking as expounded in his book *The Japan That Can Say No.*

Mindful of this background, and in order to draw a clear line of demarcation between himself and the positions espoused by Matsumoto and Ishihara, Noda has declared, "My thinking differs from Matsumoto's." For Noda, the Japan-US relationship is the absolute cornerstone. In line with this diplomatic philosophy, Noda yearned to go back to the kind of footing that characterized the Ron-Yasu era. Thus Noda was more inclined to assimilate with the first-name-basis relationship that Nagashima had developed with Michael Green, the former advisor to the president (senior director for Asian affairs at the National Security Council) and other American counterparts. For Noda, such close relationships created room for new forms of resonance and cooperation between the two countries.

On the other hand, Ishihara who was 12 years old when the war ended, was painfully aware of the gap that existed between the prewar Empire of Japan and the postwar pacifist Japan. Ishihara had come to represent an entire generation of people who had struggled mightily to square this irreconcilable gap. For those who had lived through Japan's early postwar years, MacArthur initially symbolized the United States as the victor. But this symbol eventually gave way to a succession of presidents—Eisenhower, Kennedy, and on to Nixon. As the symbol of the victor changed, so did the victor's demands and expectations of Japan. What started as the pursuit of the ideal pacifist nation gave way to American expectations that Japan should function as a bridgehead in containing Communism. In the Cold War that continued for nearly half a century, Japan failed to engage in any realistic discussions of its security issues and was permitted to busy itself in abstract theological arguments over the interpretation of the Constitution. In this environment, many chose to bask in the benefits of peace and prosperity without ever seriously examining the reality of Japan's national security requirements. This mindset certainly applied to postwar Japan's liberal left. However, at a certain level, this formulation applied equally to Ishihara and others who made up the conservative right.

During this period, the United States continued to protect Japan with its immense military and economic might. At the same time, the United States inevitably gave the impression that it looked down on Japan as it issued a long list of instructions and orders on various and sundry matters. This American attitude became a source of mental trauma and a gnawing internalized struggle for both the left and the right. Consequently, both sides of Japan's political spectrum soon began to show signs of reaction and resistance, each through its own style and arguments that eventually coalesced into such terms as "anti-American," "cutting the ties with the US," "America fatigue," and "bidding good-bye to America." Needless to say, as a proponent of a Japan that could say no, Ishihara emerged as one of the loudest voices of resistance.

The main pillar of what was called the Yoshida Doctrine that epitomizes Japan's postwar national strategy was a commitment of all of Japan's available resources to economic reconstruction and development. The other side of the coin was Japan's skewed system of national administration that depended utterly on the United States for military power and national security.

Building and maintaining this skewed system, Japan was inexorably drawn into an "anatomy of dependence" that quickly came to taint its relationship with the United States. The inconsistencies of dependence came to a head in the 1980s and 1990s at the height of bilateral trade friction when Japan came under fire in the United States for its "free rider" status in matters of national security. The twenty-first century has seen the emergent military might of China juxtaposed against the ebbing of US power. The many obsolete and shallow theories on the United States and China that continue to persist in Japan today are in many ways rooted in this dependence that remains partially in place even in the present century. While Ishihara was arguing that this dependence had to be cast aside, it is quite probable that Ishihara's own thinking on foreign affairs and national security had unwittingly been influenced by the constructs of dependence.

There was something fundamentally inconsistent and unrealistic in Ishihara's stance on national security. That is, while looking askance at the nuclear umbrella the United States provided, Ishihara had boasted, "So long as the war is fought with conventional weapons, Japan will win." This inconsistency betrays the characteristic ambivalence with which the people of Ishihara's generation viewed the United States.

"In the end, he lived in a virtual world and all of his life was a fiction.

His dramatic suicide was not a political act. It was simply an extension of the virtual world he had concocted . . . I would say that in his heart, he did not harbor true reverence for the emperor." This passage refers to the life of Mishima Yukio, to whom Ishihara has been frequently compared, and appears in Ishihara's October 2010 book *Mishima Yukio to sengo* (Mishima Yukio and the postwar period, Chuokoron-Shinsha).

Mishima ended his life in a dramatic act of *seppuku* at the SDF Ichigaya Camp. Shortly after this shocking incident, Ishihara famously took pen to paper to write, "There is no doubt that Mishima's death has greatly increased the ennui that prevails in Japanese society." Regarding the cause for which Mishima gave his life, Ishihara brushed all aside with the single word "virtual."

Around the time the book was published, Ishihara was at the zenith of his power as governor of Tokyo. Writing again on the subject of Mishima in November 2010 in a book titled *Dokyumento fukuchiji* (Document vice governor, Kodansha), Ishihara gave vent to bitter criticism. "That way of dying is of no value. It does absolutely no good. You have to live to take action—that is where meaning comes from."

There is little doubt that Ishihara has always been ready to take action as governor. And in so doing, he had frequently drawn the public's attention to himself. Without question, the greatest attention-grabbing action that he took was to announce his plan to purchase the Senkaku Islands, which came in the very last stage of his career as governor.

Ishihara boasted that Japan could trounce China in a conventional war, but he was totally oblivious to the fact that there was nothing to guarantee that such a war would remain a limited and conventional war other than the extended deterrence provided by the US nuclear umbrella, which was something that he had repeatedly called unreliable and said should be cast away. In other words, what Ishihara was doing was to disparage the reliability and efficacy of the American nuclear umbrella and advocate Japan acquire its own nuclear capability. Herein lies the absurdity of Ishihara's positions on national security and defense, and this is why the term he had used in criticizing Mishima was fully applicable to Ishihara himself. Ishihara's positions were equally the figment of an imagination that was functioning in a virtual world.

Noda, on the other hand, came from a totally different background. Noda was the product of the postwar period. His father was an officer in the SDF and a member of the first class of recruits taken in by the Police Reserve Force, the predecessor organization to the SDF. Noda's father was with the elite 1st Airborne Brigade. Camp Narashino, where the brigade was stationed, was the closest thing to home that Noda knew. The SDF and national defense had been a part of Noda's life since childhood. In many ways, they formed an integral part of his daily routine.

On days off, the small and simple government-issued Noda home would be crowded with his father's subordinates gathered for dinner. For Noda, it was a given that the young soldiers were going through extreme training to prepare for national emergencies. This was a fact of life that Noda had already fully internalized as a child. For Noda, national defense was by no means a virtual pursuit, nor could it ever be allowed to be a virtual pursuit. National defense was extremely real as it could very well involve the shedding of real blood by real people whom he had grown close to and with whom he had shared countless meals.

"Ishihara's generation views the United States through muddied lenses, but my generation is free of all that baggage, and we have a much clearer understanding of what the United States is all about." Even while providing this analysis of what separates his generation from Ishihara's, Noda says that he also more or less gets the ambivalence toward the United States that came from the mixture of admiration (Disney) and raw anger (Rikidozan) in the hearts of Ishihara's generation. Having said this, it is undeniable that, as a politician, Noda himself bore all the scars and trauma characteristic of his generation.

Returning once again to his book *Minshu no teki,* it is notable that Noda writes, "Politics was allowed to enter into the classroom." It should be remembered that when Noda was growing up in the 1950s and 1960s, Japanese intellectuals and educators were for the most part liberals commonly referred to as "progressive people of culture." For this class of intellectuals and educators, such terms as national defense, SDF, and national security were to be shunned and shunted into a corner, as were all terms and concepts that evoked war. "A student who wrote, 'Go Viet Cong. Beat America!' was praised."

Noda grew up eating the hard biscuits his father brought home from SDF encampments. And as he ate, Noda grew increasingly disenchanted with the politics taught in the classroom. As a member of the Cold War generation, there was little room to doubt that the Japan-US alliance was Japan's national defense. In Noda's mind, this equivalency was something close to a categorical truth. "It is extremely risky for Japan to look beyond the framework of the Japan-US alliance in discussing national security."

Born in postwar Japan and more specifically the product of the period of Japan's full-throated reconstruction and recovery, Noda exhibits a very clear and principled approach in his understanding of the United States. By comparison, Ishihara's view of America is, for better or worse, far more complicated and convoluted. This can be glimpsed in the spatial features of the language he uses to cynically compare himself to Mishima. "Japan became very boring after Mishima's death. Japan will become even more boring after I die. (laughter)" (From *Mishima Yukio to sengo*)

It will be remembered how Sonoda Hiroyuki provided Ishihara behind-the-scenes support in matters related to the Senkaku Islands and how he later joined Ishihara in creating the Japan Restoration Party as a new political entity. Speaking from this position of proximity, Sonoda explains Ishihara's thinking on diplomatic policies as follows. "His roots trace back to his anti-hegemonic stance. That's where everything starts with him." According to Sonoda, China is not the only country that triggers Ishihara's sense of resistance to power. The same sentiment guides him in standing up to the United States. In Ishihara's mind, Japan's relationship with the United States is not a relationship that can be easily navigated.

Ishihara is generally considered to be a strident hardliner on all matters related to China. But Sonoda adds this caveat. "It's not that Ishihara dislikes China and China alone." In other words, as an "anti-hegemonist," China is not the exclusive target of Ishihara's aversion and dislike. The same negative sentiments apply to the United States. However, from a realistic international politics perspective, Sonoda says that Ishihara has come to the following conclusion. "If he had to choose among the various superpowers, his heart is closer to the United States than to China." Sonoda explains that these sentiments and calculations lie at the core of Ishihara's view of the United States.

Where does Abe Shinzo, the politician who returned to the prime minister's office after Noda was ousted, stand in this spectrum? After all, Noda and Abe belong to almost the same postwar generation. In an interview with *Sankei Shimbun* published on May 12, 2012, Abe made the following revealing comments. "The public response to the Tokyo Metropolitan Government's plan to purchase the Senkaku Islands has been astonishing. Donations from the public are already poised to exceed 400 million yen. I suppose Tokyo Governor Ishihara simply ran out of patience with the DPJ's incredibly weak awareness of territorial sovereignty. I can just see him saying, 'I can't take this anymore!' I am fully committed to supporting Ishihara. I consider myself a moderate conservative. But Ishihara takes it a step further to advocate anti-Americanism. That's where we differ fundamentally."

Noda had identified this difference between himself and Ishihara in the course of the intense dialogue the two had had at the Kantei. Whether Noda himself was aware of this or not, there is no question that his discovery of this troubling difference soon began to propel him toward nationalizing the Senkaku Islands. While Noda self-identifies as a member of the last Rikidozan generation, Noda has also said that he more or less gets the deep reverence for territory, sovereignty, and the Japanese nation that Ishihara had nurtured in his heart as a patriot and as the standard bearer for the generations born in wartime Japan. Noda's statement was intended to convey that he was willing to understand and appreciate the positions taken by the generations that had gone before him. Noda viewed himself as being sandwiched somewhere between the prewar, wartime, and postwar generations. When the time came for him to make a final decision on nationalizing the Senkaku Islands, Noda was deeply affected and guided by his "postwar patriotism." Similarly, it was this postwar patriotism that fixated him on the idea of installing LED lamps in the lighthouse on Uotsurijima.

There was someone on the opposite side of the Pacific who had from a great distance seen through all that was going on in Noda's mind—none other than Assistant Secretary of State Kurt Campbell. In his public statements, Campbell had put a check on China by affirming that the Senkaku Islands came under the provisions of the Japan-US Security Treaty. But behind the scenes, Campbell continued to very meticulously try to determine the real story behind Japan's march toward nationalizing the Senkaku Islands. Campbell has summarized his impressions and findings on why the DPJ and the Noda administration ultimately opted for nationalization.

The DPJ was sending two very distinct messages. The first message was that there is no other option available and they were going through with this in order to ensure peaceful and stable administration. This message was conveyed to China among others. But then, from time to time, the [Japanese side] would also comment on its actions to say they are nationalists acting in Japan's national interest by ensuring the stable administration of the islands. It was as though Japan was sending two different messages to two different audiences. It did not appear that this second message was being directed to any specific someone. It seemed more like it was part of a broader campaign.

Battles Rage Inside the Kantei

As Campbell pointed out, Noda had definitively stated in his meeting with Ishihara that, "Building a moorage was absolutely unacceptable." On the other hand, shortly after the meeting, Noda began seriously considering the possibility of the government's accepting responsibility for building some sort of structure on the Senkaku Islands following nationalization.

"There is no fundamental difference between Ishihara and myself on the subject of acting resolutely to defend the nation's territory and its territorial waters. The only difference is that between my 'vigilant and cautious' approach and Ishihara's 'sudden thrusting' approach."

This is how Noda recounts his impressions from their August 19 summit meeting. As they discussed the Senkaku problem that evening, Noda and Ishihara candidly shared their views on national security. In opening up to Ishihara as representating the wartime generation, Noda had begun to feel some understanding and affinity for the philosophy that characterized the older generation. At the same time, Noda had decided to keep one thing in mind as he observed Ishihara's reactions to the discussion. Throughout the meeting, even as he endeavored to more accurately assess Ishihara's position, Noda remained focused on the single question: "How far will the government have to go to satisfy Ishihara and convince him to back off from his announced plan?" As previously noted, it was during this meeting that Ishihara had spouted, "As long as the war is fought with conventional weapons, Japan will win." Noda explains that Ishihara made this statement in the course of his assessment process.

While there is no way of knowing if Ishihara was aware of what was going through Noda's mind, the fact remains that Ishihara continued to direct an unrelenting barrage of criticism against the Foreign Ministry for its refusal to even contemplate building some structure on the Senkaku Islands out of consideration for Japan's relations with China. Even as he continued to rant and rave against the Foreign Ministry, Ishihara did not spare the United States. Referring to what the US might do as an ally, Ishihara said, "How can you expect the United States to protect us if we are not serious about protecting ourselves?" With this as his line of attack, Ishihara pressed Noda to take the occasion to manifest the spirit of Japan.

What Ishihara meant by manifesting the spirit of Japan was for the government to construct a moorage or some other port facility on the Senkaku Islands. Any such construction, Ishihara argued, would clearly underscore and reinforce Japan's effective control of the islands. But having considered the matter from all angles, Noda had come to the conclusion that he could not go along with Ishihara's demand. Having rejected the idea, Noda tried to make sure Ishihara would not lose face. At the same time, he tried desperately to find a compromise that would draw a logical and cool-headed response from China.

By this time, Noda had received numerous messages from various quarters asking him to make sure Ishihara did not lose face. "I pledge my support for nationalization. In return, please show Ishihara some consideration," these messages pleaded. The islands' owner, Kurihara Kunioki, conveyed the same request through Deputy Chief Cabinet Secretary Nagahama Hiroyuki. As for Sonoda Hiroyuki, Ishihara's comrade in arms, he delivered his request to Noda through his aide, Nagahama Akihisa. These requests soon reached a deafening crescendo. It was as if he were surrounded by a chorus calling on him to make sure the old politician did not lose face.

Even while these pleas continued to come in, the Foreign Ministry had turned the focus of its attention to the growing opposition that was heating up in China and had already committed itself to an entirely different approach—an approach that can be described as a modified version of the quiet approach initially advocated by Vice Minister of Foreign Affairs Sasae Kenichiro. In its revised form, the quiet approach featured two options that would allow the Japanese government to make the case that no change had been made in the status quo.

OPTION 1:
Allow Ishihara and the Tokyo Metropolitan Government to go through with their planned purchase and take the position that the purchase was merely the act of a local government.

OPTION 2:
Go through with the government's purchase of the islands on the premise that the act involves no more than a transfer of title, and thereafter avoid building any facilities on the islands.

Noda was now beginning to feel that Kurihara Kunioki was leaning toward selling to the national government instead of to Ishihara and the Tokyo Metropolitan Government. Thus when the Foreign Ministry presented its two options to Noda at the end of August, the prime minister chose not to make an immediate decision and allowed the matter to remain pending. Noda had already informed Ishihara that building a large moorage was out of the question. But at the same time, he was quietly mulling what other measures could be taken instead. Noda was increasingly convinced that, "Doing nothing was not a viable option," a closely guarded view that Noda quietly shared with Nagashima, his aide.

As discussed earlier, Noda had instructed a team led by Fujimura to formulate a series of compromise proposals. Hammered out on the administrative level, the compromise proposals contained multiple plans to be implemented after the islands had been nationalized. The proposals ran the full gamut of options beginning with doing nothing more than stepping up the level of maritime surveillance. More proactive measures included engaging in environmental protection programs in the waters around the Senkaku Islands, upgrading the lighthouse (installing LED lights) to enhance maritime safety, installing a communications relay station equipped to handle mobile telephone communication, and building what Ishihara had called a moorage that could serve as a harbor of refuge or some type of pier. A final and extreme measure was the possibility of inhabitation.

Noda has refused to discuss this topic in detail, arguing that his status as former prime minister obligates him to preserve confidentiality. "I cannot go into the details," Noda professes, but agrees to present a hypothetical case. "Let us suppose that a total of ten options were presented to me, going from Level One all the way up to Level Ten. Let us next stipulate that the construction of a moorage would be a Level Ten option. What I can say is that what I had in mind was something in the vicinity of level one."

Fujimura and other government officials are able to shed some light on what Noda is not prepared to discuss. According to these sources, Noda remained interested in one option until the very end. And this was the option that Fujimura himself silently favored, which was to install LED lamps in the lighthouse on Uotsurijima and make greater use of the lighthouse. Fujimura explains his preference, and likely the prime minister's preference, for this option saying: "For a number of years, Japan Coast Guard officers were landing on Uotsurijima once a year to inspect and repair the lighthouse. The Chinese side was, of course, aware of these annual landings because they monitored these activities closely. Considering this situation, it was possible to argue that switching to LED lamps is consistent with peaceful and stable administration of the islands."

On Noda's instructions, various measures were being weighed in the back rooms of the Kantei to spare Governor Ishihara a loss of face. Concurrent with this, on August 27, 2012, Noda rejected in writing the request that had been submitted by the Tokyo Metropolitan Government for permission to land on Uotsurijima for the stated purpose of surveying the island.

Issued in the name of Deputy Chief Cabinet Secretary Nagahama Hiroyuki and addressed to Governor Ishihara of the Tokyo Metropolitan Government, the rejection letter contained the following passage. "In the interests of ensuring peaceful and stable maintenance and administration of the Senkaku Islands, the request for landing is hereby rejected." Concurrently, Chief Cabinet Secretary Fujimura provided the following explanation on why the request had been rejected. "It is our understanding that the prospects for the acquisition of the islands by the Tokyo Metropolitan Government remain unsettled. Furthermore, the application was not accompanied by documents issued by the landowner." In his choice of words, Fujimura was implying that the owner of the islands was moving away from Ishihara and was now leaning toward selling the islands to the national government.

Ishihara immediately responded to the rejection with a public statement. "As a step toward purchasing the Senkaku Islands, the Tokyo Metropolitan Government sought permission to survey the site. This is in line with normal commercial practice. The decision not to allow us to enter the site absolutely defies comprehension."

Following Ishihara's highly critical statement that openly challenged the government's decision, the Tokyo Metropolitan Government opted to take countermeasures. Thus on September 2, it dispatched a chartered vessel to the Senkaku Islands to survey Uotsurijima from the sea. The survey vessel approached the islands on September 2 and spent a total of ten hours in the waters near the Senkaku Islands, during which time it primarily surveyed the coastline. The vessel returned to Ishigaki Port after 10:00 p.m.

The surveying mission consisted of a total of 25 members and included a number of experts. Among them were two experts in maritime policy, including Professor Yamada Yoshihiko of Tokai University, who was concurrently serving as a member of the Tokyo Metropolitan Government's panel of experts. One real estate appraiser and a number of Tokyo Municipal Government employees were also on board. *Koyo Maru* (2,474 tons), a maritime rescue vessel, had been chartered at a cost of about 25 million yen to transport the mission to the Senkaku area. After arriving at the target area, small boats and a rubber dingey were used to approach the islands and undertake more detailed surveys.

Upon completing the mission, the Tokyo Metropolitan Government's Sakamaki Seiichiro, who served as the head of the mission, made a statement. "The beaches and flat areas could not be surveyed because we were unable to land. Nevertheless, we were able to successfully complete most of what we had planned to do. Regarding the construction of the port of refuge for fishing boats that Governor Ishihara is advocating, we will look at the data and examine the possibilities." The statement conveyed a sense that the results needed for moving forward on the purchase of the islands had been duly obtained.

The same day, September 2, Ishihara Nobuteru, the governor's eldest son, said "I spoke with Governor Ishihara on the phone yesterday. During our conversation, the governor told me, 'I asked Prime Minister Noda what he was going to do about nationalization. I waited two weeks for an answer and finally gave up on waiting. We are going to acquire the Senkaku Islands. We will go to the Senkaku Islands in October and land. Why not give them a chance to arrest us?'"

These comments were made during a speech the younger Ishihara gave in Kanoya City, Kagoshima Prefecture. On the same day, Governor Ishihara himself appeared in a television program and emphasized the need to land on the islands. Commenting on a planned follow-up survey of the Senkaku Islands by the Tokyo Metropolitan Government, Ishihara said, "We need to have experts examine the geological features of the bedrock." He then continued, "We have to do this, and we don't care if we are arrested and put in prison." Ishihara indicated that he would join the second survey mission scheduled for October and land on the islands himself. Ishihara's words were designed to send a strong message to Noda.

While keeping a wary eye on the aggressive actions of the Tokyo Metropolitan Government, Noda had more or less made up his mind by the end of August. On the one hand, Ishihara would be allowed to save face, while on the other hand the government would leave enough room to be able to explain to the Chinese side that the status quo had been maintained. Noda would seek a compromise that would satisfy both conditions. At about the same time, as the end of August approached, the foreign policy establishment was preparing to go on the attack. Foreign Minister Gemba Koichiro would lead the attack as the minister of state with the foreign policy portfolio.

In the secret meetings held at the Kantei, Gemba consistently adhered to a position on nationalization that he called passive promoter. Meanwhile, he was always painfully aware of the alarms that were being sounded from behind him by the foreign policy establishment. Mindful of these alarms, Gemba continued to argue for "not taking any action." Finally, on August 30, Gemba made his way to the Kantei to directly make his case before Noda and to ask him to reconsider.

As a politician, Gemba was resigned to the thought that the nationalization of the Senkaku Islands was not something that could be avoided for-ever. But from his vantage point as Japan's top diplomat, he was constantly monitoring the nation's security policies and Japan's diplomatic relations with the United States as well as with China. And it was from this vantage point that Gemba judged that the prime minister had become overly com-mitted to helping Ishihara save face. His August 30 visit to the Kantei was undertaken to convince Noda he was making a mistake.

Mindful of the growing tension between Japan and China, Gemba admonished the prime minister that "We should allow more time to pass quietly and calmly so that stable administration of the islands can be achieved." Ultimately, his advice to Noda was to maintain the status quo. But Noda was adamant in rejecting this suggestion. "We can't just do noth-ing!" the prime minister rebutted testily. As previously noted, by this time Noda had made up his mind on the need to take some form of concrete action on the islands after their nationalization. Gemba picked up on the unspoken commitment that had taken form inside the prime minister's mind and became increasingly agitated. He felt all that he could do now was to lay out his arguments before former Foreign Minister Okada Katsuya, the prime minister's trusted personal advisor who had been brought into the Noda Cabinet as deputy prime minister. Gemba knocked on Okada's door to make his case.

Okada had not been involved in drafting and reviewing the territo-rial affairs speech that Noda had delivered in mid-August. But from the moment he absorbed the arguments that were being presented to him, Okada became a powerful ally for Genba and the foreign policy establish-ment, joining the forces urging Noda to reconsider.

Gemba recalls his interactions with Noda when the Kantei was approaching peak tension. "It wasn't that simple. Convincing Noda took more than one meeting." Time and again Gemba repeated his dire warn-ing: "If we go any further than nationalization and implement measures leading to greater use of the islands, there is no telling what the outcome will be." Feeling that his words did not carry enough weight with Noda, Gemba recruited Okada and arranged for the two of them to meet with the prime minister. It was during this meeting that Noda finally relented. This marked the moment of final decision on the Senkaku Islands. "Yes on nationalization. No on the construction of additional facilities."

Nagashima expressed shock when he learned of Noda's final decision, rendered on August 31. "In a single night, all of earlier discussions were simply thrown out the window." Nagashima had not participated in the last-minute counter-attack mounted by the foreign policy establishment and had instead watched the fray from the sidelines. The prime minister had already instructed him to, "Go to Ishihara and explain the situation." Nagashima smiles wryly as he reveals what went through his mind when he heard the details of Noda's decision. "That very moment, I descended into the depths of depression."

Shortly before this, Nagashima had flown to Okinawa to engage in behind-the-scenes discussions with local residents and leaders on the relocation of the US military's Futenma Air Station. Just as his plane was touching down at Naha Airport, Noda contacted Nagashima to inform him that negotiations with Kurihara had reached a successful conclusion. Noda added, "I want you to meet with Governor Ishihara immediately. This should be explained to him at the earliest possible time." Nagashima hopped right back on the next flight to return to Tokyo.

On September 3, Ishihara contacted Nagashima with a terse message. "Be at my house tomorrow morning." This was only three days after the conclusion of the battles that had been raging inside the Kantei. On the same day, September 3, the Noda Cabinet had finally succeeded in reaching a final agreement to buy the islands from their owner, Kurihara Kunioki.

Kurihara conveyed his acceptance of the terms of sale to Nagahama, who had acted as Noda's proxy throughout the negotiations. "I accept. I am leaving the details to you. I am leaving my house now to meet Ishihara and apologize." Kurihara had refrained from signaling his consent until the last possible moment. But by closely observing Kurihara's words and deeds, Nagahama already had an inkling that the end was near. "On one occasion in the final stages, Kurihara brought his sister to the meeting. This was of course the sister that owned Kubajima [another of the Senkaku Islands]. I was very surprised to see her because Kurihara had told me previously, 'My sister says she does not want to sell Kubajima.' So I was very surprised."

According to Nagahama, Kurihara introduced the woman that had accompanied him saying, "This is my sister." He proceeded to negotiate with Nagahama so that his sister would be able to hear everything that was being said. Nagahama explains the importance of the meeting: "It was clear to me that Kurihara wanted someone very close to him—in this case, his sister—to hear our conversation. Her presence there had a definite purpose, and it had nothing to do with buying time or wasting time. This is what I surmised."

Nagahama's intuition was correct. Shortly after this encounter, Kurihara again met secretly with Nagahama. It was on this latter occasion that

Kurihara informed Nagahama of his decision to sell the islands to the government. However, even after receiving Kurihara's pledge to sell, Nagahama was unable to fully rid himself of anxiety. The reason had to do with the owner's persistent demand throughout the negotiations. "You must not cause Ishihara to lose face." But every time this demand had come up, Nagahama had responded in a firm tone that implied there was no room for compromise. "I appreciate your feelings, but no conditions can be attached to the sale."

This tug-of-war had been repeated on every occasion that the two had met, and judging from the atmosphere that prevailed, Nagahama had more or less resigned himself to an endless repetition of the same go-no-where argument. "I had come to believe that this was going to continue for quite a while." Nagahama theorized that while Kurihara would eventually find himself convinced at some juncture in the negotiations, more time was needed for him to arrive at that critical point.

But contrary to Nagahama's bleak prognosis, Kurihara finally came around to choose the government as the party he would sell the islands to. Nagahama describes what he sensed was going on in the seller's mind. "I could see that the islands were weighing heavily on him. In a sense, he wanted to unburden himself. He was looking back through a long history in search of the right time to unburden himself. I suppose he had concluded that the right time was approaching."

The Last Supper

"We have finally managed to come to an agreement for the government to purchase the islands. But under the current conditions, it is impossible for us to do any more than that. I am so sorry to have to admit that I was powerless to meet the conditions that you requested."

On September 4, 2012, Nagashima went to Governor Ishihara's home in Tokyo's Denenchofu to report to his host. Nagashima bowed deeply in apology. The intent of his words was clear. The Senkaku Islands would be nationalized but Ishihara's persistent demands for the construction of a moorage or some other form of harbor facility would not be met. According to Nagashima, the governor responded as if disappointment were oozing out of every pore. "So, what are you waiting for? Hurry up and get your agreement signed and make the announcement!"

As Nagashima remembers this strained encounter, the Noda Cabinet was not the primary target of Ishihara's ire. Rather, the governor's fury that day was directed at the Foreign Ministry and the landowner, Kurihara

Kunioki. A week after this exchange, Ishihara held a press conference at the Tokyo Metropolitan Government building. "Nagashima came all the way to my house with all kinds of explanations that explained nothing and all kinds of excuses that excused nothing. I really feel sorry for the man for the position that he was put in." Ishihara showed that he was willing to turn a sympathetic eye to Nagashima.

While scorning Nagashima to his face with "The Foreign Ministry defeated you. That's what happened. What a bunch of losers you are." Governor Ishihara repeatedly muttered, "Kurihara tricked me. I was betrayed." As the meeting with Nagashima came to an end, Ishihara could not resist a parting shot. "Just prepare yourself for how I'm going to repay you for this. I am going to walk into the Foreign Correspondents' Club and tear the DPJ apart. I am going to criticize Kurihara mercilessly!" After pouring out his anger to Nagashima, Ishihara turned to Sonoda Hiroyuki, who was also at the meeting. The two immediately became engrossed in discussions on launching their new political party. Although he felt increasingly uncomfortable, Nagashima stayed put in his chair as the two engaged in a lively exchange. Suddenly, Ishihara turned his gaze toward Nagashima to bark out an order, "Why are you still sitting there? You're dismissed!" As Nagashima walked alone toward the door, Ishihara barked out another order at his slumped back. "Make sure the government does its job right. And make sure you spend that 1.5 billion yen wisely."

As he had promised Nagashima, Ishihara spoke at Tokyo's Foreign Correspondents' Club on November 20, 2012. He was there representing the Japan Restoration Party. Ishihara took the occasion to rehash his long-standing positions. "Japan should at least run some simulations on going nuclear. That in itself would serve as a form of deterrence. The question of whether or not to actually acquire nuclear weapons can be addressed later." Ishihara proceeded to explain why he used the word "Shina" to refer to China, which was becoming increasingly assertive in its opposition to the nationalization of the Senkaku Islands. "There is nothing wrong with this term. There is nothing derogatory. It was coined by Sun Yat-sen. For the people of Japan, the Chugoku region means Hiroshima and Okayama Prefectures." Commenting on Japan-China relations, he said, "The Dalai Lama is my close friend. I feel terribly sorry for Tibet. Sure, it would be preferable to maintain friendly and cooperative ties with China. On the other hand, I won't allow my country to be violated by the Shina hegemonists who would turn Japan into a second Tibet." Ishihara's familiar vitriol and bombast were on full display that day.

Ishihara began his speech with a solemn vow to "remake Japan into the 'strong and resilient' nation that it once was." From there, he went on to review his political credo as the Japan Restoration Party co-representative. "The central bureaucracy represents nothing more than a feudal system. We are going to destroy it." Ultimately, however, Ishihara did not make good on the threat that he had made to Nagashima, and there was almost no criticism of the owner of the Senkaku Islands, the DPJ, or the Noda Cabinet.

On the subject of the nationalization of the Senkaku Islands, Ishihara categorically stated that he had not uttered a single word about being prepared to go to war with China in his meeting with Noda. Other than this weak excuse, Ishihara had very little to say on the subject.

Commenting on why the Chinese side had actively pushed the Noda-Ishihara conspiracy idea in attacking the nationalization of the Senkaku Islands, Noda had conjectured that this was because "Against all expectations, Governor Ishihara did not raise a big fuss [after nationalization]." True enough, by this time, it seemed that Ishihara was treating the Senkaku problem as something from the distant past. At the start of the race for the purchase of the Senkaku Islands, Ishihara had enjoyed an overwhelming lead. He had been able to protect that lead for a considerable time, but was finally overtaken by his rival in the last lap of the race. The problem for Ishihara was that he never viewed the opposition as a worthy rival, thinking the opposition was beneath him. Considering the special bitterness that came with losing to such an unworthy rival, it is understandable that Ishihara wanted to put the whole incident behind him as quickly as possible.

The Noda Cabinet formally approved the nationalization of the Senkaku Islands on the evening of September 11. At approximately the same time, LDP Secretary General Ishihara Nobuteru was appearing on a TV Asahi program. Asked about the possibility of China's use of force over the Senkaku Islands, Ishihara responded, "No, they will not attack. Why would they? No one lives on those islands." This response, which on the surface appeared to indicate a facile and immature understanding of national security, caused a storm of criticism. During the same program, he was asked to explain why he had been present at the secret meeting between his father (Governor Ishihara) and Kurihara, who owned the Senkaku Islands. "I was there as a son to assist my father," was his tortured excuse.

On September 14, Governor Ishihara appeared before reporters in his regular press conference to defend the statement that his son had made. "A member of the Diet, Nobuteru said that Shina [China] will not attack.

This statement has to be viewed in the context of a much larger issue. I believe other politicians know about this, and I'm sure Ishiba [Shigeru] knows. But others don't know because it is not talked about. You have to compare combat capability. That's what you have to consider in this case. Who has the upper hand? Shina is the one that knows the answer to this question better than anyone else. I think that he had this in mind when he answered the question." Governor Ishihara reiterated that "there was no error of judgment" in his son's statement.

Governor Ishihara also provided the following rationale in defending his son. "What I mean to say is that you have to examine our combat capability against theirs." It was as though Ishihara was signaling that, "Japan doesn't have to be scared." This was a message that was in complete agreement with what Ishihara had told Noda in their meeting at the Kantei on the evening of August 19. "As long as the war is fought with conventional weapons, Japan will win."

Ishihara received Nagashima's final notice on the nationalization of the Senkaku Islands on September 4, 2012. Three days later, on the evening of September 7, Ishihara met with Kurihara, who owned the islands. This would be a "last supper" occasion for them. In addition to the two principals, two witnesses were present that night for the dinner hosted at the American Club in Tokyo's Azabu district. Ishihara had invited his son, Nobuteru, who was the LDP secretary general. The second witness was Santo Akiko, the House of Councilors member who had been the intermediary between the two parties. "So, what happened? You know how impatient I am. So, just come out and say it."

According to Santo, this is how Ishihara started the conversation. Kurihara lowered his head as he sat at the table and squeezed these words out of his mouth. "I am sorry. I have decided to sell the islands to the government." Ishihara jumped in with a question. "When did you decide?" Kurihara answered evasively, "A little while ago." He then continued, "I was thinking of dividing up the three islands. Uotsurijima would be sold to the Tokyo Metropolitan Government while Minami-kojima and Kita-kojima would go to the government. But there were problems . . ."

Ishihara provided a detailed description of the exchange during his regular press conference at the Tokyo Metropolitan Government building on September 11.

> Suddenly, Kurihara placed his hands flat on the table and apologized. "Please forgive me. I am very sorry." So, I asked, "What do you mean?"

and he said, "Well . . ." So, I said, "Wait a minute. Nobuteru is supposed to be here. When he arrives, the three of us will listen to what you have to say." When Nobuteru arrived, Kurihara again bowed down and pressed his forehead to the table. "I am sorry. Please forgive me." I countered with a question, "What is there to forgive you for?" He then answered, "I have sold the islands to the government." I asked another question, "Is that right? When was the sale made?" Kurihara replied, "A little while ago." I am wondering how this whole affair will be presented in the official statement.

Thirty minutes before meeting Ishihara for dinner that night, Santo and Kurihara had a tete-a-tete to review all that had happened. Santo, who had served as the go-between for Ishihara and Kurihara throughout their negotiations, demanded a detailed report of all the relevant facts. Santo recounts their short meeting beginning with her question, "How do you square what you have done from a moral perspective?" According to Santo, Kurihara tried to hand her a piece of paper on which he had listed a litany of excuses, among which was this explanation. "The weekly magazines have been hounding me and heaping criticism on me, and I have been made the victim of reputational damage related to the sale of the Senkaku Islands."

Unable to contain her anger at the sudden change in direction, Santo pushed the piece of paper back. "I don't need this!" Santo explains that even after being rebuffed, Kurihara continued on about the written statements he had prepared to explain his decision. "I wrote a long version and a short version, and have brought both to explain myself." Kurihara appeared obsessed with the statements he had written, but Santo did not relent in her refusal to receive them. As a result, Ishihara never saw the statements that Kurihara had prepared.

The government's purchase and nationalization of the Senkaku Islands had become a virtual *fait accompli* by September 7. Responding to an *Asahi Shimbun* reporter that day, Ishihara said, "It is regrettable. But I suppose you have to understand the owner's situation." Ishihara had hoisted the white flag of surrender. Asked about the follow-up survey that the Tokyo Metropolitan Government had scheduled for October, Ishihara indicated that the survey mission would be cancelled. "The islands now belong to the government. So that's the government's responsibility. It's their business."

All that was left was the matter of Kubajima, which Ishihara had initially hoped to acquire together with the other three islands. Speaking to reporters at his regular press conference, Ishihara revealed that he had given up on acquiring Kubajima as well. "That island can stay the way it is now. In any case, this is not an issue for us to comment on."

It is questionable whether either the government or the Tokyo Municipal Government could have successfully acquired Kubajima in the first place. After all, whereas the three islands purchased by the government were owned by Kurihara Kunioki, Kubajima was held in the name of his sister who was adamantly opposed to selling her island. As a result, to this day, Kubajima remains in her name and is leased to the Ministry of Defense.

Ishihara was heard muttering "Maybe I'm going to be made a fool of" at his regular press conference shortly before going to that last supper with Kurihara. At this press conference at the Tokyo Metropolitan Government building on September 7, Ishihara offered the press the following confession on the exchanges that he had had with Kurihara. "You have to understand that we had not gone beyond a verbal promise. I have been suggesting that we exchange a memorandum, and a draft has already been prepared. I never expected this to become such a convoluted and drawn-out affair."

Ishihara had first announced his intent to purchase the Senkaku Islands in April, and he had always exuded full confidence since that first announcement that, "The owner will sell to us and to nobody else." As Ishihara's trusted confidante in matters related to negotiations with the owner of the islands, Sonoda affirms that Ishihara's confidence was genuine. "Until the very end, he firmly believed the owner would not sell to anyone but him. There was no trace of doubt in his mind. I am sure he never dreamed the government would step in and nationalize the islands."

Santo, the intermediary, had gone to great pains to push the negotiations forward. On one occasion, she had invited all the parties to her home for a homemade dinner. The Ishiharas, both father and son, were there, as were Kurihara and his sister. Santo clearly remembers that during the evening, Kurihara offered Ishihara some of the vitamin supplements that he carried and repeatedly affirmed, "Everything will be fine. I am selling the islands to you." In light of all that she had seen and done, the disappointment that she now saw in Ishihara affected her as if she herself had been betrayed.

"For our part, we had prepared a memorandum and wanted to talk to Kurihara about it. But the conversation tended to meander directionless. I thought we would use the time to go through these motions until finally settling on something that would be acceptable to both sides."

Normally noted for his bombast and bullish tone, Ishihara sounded

oddly diffident and weak during much of his September 7 press conference. While he did not explicitly voice disappointment or resentment,
these emotions could be clearly inferred from what he said that day. "I'm
not quite sure what Kurihara is thinking."

From Ishihara's perspective, Kurihara's abrupt reversal had suddenly
cast him in the role of a hapless clown. Furthermore, there are indications
that all sorts of contrary information and theories were being cast about
within the Ishihara camp right up to the moment when Kurihara directly
presented his apologies to Ishihara.

"What would you expect? 'I have at no time engaged in such discussions
with the government.' This is what Kurihara had been telling us through
Santo, a member of the Diet. I heard these words and proceeded to make
my judgment and plan my next move on that basis. What else could I do?
I am going to meet with him directly and speak to him directly."

Judging from this statement by Ishihara at the September 7 press conference, it appears that somewhere in his heart Ishihara had not yet given
up hope. There was something that continued to tug at him, urging him to
cling tenaciously to the last ray of hope that emanated from the relation of
trust that he had developed with Kurihara.

This is borne out by Ishihara's actions following the government's September 11 formal decision to nationalize the Senkaku Islands. On this day,
Ishihara vented his anger saying, "I was feeling very honored and happy
that Kurihara was mentioning my sincerity and my true friendship. But
then, he suddenly bowed deeply, pressed his forehead to the table, and
began to apologize. Even now, I feel lost in a fog and do not completely
understand what happened." From there, Ishihara proceeded to summarize the end of the affair. "I had believed that my counterpart was sincere,
and I had believed the words that he spoke. So my sense of the entire affair
is that I was knocked out of the ring at the last moment. I was really suck-
er-punched."

Nagahama, who was carrying on parallel negotiations with Kurihara
on behalf of Noda, has added his own cryptic comment on the negotiations. "At the end of the day, it was never clear how many 'buyers' were
sitting around the table." Nagahama used this comment to reveal that in
addition to the Tokyo Metropolitan Government and the government of
Japan, information had been received about others who were promoting
their own plans to acquire the Senkaku Islands, including a Chinese entre-
preneur. Nagahama went on to sympathize with the difficult position that
Kurihara had been placed in. "This was a real estate deal, plain and simple.

The owner was always free to decide whether to sell or not to sell. That is why Kurihara found it so stressful." Finally, Nagahama commented on the despondency that Ishihara exhibited at the end of the process. "Ishihara wanted to do something and he was in a very good position to pull it off. It may sound strange for me to say this, but I can well understand his disappointment."

It was now the first day of 2013, and Ishihara and Santo were both present at New Year ceremonies at the Imperial Palace. Considerable time had passed since the two had last met. Ishihara appeared to be totally relaxed and refreshed when he turned to speak to Santo. "I would have had to stay on at the Tokyo Metropolitan Government [as governor] if it had not been for that incident. That thought helped me disentangle myself from the whole affair." Ishihara continued to speak his mind. "Once the plan collapsed, there was really no reason for me to stay on as governor. I guess that provided the impetus for me to switch over to this Japan Restoration Party project."

CHAPTER

6

Breakout of the Political Battle

Japanese fishing vessel shadowed by China Marine Surveillance and Japan Coast Guard
patrol boats in waters bordering Japan's territorial waters
(April 23, 2013)
Kyodo

Today again, Chinese vessels ply the waters near the Senkaku Islands.

A Chinese warship trains its fire-control radar on a Japanese target.

The Japan-China diplomatic dispute involves the United States with no clear roadmap in sight.

A Parting Gift

"We acknowledge they are under the administration of Japan. We oppose any unilateral actions that would seek to undermine Japanese administration, and we urge all parties to take steps to prevent incidents and manage disagreements through peaceful means." This reassuring statement from Secretary of State Hillary Clinton was directed to Foreign Minister Kishida Fumio. The date was January 18, 2013, and Kishida was in Washington, DC, representing the Abe administration. It should be added, however, that Secretary Clinton was at this time already scheduled to leave her post very soon.

Clinton's statement on this occasion was significantly more forward leaning in its criticism of China than earlier statements, a reflection of the sense of urgency engendered by China's frequent provocations in the territorial waters and airspace around Okinawa Prefecture's Senkaku Islands. One misstep, it was feared, could lead to unintended consequences that would embroil Japan and China in a hot conflict.

With the end of her term in sight, it seemed Clinton had chosen words that would clearly agitate the Chinese side. Nagashima Akihisa, who had been directly involved in the process leading to the nationalization of the Senkaku Islands as an advisor to Prime Minister Noda under the preceding administration, offers an analysis of Clinton's statement by saying that he could clearly make out the shadow of Assistant Secretary of State Kurt Campbell (East Asian and Pacific affairs) looming in the background. The United States certainly had some reservations about nationalization, but in the end, it had chosen to express understanding for nationalization in a nod to the importance of the Japan-US alliance.

"As a seasoned Japan hand, Campbell fully understood the circumstances that had pushed Japan to make this difficult decision. It was exactly for this reason that Campbell had Secretary Clinton mention Article V of the Security Treaty."

Nagashima explains the background to this parting gift that was left behind by the duo of Clinton and Campbell. Campbell himself would soon join Clinton in leaving the Obama administration. Already favored in the upcoming presidential election of 2016, Clinton left a critically important message for Japan as she left the office of secretary of state. It was a message that went beyond the "We shall not, as a matter of principle, intervene in territorial disputes" principle that the United States had long adhered to. Clinton had effectively stated that the United States would defend Japan's "right of administration" in the Senkaku Islands.

In advance of this statement, President Obama had signed the Fiscal 2013 (October 2012–September 2013) National Defense Authorization Act containing a provision that was meant to reaffirm that the Japan-US Security Treaty did in fact apply to the Senkaku Islands.

The bill had been crafted by Senator John McCain (Republican), a former US Navy officer and prominent member of the Senate, and Senator Jim Webb (Democrat), a former Marine. The wording that the two had formulated referred to the Senkaku Islands in the following terms. "The unilateral action of a third party will not affect the United States' acknowledgement of the administration of Japan over the Senkaku Islands." The bill went on to declare, "The United States reaffirms its commitment to the Government of Japan under Article V of the Treaty of Mutual Cooperation and Security."

The National Defense Authorization Act is a comprehensive legislative action pertaining to the defense budget. The inclusion of a clause that does not directly relate to the defense budget is normally used by Congress as a means of expressing its will and position on a specific diplomatic or security issue. In other words, the acknowledgement that the Senkaku Islands come under the provisions of the Japan-US Security Treaty had now been explicitly affirmed not only by the White House (the executive branch) but also by Congress (the legislative branch). There is no question but that the escalation of Chinese physical harassment in Japan's territorial waters and airspace around the Senkaku Islands had motivated the United States to adopt this stance.

What was China's aim in sending government vessels and surveillance aircraft to these waters and airspace almost daily? Kawashima Shin, associate professor at the University of Tokyo, says China's purpose was to strike an international pose that, "Japan was not alone in exercising effective control over the Senkaku Islands, and that China also had effective control." This, Kawashima explains, was intended to create a new reality in the Senkaku Islands. It was hoped that the repetition of such actions would foster the impression in the international community that Japan was not

alone in exercising effective control and would thereby open a path leading to effective control by China.

If China were to succeed in achieving this objective, the US commitment to non-intervention in territorial disputes would perhaps have made
it impossible for the US to even refer to the problem of the Senkaku Islands.
Japan could not afford to see any ebbing in the international view that
it was in fact Japan that exercised effective control over the islands. Any
international acknowledgement of China's claims would fundamentally
undermine the two-part argument that the United States currently adheres
to. This American argument first posits that the "Senkaku Islands are under
Japanese administration," and then follows it up with "Therefore, the Senkaku Islands come under the provisions of the Japan-US Security Treaty."

However, the American side had no difficulty in seeing through the long
game that the Chinese were playing. Having read China's hand, Congress,
Obama, and Clinton acted in unison to fundamentally refute the premise
of the Chinese argument. In other words, they were unambiguously stating that it did not matter how frequently China infringed upon the territorial waters and airspace around the Senkaku Islands. The repetition of such
unilateral actions would not change the fact that administration of the
Senkaku Islands rested in Japanese hands. In so doing, the United States
was clearly sending a very strong signal in response to China's dangerous
and provocative actions.

"When it became clear that China was not going to back down on this
issue, we began to feel that it was time for us to step up." Campbell, who
left the Obama administration with Clinton in early 2013, provides this
explanation of what was going on behind the scenes in the United States.
Campbell states that, during this period, he was briefing Clinton on the
Senkaku Islands almost daily. Clinton herself explains the intent behind
her statement. "It would be undesirable for unintended consequences [e.g.,
military confrontation between Japan and China over the Senkaku Islands]
to undermine stability and economic growth in the Asia-Pacific region."

From the US perspective, the Japan-China dispute over the Senkaku
Islands was just another example of China's rapid military expansion in the
Asia-Pacific region and its growing ambitions for territory and resources.
The plain fact was that, in addition to the Senkaku Islands, China was also
locked in territorial disputes with Vietnam and the Philippines involving
the Spratly Islands and other maritime formations.

However, it was obvious to all observers that the hottest issue at this
time was the Senkaku Islands, where the Japanese government had decided

to go forward with nationalization. "These flare-ups run the risk of involving the United States in an armed conflict in the region." This shocking warning appeared in a reference report prepared for Congress by the Congressional Research Service (CRS).

In February 2013, CRS issued its latest report on Japan-US relations. On the subject of the Senkaku Islands, its pages contained what many members of the US military and diplomatic services as well as security experts and political leaders were thinking in their hearts but had refrained from stating openly. Their deep-seated concern had been committed to paper in very straightforward language.

To explain the possibility of US involvement in armed conflict, the CRS report pointed out that China had been engaged in provocations such as dispatching government vessels to the waters around the Senkaku Islands ever since the nationalization of the islands. Among various provocative actions, the report assigned special significance to the incident when a Chinese navy ship had locked its fire-control radar on a Japanese destroyer in the waters off the Senkaku Islands.

Fire-Control Radar Lock-on

"This is an extremely abnormal move. We understand that a simple misstep could create a very dangerous situation."

These words were spoken at an emergency press conference called on February 5, 2013. Facing the press that day was Onodera Itsunori, who had been appointed defense minister in the Cabinet newly formed by Prime Minister Abe Shinzo. Onodera announced that a few days earlier, on January 30, a Chinese naval ship had locked its fire-control radar on a Japanese Maritime Self-Defense Forces (SDF) destroyer. He added that the incident had occurred in international waters in the East China Sea. It was also suspected that a Chinese naval ship had similarly locked its fire-control radar on a Maritime SDF helicopter on January 19.

Fire-control radars are activated to accurately determine the target's position and speed prior to firing shells or missiles from aircraft or vessels. To avoid the first wave of enemy attack, Japanese naval vessels and aircraft, as well as those of other countries, are equipped with systems to detect fire-control radar lock-ons. Such systems are also capable of instantaneously determining the position of the source of the lock-on.

According to Onodera, the January 30 incident was the work of a Type 053H3 (Jiangwei II) Chinese frigate and occurred around 10:00 a.m. in waters located more than 100 kilometers from the Senkaku Islands. The targeted Japanese destroyer, *Yudachi* (based in Sasebo, Nagasaki Prefecture), was on patrol in these waters. It was reported that the Chinese frigate locked its fire-control radar on the *Yudachi* for a period of several minutes from a distance of about three kilometers.

On the other hand, the January 19 incident occurred around 5:00 p.m. in the East China Sea and involved a SH-60K patrol helicopter with the Japanese destroyer *Onami* (based in Yokosuka, Kanagawa Prefecture). Here, the fire-control radar from a Type 053H2G (Jiangwei I) Chinese frigate locked on a helicopter while it was in flight.

Conventional military wisdom says that when a fire-control radar is locked onto a vessel or aircraft, it would be logical to expect a volley of shells or missiles to follow within a few seconds. This is why Onodera criticized China so sharply at his press conference. "Usually any country that owns ships like these would not do anything like this unless in extreme circumstances." Onodera made a point of emphasizing that responsibility lay with China. "This immediately raised the tension level on the site. We were not at fault."

Asked whether the radar lock-on indicated the intent to attack, Onodera immediately denied this possibility by stating, "We do not believe the incident went that far." However, he did add a dire warning. "This can become a matter of extreme concern if proper restraint is not exercised." This was his way of strongly suggesting that the situation in the vicinity of the Senkaku Islands was far more sensitive than the Japanese side had assumed.

Since the nationalization of the islands in September 2012, China was sending State Oceanic Administration surveillance vessels to the waters around the Senkaku Islands almost daily on what it called patrol missions. The Chinese tactic seemed to be to try to normalize this behavior. However, it should be noted that the Chinese frigate that locked its fire-control radar on the Japanese destroyer was armed with naval guns and missiles. This frigate was not under either the State Oceanic Administration or the Bureau of Fisheries of the Ministry of Agriculture. It was a People's Liberation Army (PLA) frigate.

The United States responded immediately to this development, the Pentagon releasing an emergency statement on February 5 (Eastern Standard Time). "There is no change in US government policy on the Senkaku Islands." Speaking at her regular press conference, State Department Spokeswoman Victoria Nuland criticized the actions taken by China. "Actions such as this escalate tensions and increase the risk of an incident or a miscalculation." She then went on to add, "These actions could undermine peace, stability, and economic growth in this vital region. So we are concerned about it."

As previously noted, the Japanese and US foreign ministers had met in Washington at the beginning of the year and Secretary of State Clinton had taken the opportunity to move beyond her previous statement and to check China. "We oppose any unilateral actions that would seek to undermine Japanese administration." China wasted no time in responding with a comment by Qin Gang, chief spokesman for the Foreign Ministry. "We express our extreme dissatisfaction and resolute opposition," he railed.

In its statement, the Chinese side gave the following explanation for the source of bilateral tension. "The Japanese government insisted on taking the wrong action in purchasing the Diaoyu Islands [Chinese name for the Senkaku Islands] and has constantly escalated its provocation, which is the root cause of continued tension." The statement then proceeded to directly rebut the United States. "Comments made by the US side disregard the facts and confuse right and wrong. The US has an unshirkable historical responsibility on the Diaoyu Islands issue [arising from the 1972 US reversion of administration of the islands as part of Okinawa]. We urge the US side to be judicious in word and deed."

There appeared to be an additional reason for China's nervous response. After a Chinese propeller aircraft violated the airspace over the Senkaku Islands in December 2012, US forces had launched their own airborne surveillance and patrol activities featuring AWACS (airborne warning and control system) beginning in January 2013.

The fire-control radar lock-on by a Chinese frigate had been conveyed to the Kantei the same day as it occurred. However, the Abe administration did not release the information for six days. Onodera explained the reasons for the delay during his press conference by saying. "Because it was critical to respond with due caution, the data was sent back to Tokyo for verification. Time went by because we exercised caution upon caution. The results were reported to Prime Minister Abe Shinzo today. The prime minister directed that the issue be addressed firmly and that protests be lodged through diplomatic channels."

Shortly before this, Yamaguchi Natsuo was visiting Beijing as president of the New Komeito Party, Prime Minister Abe's coalition partner. Five days before the incident, Yamaguchi had met with President Xi Jinping, China's new supreme leader. During the meeting, Xi Jinping referred to deteriorating Japan-China relations brought on by the problem of the Senkaku Islands and emphasized the importance of resolution through dialogue. He also seemed to take a positive stance on holding a summit meeting with Abe.

The fire-control radar lock-on incident not only threatened to ruin this opportunity for bettering Japan-China relations but also had the potential for triggering further escalation in the bilateral tension over the Senkakus. Thus the Japanese side exercised the utmost caution throughout the entire process of verification, announcement, and diplomatic protest. The decision to go public with the lock-on incident was made only after thoroughly weighing the possible gains and losses from a diplomatic perspective.

According to newspaper reports at the time, some members of government initially argued against making an announcement. However, in consideration of the gravity of the fact that two similar incidents had occurred, Prime Minister Abe ultimately decided in favor of releasing the information. His purpose, it was reported, was to appeal to the international community and let the whole world know that China is a country that ignores common-sense norms. Some time later, Onodera had occasion to release the following comment on this point. "It is highly probable that extremely dangerous acts were repeated over a short period of time. The announcement was made in light of the fact that this was a very unusual case."

One day following the release of this information, Prime Minister Abe stood before the plenary session of the House of Councillors to answer questions and took the opportunity to express his strong displeasure. "It is highly regrettable that China has taken unilateral and provocative actions at a time when we were seeing positive signs for Japan-China dialogue." During this session, Abe stated the Chinese actions "were extremely dangerous as they could easily have unintended consequences." He then explained the Japanese government response: "We have protested through diplomatic channels and have demanded that the recurrence of similar incidents be prevented." Abe further continued, "We strongly urge the Chinese side to return to the starting point of mutually beneficial relations based on common strategic interests and to exercise due restraint so that the situation does not escalate unnecessarily."

On May 12, 2012, the *Sankei Shimbun* had run an interview with Abe. This interview predated the decision by his predecessor, Noda Yoshihiko, to nationalize the Senkaku Islands by several months. In the interview, Abe had made the following comments.

The situation today is completely different from what it was ten years ago. China is enhancing its military as a maritime power. Since the beginning of this year, the *People's Daily*—the official newspaper of the Chinese Communist Party—has been referring to the Senkaku Islands as a core national interest. In other words, China is now treating the Senkaku Islands the same as it treats Taiwan, Tibet, and the Xinjiang autonomous region. We cannot afford to lose even a moment. The time has come to clearly express the nation's will.

It is very likely that disclosing the fire-control radar lock-on incidents constituted one form of what Abe had referred to as clearly expressing the nation's will.

At this point, however, the Japanese side was unable to determine if the Chinese Communist Party and the PLA were united on this matter. On the morning of February 5, 2013, the day Onodera made his announcement, Deputy Minister for Foreign Affairs Saiki Akitaka had summoned Chinese Ambassador Cheng Yonghua to the Foreign Ministry to strongly protest the longest incursion (14 hours) into Japan's territorial waters by Chinese government ships, which had occurred on the previous day. "This runs completely contrary to the wish of both sides to improve bilateral relations," Saiki had said. However, at this point, the Foreign Ministry had not yet been told about Onodera's announcement. As a result, Japan missed an excellent opportunity to gauge the Chinese position.

For Abe, announcing the radar lock-on incident was not the only opportunity for "expressing the nation's will." Shortly after learning of the radar lock-on incident, Abe had flown to Okinawa on February 2 for his first visit there. Addressing members of the SDF and Coast Guard engaged in patrolling and defending the Senkaku Islands, Abe said, "Our territory, territorial waters, airspace, and sovereignty are being constantly challenged." Clearly, he had the Senkaku Islands in mind as he spoke.

Approximately a month before this, on January 8, Abe had met with *Sankei Shimbun* Chairman Kiyohara Takehiko and President Kumasaka Takamitsu for about two hours over dinner at the ANA Intercontinental Hotel in Tokyo's Akasaka district. Abe was in the habit of publicly saying that *Sankei Shimbun* was the "only paper that I subscribe to at home." The next day, January 9, *Sankei Shimbun* published an article that contained the following passage.

On January 5, Prime Minister Abe Shinzo instructed Deputy Chief Cabinet Secretary for Crisis Management Yonemura Toshiro and others to examine beefing up territorial patrol and surveillance. Specifically, the principal measures to be considered included firing tracer rounds as warning shots at aircraft in violation of Japan's airspace that do not respond to radio warnings and deploying Maritime SDF ships within a certain range when naval vessels are approaching Japan's territorial waters. In a prior case that occurred in 1987, the Air SDF fired tracer rounds at a Soviet patrol aircraft that had violated Okinawan airspace.

Former Defense Minister Morimoto Satoshi was dismayed by what he read. Noted for his many connections with the Liberal Democratic Party (LDP) defense establishment, Morimoto felt very strongly that the response he was seeing from Abe and the LDP was inappropriate. Previously a professor at Takushoku University, Morimoto had been appointed defense minister by Prime Minister Noda in an effort to make up for the string of bizarre statements that Tanaka Naoki, the defense minister before Morimoto, had made in the Diet.

Prior to this, Morimoto had been an Air SDF officer and had also spent some time in the Ministry of Foreign Affairs. With this background, Morimoto was widely recognized as a specialist in the diplomatic and national security areas and was particularly well known for his wide network of personal contacts in the United States. Banking on these credentials, Noda had enthusiastically wooed Morimoto to join his Cabinet. Once Morimoto accepted, Noda made a point of keeping him informed on the behind-the-scenes developments leading to the nationalization of the Senkaku Islands. This sharing of information is said to have started at a very early stage of the nationalization initiative.

Morimoto was appointed defense minister on June 4, 2012. A week later, Noda called him to the Kantei for lunch with Noda and Chief Cabinet Secretary Fujimura Osamu. Over lunch, Noda said, "We are going to nationalize the Senkaku Islands" and outlined his plans. The moment he heard these words, Fujimura began to wonder, "How is this going to happen?" At the time, Governor Ishihara was still a few laps ahead of the government in the race to acquire the islands and over 100 million yen had already poured in from the public in response to the governor's call for donations. But at this meeting, Morimoto refrained from expressing any definite opinion. He did not say, "Yes, this should be done." Nor did he counsel caution saying, "We should carefully monitor China and the United States to see how they react."

Morimoto recalls, "Advising the prime minister was not my job.

I believed my responsibility was to deliberate on a wide range of issues within the Ministry of Defense and to create a robust system." Although he kept his silence, Morimoto was thinking to himself, "This is a natural move. It makes sense." But at the same time, he was taken by surprise.

"I have to be honest. At that point in June 2012, my mind was 100 percent occupied with the question of what to do with the Osprey [the new military transport aircraft introduced by the Marine Corps to Japan]. I had not thought that I would be so involved in the defense ministry so soon."

The US Defense Department had decided to deploy its MV-22 Osprey at the Futenma Air Station in Okinawa. The problem was the issue of safety that loomed over the new accident-prone piece of equipment. Serious safety concerns were being heard not only from Okinawa but also from Iwakuni in Yamaguchi Prefecture and many other municipalities that would be affected by the activity at US military bases in Japan—their training exercises and their flight paths. Everything had come to a boiling point, and it was Morimoto's task to cope with this quickly escalating crisis.

More than anything else, Noda had expected Morimoto to put the Japan-US alliance back on track. The Osprey problem was one of the first hurdles he would have to clear. Morimoto was thought to be superbly suited for the task, given his close ties not only with the Obama administration but also with the bipartisan group of Japan hands headed by former Deputy Secretary of State Richard Armitage. This is why Noda did not ask Morimoto "What do you think?" when he revealed the plans for nationalizing the Senkaku Islands and instead limited himself to saying "This is what we are going to do."

"Having made the claim of territorial sovereignty, China will now repeatedly challenge us over the coming decades to translate this into reality. In this process, on our side, we must strictly avoid provoking China. By the same token, we must not let China do anything that provokes Japan."

After being informed by Noda of his plans for the Senkaku Islands, Morimoto repeated this warning in various private and confidential discussions with the top echelons of the Defense Ministry, including the top members of the Defense Ministry's civilian officers and the elite uniformed officers of the Joint Staff. Among the participants was Iwasaki Shigeru, SDF chief of staff, Joint Staff. Iwasaki was the first chairman to be appointed from the Air SDF and had been instructed by Morimoto himself in his first year in the Air SDF.

As the end of 2012 approached, the Diet dissolution Noda had promised became a reality and the whole country was thrown into the excitement of a general election. It was at this time that Morimoto's concern also became a reality.

Violation of Japan's Airspace

The incident occurred at 11:06 a.m. on December 13, 2012. Four vessels from China's Marine Surveillance had entered the territorial waters near Uotsurijima in the Senkaku Islands, and a Japan Coast Guard patrol ship was monitoring their movement. It was then that the patrol boat spotted a Chinese propeller aircraft flying through Japan's territorial airspace about 15 kilometers south of Uotsurijima. The patrol ship warned the aircraft to leave. Before flying off in a northeastern direction at around 11:10 a.m., the aircraft responded in English, "This is Chinese airspace." The aircraft bore Marine Surveillance markings and was thought to be a transport plane used for the surveillance of fishing boats.

When news of this incident reached the Air SDF, two F-15 fighters that were patrolling the nearby skies for airspace violations rushed to the scene. An additional six F-15 fighters and one E-2C early warning aircraft also scrambled. By the time the two contingents arrived, the Chinese aircraft had already left Japan's airspace. At around the same time, one Chinese Marine Surveillance vessel was found to have entered Japan's territorial waters off the coast of the Senkaku Islands. This marked the third consecutive day of violation and the 17th maritime violation since the islands had been nationalized.

"We are engaged in patrol and surveillance activities on high alert, and we have lodged a serious protests with the Chinese government. Going forward, we will maintain full-preparedness in our crisis management systems."

Prime Minister Noda was campaigning on this day in Sagamihara City in Kanagawa Prefecture when he was informed of the incident. Turning to the crowd gathered to hear his stump speech, he interjected this comment that related to Chinese violations of Japan's airspace and territorial waters. As Noda had indicated, Han Zhiqiang, the charge d'affaires ad interim at the Chinese Embassy in Japan was summoned to the Foreign Ministry to be given the Japanese government's strong protest. The task of delivering the protest was assigned to Vice-Minister of Foreign Affairs Kawai Chikao, a close Noda aide in carrying the nationalization process forward. Kawai was blunt in making his protest, as he demanded China restrain itself. "It is Chinese actions that are escalating the situation."

China responded in a press conference on December 13, 2012, at its

Ministry of Foreign Affairs. Addressing the press was the ministry's Deputy Chief Spokesman Hong Lei. "Diaoyu Island (Chinese name for Uotsuri-jima) is the sovereign territory of China, and therefore it is completely normal for Chinese aircraft to fly in these skies." Having rebutted the Japanese position head on, Hong Lei next commented on the Air SDF aircraft that scrambled and endeavored to justify China's actions. "We urge the Japanese side to stop all activities that violate or infringe on China's territorial sovereignty."

This marked the first time a Chinese aircraft had violated Japanese airspace since the SDF had begun compiling official statistics in 1958. The news shook the Japanese government seriously. This was soon followed by a disturbing new fact that came to light. SDF radar deployed in Okinawa had failed to function as expected and had not picked up the airspace violation. Consequently, nobody had noticed anything until the crew of the Coast Guard patrol ship visually spotted the Chinese aircraft in Japanese airspace.

The Air SDF has a total of 28 radar bases throughout Japan and is engaged in round-the-clock surveillance of "aircraft of unknown nationality" that approach Japanese airspace. The Nansei Islands are covered by Japan's westernmost radar base located on Miyako Island in Okinawa Prefecture. Because Miyako Island is approximately 200 kilometers from the Senkaku Islands, low-flying aircraft can fly below the visible horizon and avoid being detected by linear radar.

Considering the distance that separates the radar from the Senkaku Islands, the Defense Ministry estimates that any aircraft flying at an altitude of under 2,000 meters can hide in this "blind spot." The fact that China had taken advantage of this weakness in Japan's radar surveillance served to further heighten the sense of urgency on the Japanese side.

"Going forward, we intend to take measures to avoid any recurrence," stated Chief of Staff, Joint Staff Iwasaki. With this statement, Iwasaki was announcing the intent to re-examine Japan's surveillance system for the Senkaku Islands and the East China Sea. "We are considering how to utilize the AWACS and the E-2C more effectively. All available measures will be implemented to ensure the effectiveness of our air defense system," he explained. Iwasaki was suggesting that similar incidents could be avoided in the future by deploying AWACS and E-2C aircraft and using them to conduct round-the-clock radar surveillance.

China's State Oceanic Administration, the principal actor in the incident, had this to say about the airspace violations. "We were simply engaged in three-dimensional patrol activities coordinated from sea and sky." Chinese media gave extensive coverage to the incident. "Airspace over Diaoyu Island patrolled for the first time." (*Global Times*, China's international newspaper) Referring to the fact that eight Self-Defense aircraft had scrambled and raced to the scene, some reports added this criticism. "Ours was neither a military aircraft nor a surveillance aircraft." In an editorial appearing on December 14, 2012, *Global Times* took up the fact that Japan had sent F-15 fighters to the scene. "China has the right to do the same."

According to Morimoto, the Air SDF dispatched AWACS stationed at its Hamamatsu Base in Shizuoka Prefecture to the Senkaku Islands the day following the incident. Parallel to this, E-2C aircraft stationed at Misawa Base in Aomori Prefecture were flown to the Naha Base in Okinawa Prefecture. The problem was that there were only four AWACS available at Hamamatsu. As Morimoto explains, sending these planes to the Senkaku Islands every day for surveillance activities placed a "very heavy burden" on the frontlines of national defense and threatened to cause all kinds of tangible and intangible problems for Japan's defense policies.

It is reported that the AWACS takes 90 minutes to fly from Hamamatsu to the Senkaku Islands. Assuming it can remain airborne for ten hours, this means that each plane can remain on site in the Senkaku area for no more than six or seven hours. The situation was even more difficult for the E-2C, a propeller-driven aircraft. Given the distance it had to fly from Misawa and fuel limitations, the E-2C had to make a stop at Naha before taking off for the Senkaku Islands. Of the total 13 available E-2C aircraft, four were to be reassigned to Naha to support surveillance and patrol operations. It would be no exaggeration to say that this deployment represented a very precarious shoe-string operation.

As the person charged with the nation's defense, I constantly reminded the Defense Ministry civilian officers as well as the Joint Staff, "We must at all times avoid over-reacting. We must avoid ill-considered reactions as well. We must endure and be patient to the end and protect our territory. It is critically important we enhance our surveillance and patrol operations so that we know in detail what China is doing. Finally, we must concentrate our efforts and energies on strengthening our monitoring capabilities." This is what I said over and over again as long as I was there.

Morimoto explains this as the "last will and testament" that he left behind for the defense establishment when he resigned as defense minister. In light of this principle and from Morimoto's perspective, there was one thing that Japan had to make the greatest effort to avoid after the nationalization of the Senkaku Islands. "It does not matter even if an action has been taken purely in self-defense. Japan must never give China an excuse for saying, 'Japan has taken provocative actions.' Japan must not take any action that China can interpret in this manner. We must not give them any excuses."

Oriki Ryoichi, the former chief of staff (currently, special advisor to the minister of defense), had returned to the Ministry of Defense to work as an aide to Morimoto. Looking back on those days, Oriki says, "The basic stance that Morimoto subscribed to was 'don't provoke.' This is what he told everyone at the Monday meetings of top officials. His thinking was that Japan had to avoid any act of provocation under all conditions."

On the other hand, Oriki with his career in the Ground SDF, admits that he was uncomfortable with the course taken by Noda. Speaking in the plenary session of the House of Representatives on July 26, 2012, Noda had stated, "In case of illegal acts perpetrated by neighboring countries in Japan's territories and territorial waters, including the Senkaku Islands, we shall act resolutely. This will include the use of the SDF when necessary." Oriki was extremely uncomfortable that Noda had failed to consult the SDF on this matter beforehand and had likewise failed to issue any specific instructions.

Noda's statement of July 26, 2012, was thought to refer to the violation of Japan's territorial waters by Chinese fishing surveillance vessels. In this context, the statement was interpreted to mean that, in addition to using the Japan Coast Guard to respond to such territorial violations, Noda was indicating that Japan was also prepared to deploy SDF warships. However, as Oriki remembers it, there is no evidence that Noda followed up with any instructions to the Ministry of Defense or the SDF. Moreover, no orders were issued for conducting desktop exercises and simulations in preparation for such actions. "The point Noda was making was that the entire government would act resolutely, including the use of the SDF as needed. It is only natural to expect some kind of consultation or instructions or something by way of preparation."

Nagashima, who was serving as an aide to the prime minister, offers a different interpretation of Noda's statement in the House of Representatives. Although he was not tasked with checking the prime minister's comments in advance, Nagashima presents this analysis. "The prime minister was simply explaining the sequence of responses as stipulated under Japan's current national defense legislation. The first line of response is the Japan Coast Guard. Further escalation would result in maritime security operations. That's what he was explaining." However, Nagashima is honest enough to express his dissatisfaction with what the prime minister had said. "In hindsight, it would have been better if Noda had given a little more thought to how unnatural it was to include the SDF in the statement."

"We have to consider how we can create and deploy a virtual network of warning and surveillance capabilities to confront China's activities." This is the task that Morimoto assigned himself as minister of defense. He then concentrated on enhancing Japan's surveillance and warning capabilities in the Senkaku area. Moreover, Morimoto actively solicited ideas from within the ministry.

Morimoto laid out all the available options: improving the radar deployed on the Maritime SDF's escort fleet; leasing out radar-equipped vessels to the Coast Guard; installing motion-detecting warning radar on isolated islands; deploying the unmanned reconnaissance drones that US forces had shown to be effective in Iraq; adding to the four AWACS currently in deployment; and replacing Japan's E-2Cs with the upgraded E-2D version of the aircraft.

He then proceeded to categorize the options as either goals that can be immediately implemented or medium- and long-term goals. His basic philosophy was to enhance surveillance and warning capabilities in the area around the Senkaku Islands to the highest level possible and to thereby create systems that would enable rapid response whenever China approached the Senkakus.

Given his commitment to this approach, Morimoto found the hardline stance taken by Abe's LDP Administrative increasingly disturbing. To Morimoto, it seemed as though the Abe Cabinet had become intoxicated with the sheer excitement of returning to the seat of power.

"Suppose Japan reacts immediately and China then uses this as a reason for sending in its fighter jets. As these fighters approach our territory, Japan scrambles its own fighters. This leads to an extremely risky situation where Japanese and Chinese fighters may encounter each other within the narrow confines of our territorial waters and skies. This is exactly why we must not under any circumstances take any action that might accidentally provoke China."

In light of Morimoto's fundamental philosophy in defending against China, it is abundantly clear that he would not be able to accept the notion of firing tracer rounds as warning shots as mentioned in the January 9 *Sankei Shimbun* article.

Morimoto's fears were soon realized. On the afternoon of January 10, the SDF confirmed that Chinese fighters had crossed into Japan's air defense identification zone (ADIZ) on multiple occasions. Although this occurred outside Japan's airspace at a distance of about 170 kilometers north of the Senkaku Islands, fighter jets from the Air SDF scrambled to meet the approaching Chinese fighters. While Japanese airspace ultimately was not violated on this occasion, Morimoto notes the significant escalation that had occurred. The situation had gone from sending unarmed propeller aircraft to the skies near the Senkaku Islands to making this sudden and significant jump to dispatching fighter jets. Morimoto speculates that this escalation was very probably in connection with the previous day's *Sankei Shimbun* article reporting Prime Minister Abe's aggressive instructions for territorial patrol and surveillance.

"China saw the article and responded immediately. Instead of deploying government vessels, they dispatched fighter aircraft with no purpose other than military use. They have not gone so far as to breach the contiguous zone, but they are appearing near the gas fields in the East China Sea. It started with one fighter flying alone. More recently, the situation has escalated to a wing of fighters circling these skies."

As Morimoto had anticipated, the Chinese Ministry of Defense commented the next day, January 11, on the Japanese fighter jets that had scrambled in response to the approaching Chinese fighters. "The Chinese military responded to the movements of Japan's SDF and scrambled its mainstay fighter aircraft." The sequence of events outlined in this statement directly contradicts the Japanese account of events. According to the Chinese side, Chinese fighter jets were engaged in routine patrol duty in an area southwest of the East China Sea gas fields when, "two Japanese F-15 fighters approached and began to tail the Chinese aircraft." Additionally, one Japanese reconnaissance plane was also flying in the same zone. The Chinese side claims it responded to these developments by "dispatching two Chengdu J-10 fighters to the scene to monitor their movements."

China's claims and its operating principle are exactly as advocated in the article that appeared in the *Global Times* following an incident in which Japanese fighters had scrambled to head off a Chinese propeller plane. "China has the right to do the same," the article had warned ominously.

China was providing an account that contradicted the account given by the Japanese Ministry of Defense, which claimed that its fighter aircraft had been scrambled in response to Chinese military aircrafts crossing over into Japan's ADIZ. If the Chinese claim were to be taken at face value, this would mean that both Japan and China had scrambled their fighter aircraft without clearly understanding the other side's intent.

"The *Sankei* wrote that the measures to be considered include firing tracer rounds as warning shots. I don't know whether this was speculation or whether someone in the Abe administration had said this. In any case, it certainly presented China with an incredibly valuable excuse."

Morimoto had always advocated a policy of steadfast endurance. Indeed, this was a basic philosophy shared by the principal officials and leaders in the Noda administration who preached "strategic patience" in Japan's relations with China. An example can be found in the speech delivered by Maehara Seiji, a hardliner on Chinese affairs who had been given the Cabinet post of minister of state for national policy in the Noda administration. Before assuming this post, Maehara delivered a speech on September 29 in Kobe in which he commented on China's claim of territorial sovereignty over the Senkaku Islands with biting sarcasm. "This distorts the facts and is devoid of reason. China has begun to manufacture history and to claim the islands belong to them."

Maehara continued his criticism of China. "We must not allow ourselves to be provoked. The important thing is for Japan to maintain effective control. [China] is just waiting for Japan to declare the launch of maritime security operations. They are just waiting for us to deploy our SDF. The important thing is not to be provoked. So let us allow the Coast Guard to take care of the situation steadily and earnestly. Let's leave it to the Coast Guard." As the commander-in-chief of the SDF, Noda was in complete agreement.

At one point, the Japanese government ran desktop exercises and simulations on how it could respond if China were to dispatch a large helicopter-carrying maritime surveillance vessel to the waters around the Senkaku Islands. Discussions took place after the simulations were completed. Normally, it is not possible to visually determine whether a vessel is actually transporting a helicopter, and a definitive determination on whether or not a helicopter is going to be deployed can only be made after the hangar doors have been opened. In light of this problem, discussions focused on the timing at which an order to scramble should be issued to Japanese interceptors. The discussants felt that there were two factors to be considered.

First, violation of airspace may not immediately occur when a helicopter begins to lift off. However, if the vessel is already very close to Japan's territorial waters, lift-off can soon develop into an airspace violation.

"My view was that this naturally called for an order to scramble. But someone else thought this was a 'No way' situation." When he recounts this discussion, Morimoto refuses to say who made the comment against ordering a scramble. But we later learned from Noda himself that it was Noda who said this.

"Assume, for example, that a helicopter lifts off from a government vessel. The question is whether or not to order a scramble intercept. If an order is issued, should this be for F-15 fighters? We ran some simulations on these questions, but I belonged to the more cautious group. If the aircraft taking off is a helicopter, let's see how things work out. Let's take a wait-and-see attitude. That's what I said." Noda went on to explain why he took this cautious position. "China is not a monolithic structure. There is the party, the military, and the government, which may not necessarily share a consistent view. The unforeseen can happen. This was my reason for caution." Noda concludes, "Abstract discussions are no good." He reveals that a helicopter did in fact take off from a Chinese government vessel, an incident that occurred at the end of 2012 during Japan's general election campaign. "I felt the intent was to sow confusion in Japan. They want to provoke the dispatch of an Air SDF aircraft as part of their attempt to build up a series of *faits accomplis*."

On January 24, 2013, the Ministry of Defense and the Joint Staff Office announced the number of times that the Air SDF had scrambled between April and December 2012. According to this report, Japanese aircraft scrambled 160 times during this period to head off Chinese intrusions. Although the fiscal year (ending on March 31) was far from over, this number already exceeded the total for any previous year.

On a quarterly basis, the total number for the first quarter (April-June) was only 15. But straddling the nationalization of the Senkaku Islands in September, the figure for the second quarter (July-September) increased more than threefold to 54. Coming after nationalization, the third quarter (October-December) saw a further near-doubling to 91. This included the afore-mentioned case in which a Chinese State Oceanic Administration Y-12 propeller aircraft violated Japanese airspace.

The total number of scrambles ordered during this nine-month period came to 349, a majority of which (180) involved Russian aircraft. However, during the October-December quarter that immediately followed nationalization of the Senkaku Islands, the number of scrambles involving Chinese aircraft (91) was nearly double those involving Russian aircraft (46), a remarkable increase.

In light of these figures, Noda stuck to the position that "We shall not be provoked." Commenting on Noda's policy, Morimoto offers this analysis. "The Noda administration's China policies after nationalization may appear to have been weak, but the truth is that a high level of restraint was shown, and this effectively robbed China of any room to act."

The LDP's platform for the House of Representatives election at the end of 2012 included a commitment to "stationing civil servants permanently" on the Senkaku Islands. But once the election was over, Prime Minister Abe himself began to walk this back. "It's just an option," he declared in the plenary session of the House of Councillors, exhibiting a more cautious stance in certain situations. But this did not quell Morimoto's concerns. Abe repeatedly used the phrase "diplomatic defeat" to describe and criticize the Democratic Party of Japan (DPJ) for its "weak-kneed diplomatic stance and its inability to act effectively." Morimoto loudly protested these accusations saying, "These comments miss the mark completely." He then proceeded to sound the alarm against playing politics with the Senkaku Islands.

Morimoto offers this assessment when asked to evaluate the actions the Abe Cabinet and the LDP took on the Senkaku issue immediately after coming to power. "Neither wise nor cautious." Lending no ear to Morimoto's concerns, Abe chose instead to up the ante in his criticism of the DPJ. "The previous administration was overly fearful of discord and conflict. Where surveillance and defense activities should obviously have been implemented against actions that infringed upon our territory, territorial waters, and airspace, the previous administration chose to narrow its options in the extreme . . . We undertook a fundamental review of the previous administration's policies to overcome this crisis."

This is how Abe responded to a question posed by Hagyuda Koichi, an LDP member of the House of Representatives Budget Committee, on the morning of March 7, 2013. Abe's direct criticism of the DPJ proved to be more than Okada Katsuya, who had served as the Noda administration's deputy prime minister, could bear. Okada immediately protested, "That statement is not at all true!" The following exchange then ensued between Abe and Okada.

Okada: I have written a letter to the *Sankei Shimbun* protesting the article it published on the fifth. Do you recognize the article as being true?

Are you claiming that it is true that the DPJ administration decided to maintain a distance of 15 nautical miles between Chinese warships and Maritime SDF ships?

Abe: I prefer not to reveal any details because this relates to the level of Japan's preparedness. What the Abe administration has done is to totally review and revamp all previous positions. In my judgment, the previous administrations showed excessive deference to China, and as a result were not able to respond properly and adequately. It is true that this is my judgment.

Okada: To the best of my knowledge, there was nothing about keeping a distance of 15 nautical miles. If you know of such a decision or policy, I ask you to come out without waffling and say so directly. All you have to do is check with the Ministry of Defense administrators and you will get the answer.

Abe: I heard this from the Ministry of Defense administrative side and from the Japan Coast Guard as well. It was obvious to us that this decision was the result of excessive deference, and therefore we reviewed this decision and completely overturned it.

Okada: You said, "overly fearful of discord and conflict." What evidence do you have for saying this?

Abe: I say this because this is my conviction.

Okada: It is true that we judged everything on a case-by-case basis because we believed confrontation between the Chinese military and the SDF could lead to who knows what situations. The prime minister should refrain from using emotion-laden expressions.

Abe: I am not speaking from my emotions. I have merely stated the facts. There is no need to bring up what past administrations have done or for me to criticize you and your party.

Abe returned to this subject later in the Diet debate, brushing off the criticism and saying, "In our judgment, this can send the wrong message to the other side. Sending the wrong message can in fact invite contingencies and other unintended consequences." Okada responded with a new round of criticism. "The prime minister is resorting again to the same pattern. He starts with groundless criticism of the DPJ, then proceeds to brag that he has changed things." The implication of Okada's criticism was that Abe was using the Senkaku problem for political purposes.

As Okada pointed out, the cause of the Abe-Okada debate was an article in the *Sankei Shimbun*—the newspaper that Abe loved to say was the only newspaper he subscribed to at home. The article in question had appeared on the front page on March 5, 2013, and contained the following passages.

It became known on the 4th that the Noda Yoshihiko administration had issued instructions calling for a policy giving excessive deference to China in connection with Chinese naval ships that have frequently engaged in provocative actions in the waters around the Senkaku Islands since the islands were nationalized on September 11 last year. In line with these instructions, Maritime SDF ships were ordered to maintain a distance of at least 15 nautical miles (about 28 kilometers) from Chinese naval ships and to retreat if Chinese naval ships came closer than this. Orders also prohibited them from moving into position in advance to forestall intrusion into our territorial waters when such intrusions were considered likely. According to multiple government sources, former Deputy Prime Minister Okada Katsuya played a central role in issuing these instructions.

Following nationalization, Chinese naval ships began to frequently appear in the waters to the north of the Senkaku Islands. A meeting of Cabinet ministers concerned was called on October 3 last year to deliberate the Senkaku situation with then Prime Minister Noda, Okada, Chief Cabinet Secretary Fujimura Osamu, Foreign Minister Gemba Koichiro, and Defense Minister Morimoto Satoshi in attendance.

According to government sources, during this meeting, Okada proposed that Japan not provoke China, and asked that Maritime SDF ships be prohibited from coming closer than 15 nautical miles to Chinese naval ships. As visual observation is difficult at this distance, surveillance activities must rely on radar, which may delay actions for preventing intrusion into territorial waters.

Okada also gave orders as if to tacitly allow Chinese naval ships to enter Japan's territorial waters. Although the standard method for forestalling intrusion into territorial waters by foreign warships is to move into position in advance within one's own territorial waters, Maritime SDF ships were ordered to stand by outside of Japan's territorial waters until confirming intrusion by Chinese ships.

Excessive restraint was also sought in response to airspace violations.

Haijian 50, a helicopter-carrying China Marine Surveillance ship, repeatedly violated Japan's territorial waters immediately after the nationalization of the Senkaku Islands. Were the helicopter to take off, that would have immediately been an airspace violation.

This makes it essential we prepare to scramble interceptors as soon as this ship enters the territorial waters. Okada rejected this preparation saying, "Don't upset the Chinese because this is only a minor intrusion. This can be left to the Coast Guard."

In the February 27, 2013, session of the House of Representatives Budget Committee which preceded the Abe-Okada Diet debate, former Deputy Chief Cabinet Secretary Fukuyama Tetsuro, who had engaged in top-secret negotiations with China during the 2010 Chinese fishing boat collision incident, charged: "It would be an extremely serious matter if this were planted for the purpose of deflecting criticism of the delayed announcement on the fire-control radar lock-on incident in January." Here, Fukuyama was talking about articles that had appeared in quick succession in the *Asahi Shimbun* and the *Nihon Keizai Shimbun* reporting that, "A radar lock-on incident by a Chinese warship also occurred during Noda's DPJ administration." Some reports included wording that could be construed to mean, "In consideration of relations with China, Noda, Okada, and others concealed this." In light of these reports, Fukuyama was pushing back and suggesting that Prime Minister Abe and his LDP administration had intentionally leaked national security related information and had used this for the political purpose of disparaging the Noda administration.

Chief Cabinet Secretary Suga Yoshihide, Abe's right-hand man in the Cabinet, took the podium to deny the allegation. "It is impossible for this information to have come from us." Throughout his rebuttal, however, Suga sounded uncomfortable and evasive. This was because Defense Minister Onodera Itsunori had stated in the course of Diet debate that, other than the two incidents that had taken place on the Abe administration's watch, "I don't believe there were any notable incidents in the past that needed to be announced." There was a subtle difference in nuance between this and what Abe himself had said to Okada.

Immediately following the series of newspaper reports, Noda released a full denial on February 7. "I never received any such report at the time. This fact has been confirmed by the Defense Ministry." A similar denial was issued by Okada, who was Noda's close confidante as deputy prime minister at the time. "We never received any reports of a radar lock-on. Therefore, it is impossible for me to have decided to prevent the release of such information."

This debate, which seemed to be more about the back and forth than about national security, was put to rest with the Abe administration's lodging a formal protest with the Chinese government concerning the January 2013 lock-on incident that had taken place on Abe's watch.

It is notable that Defense Minister Onodera had stated in the heat of the debate (February 8 session of the House of Representatives Budget Committee), "The question of whether a radar lock-on occurred or not is a matter that pertains to top-secret information on our patrol activities. When we announce that this radar lock-on or that radar lock-on has occurred, we may inadvertently be sending the message that we have failed to notice some other lock-on that has occurred." Referring to this statement, Morimoto says in praise of Onodera, "This is a very reasonable man speaking very reasonable words."

It is highly likely that the actual message that Onodera wanted to convey in this statement was that, from a national security perspective, no further details should be released. If evidence supporting Japan's claims were to be released, that would certainly upset China. At the same time, it could unwittingly tell the Chinese side about the SDF's information gathering and analytical capabilities. To avoid falling into this trap, Japan had no choice but to keep mum.

However, multiple sources in the Defense Ministry and SDF, as well as media reports, agree that there are some indications that Prime Minister Noda and his administration made a concerted effort not to aggravate China unduly. After Prime Minister Noda and his DPJ administration nationalized the Senkaku Islands in September 2012, Maritime SDF warships on patrol and surveillance duty consistently remained beyond visible range of Chinese naval ships. Abe stated in the Diet debate that Japanese warships went as close as three kilometers to the Chinese ships prior to nationalization but that this distance had been increased to 15 nautical miles after nationalization. There is no concrete evidence to support this claim. On the other hand, the veracity of this statement was indirectly attested to by an SDF officer who said, "We were being extremely careful."

Abe himself has admitted to an interesting fact. After Abe formed his cabinet in December 2012, the distance between the two countries' ships was reduced back to the pre-nationalization distance. It was shortly after this re-adjustment that Chinese warships locked their fire-control radar on a Japanese destroyer and helicopter in two separate incidents. As Morimoto had constantly warned, it is quite possible that the return of Japan's surveillance stance to its pre-nationalization level was seen by the Chinese as a provocation and that the threatening lock-on incidents were undertaken as acts of retaliation. If this is true, it would mean that the Abe administration was beginning to go beyond the framework that Morimoto had consistently preached. "We must endure and be patient to the end."

Since regaining the reins of power, Abe and the LDP were going out of their way to highlight the differences in their national security policies as compared to those of the previous DPJ administrations. Observing this tendency, Morimoto points to the questionable value of this tactic and to its underlying danger. "I do not know what the LDP intends to do, but you have to understand that China has been looking from the very start for an excuse to up the ante against Japan."

"Chinese Dream"

"We must follow the leadership of the Chinese Communist Party and resolutely protect our national sovereignty, security, and development interests." Thus declared President Xi Jinping on March 17, 2013, in the first session of the 12th National People's Congress, raising his voice to laud the men and officers of the PLA who were at the session.

This was the first speech that Xi Jinping delivered after becoming president, and he repeatedly emphasized this phrase: "the Chinese dream of the great rejuvenation of the Chinese nation." As concrete examples of this dream, he named "prosperous and strong country," "rejuvenation of the nation," and "well-being of the people." In a press conference held at the close of the National People's Congress, Li Keqiang—the newly appointed premier—echoed Xi's words. "We shall never waver in our determination to defend the nation's sovereignty and territory."

Speaking at the same time, Xi Jinping made a point of exuding confidence as the "world's second superpower," second only to the United States in terms of both economic and military might. "Today, our nation stands tall and firm in the East." The new president went on to emphasize the spiritual aspects of the dream. "Patriotism is the spiritual force that powerfully unites the Chinese people." He then concluded by citing the goal of creating a powerful military that will surely emerge victorious if it fights under the leadership of the Party.

This was the Chinese version of "prosperous country, strong army" that Xi Jinping was committing to. The speech also clearly indicated that China was ready to resort to force if necessary in various confrontations, including that with Japan over the Senkaku Islands. Xi Jinping had clearly laid out his inflexible hardline stance.

The appointment of Yang Jiechi as state councilor with vice premier status was very much in line with this stance. Having served as foreign minister for six years, Yang Jiechi had been brought in to succeed Dai Bingguo. During his years at the Foreign Ministry, Yang Jiechi had consistently taken a hardline stance on Japan, and he was now being put in a position to wield even greater power over Chinese foreign affairs. In effect, the Xi Jinping administration had endorsed Yang's hardline policies.

For a while, there was a growing sense among China experts in both the United States and Japan that this post would go to Wang Yi, the former ambassador to Japan. Wang Yi, the director of the Taiwan Affairs Office, was known as a Japan hand with an extensive network of connections in Japanese political circles. However, as previously discussed, Xi Jinping and Li Keqiang had decided to distance themselves from the policy of pursuing mutually beneficial relations based on common strategic interests with Japan—the policy that Hu Jintao and Wen Jiabao had espoused. Thus the new leadership decided to delegate the responsibility for implementing its foreign policies not to Wang Yi but to Yang Jiechi.

On March 9, Yang Jiechi held a press conference in Beijing's Great Hall of the People where the National People's Congress was in session. Chinese criticism of Japan had been muted during the "appointment season" that extended from the end of the previous year to the start of the new. But now that the appointment season was over and everyone had been allotted his position, Yang Jiechi proved that he was not shy about attacking Japan to make his presence known.

"Japan has stolen and is now illegally occupying our territory. The present situation is entirely Japan's responsibility." Since the nationalization of the Senkaku Islands, Yang Jiechi had maintained the most militant stance against Japan. Having vented his anger at Japan, Yang Jiechi switched to a much more flexible tone as he addressed China's relations with the United States. "We must set aside old ideas of animosity based on differences in political systems and respect each other's core interests." Yang Jiechi also expressed a positive attitude toward the concept of a "new relationship among great powers" that had been set forth by his predecessor, Dai Bingguo, during the Hu Jintao administration. As for Taiwan—the thorn stuck in the throat of China's relations with the United States—Yang Jiechi did not venture beyond the safe and formulistic reference to the problem. "The US should act appropriately." It was as though Yang Jiechi were sending kisses to the Obama administration.

His attitude toward Japan stood in stark contrast to the reconciliatory tone that he had assumed toward the United States. "Japan has no future unless it accepts and respects its history of having brought calamity and suffering upon the people of Asia." In saying this, Yang Jiechi showed that he was more than willing to play the historical awareness card—the Abe administration's Achilles heel—to stir things up. Finally, Yang Jiechi also issued a stern warning to the Abe administration on the subject of the Senkaku Islands. "The Japanese side must avoid escalating the situation to the point that it spins out of control."

This was Yang Jiechi's standard approach to censuring Japan. He habitually said Japan had "illegally stolen" the Senkaku Islands and decried this as "a challenge to the postwar international order." His claim harks back to the language of the 1943 Cairo Declaration's demand for reversion of "all territories Japan has stolen from the Chinese." Taking this a step further, Yang Jiechi was making the untenable argument that recognizing Japan's claim of territorial sovereignty over the Senkaku Islands was therefore equivalent to negating the international order that had been constructed after the Second World War.

Yang Jiechi had repeated much the same argument in his September 2012 speech at the United Nations (UN) General Assembly when he presented China's position on the Senkaku Islands. Yet the international community has to take him more seriously now that he is Dai Bingguo's successor.

However, this was not the only key message that China was conveying internally and internationally as the new Xi Jinping administration began to function in earnest. The consolidation of China's government departments tasked with maritime administration was a key component in the proposed organizational reforms submitted to the 12th National People's Congress. A few days before this plan was submitted, Deputy Director Wang Feng of the Central Institutional Organization Committee, the body in charge of reforming the Chinese government organization, held a press conference on March 11, 2013. During this press conference, he made the following statement regarding the proposed revision. "Following the examples of other countries, the various departments responsible for maritime safety will now be unified. Japan calls theirs the Coast Guard. What we mean by China Coast Guard is 'maritime police.'"

Prior to the reorganization, China's maritime surveillance vessels and fisheries surveillance vessels were separately and independently directed by the State Oceanic Administration and the Ministry of Agriculture Bureau of Fisheries. The proposed revision was designed to bring these separate agencies under the unified command of the State Oceanic Administration and to rename the organization the "China Coast Guard." Parallel to this revision, the "State Oceanic Commission" was formed and put in charge of formulating national maritime strategies and coordinating related policies within the government.

One year before this, the Party National Congress had adopted the goal of transforming China into a "maritime power." The various reforms introduced in March 2013 should be understood as having originated in this earlier decision. The revisions that were made were designed to facilitate a stronger stance on China's various territorial disputes with neighboring countries, including the face-off with Japan over the Senkaku Islands and the disputes with the Philippines and Vietnam in the South China Sea.

Director-General Kitamura Takashi of the Japan Coast Guard explains that, prior to this reorganization, the Japan Coast Guard had the most interaction with the China Coast Guard, or Maritime Police, which functioned under the jurisdiction of Ministry of Public Security. There was also a degree of interaction with China's Maritime Patrol, an organization under the jurisdiction of the Ministry of Transportation for maritime rescue operations. The Japan Coast Guard had established hotlines with both of these organizations to be used in case of emergency. On the other hand, the Japan Coast Guard had somewhat less contact with the Ministry of Agriculture Bureau of Fisheries and the Chinese Customs Port Customs Administration.

Of these four organizations, the Japan Coast Guard had very little prior contact with the State Oceanic Administration (Marine Surveillance), which the reorganization designated as the lead authority. Kitamura says, "Of course, when we are at sea, we do contact each other by radio. However, we have no hotline with the State Oceanic Administration in case of trouble."

While there is no way of knowing if this factored into the Chinese decision to concentrate authority in the hands of the State Oceanic Administration, it is clear that, as a result of the reorganization, the Japanese and Chinese Coast Guards were now operating in close proximity without a hotline. The two maritime patrol organizations would have no choice but to feel their way and play it by ear if they encountered each other in a border area.

Kitamura says that, following the nationalization, China has been sending four to five ships to the waters around the Senkaku Islands almost daily beginning around the middle of October 2012. During the earlier part of this period, the normal pattern was for Marine Surveillance and Fisheries Surveillance ships to form separate groups as they traversed these waters. However, in a move that seems to have anticipated the reorganization, the majority of the ships are now Marine Surveillance ships.

"I believe this trend will remain unchanged in the future. The number of ships has increased, the number crossing over into Japan's territorial waters is increasing, and the time they spend inside our territorial waters is also increasing. In some instances, the ships remain in our waters for up to 14 hours until very late at night. The pattern of Chinese actions is gradually changing, but our task remains unchanged. We must perform our duty calmly and rationally and make sure we defend our territorial waters."

Having outlined the current situation, Kitamura goes on to explain that it normally takes twice as many ships to guard as there are ships being guarded against so long as Japan remains committed to a defensive stance. To use a soccer metaphor, tailing individual Chinese ships certainly demands a man-to-man defense, but defending the (territorial waters) goal requires multiple ships in a zone defense.

The Senkaku Islands are located in the open seas where the waves tend to be rough and high. Consequently, it takes a ship of at least 1,000 tons to properly patrol these waters. The problem is that Japan's 11th Regional Coast Guard Headquarters, which is responsible for the Senkaku area, has only seven vessels that exceed 1,000 tons (as of 2013). Nationwide, the Coast Guard has only 51 vessels exceeding 1,000 tons. Since the nationalization of the Senkaku Islands, the Coast Guard has had to dispatch whatever large vessels it can spare to Okinawa on temporary Senkaku duty.

Some vessels have been sent to Okinawa from as far as Hokkaido, a move that inevitably places a very heavy burden on Japan Coast Guard personnel. The Coast Guard is thus working to upgrade the 11th Regional Coast Guard Headquarters assets to include a total of 14 dedicated vessels exceeding 1,000 tons. Additional budget has been requested to make this possible. If all goes according to plan, Kitamura says, the 11th Regional Coast Guard Headquarters will become self-sufficient by fiscal 2015.

Kitamura assumed the Coast Guard directorship on September 11, 2012, the same day the decision was finalized to nationalize the Senkaku Islands. Strangely enough, he says that he had absolutely no idea what was going to happen until a week before taking office.

Kitamura recalls his early days as Coast Guard director-general. "There was quite a bit of criticism in the beginning. We were receiving information that a thousand Chinese fishing boats were coming to storm the shores.

What's going to happen, I wondered." Immediately after taking office, he made a firm commitment on how he would perform his duty. "We must not allow our wider relationship with China to be damaged. We will act calmly and rationally in defending our territorial waters. Everything begins and ends there."

To underscore its claim of territorial sovereignty in the Senkaku Islands, China began to make ostentatious displays by sending government ships to the Senkaku area almost daily. Under the provisions of the UN Convention on the Law of the Sea, the Japanese side cannot seize these government ships. If they wish, these ships can sail through Japan's territorial waters under the "freedom of navigation" guaranteed in the UN Convention. However, Kitamura declares that the seemingly aimless meandering of Chinese government ships in the waters around the Senkaku Islands "can in no way be equated to freedom of navigation." He follows this statement up by saying, "The Japan Coast Guard will take all necessary measures. The first step is to warn. If that doesn't work, we will regulate their course of passage. What is happening is that we are engaged in 'preliminary skirmishes.'"

The US Bottom Line

As noted above, information on the fire-control radar lock-ons by Chinese warships was declassified by Prime Minister Abe. These unnerving incidents had two ramifications for security in the Asia-Pacific region. The first was that China had ratcheted up its provocation against Japan one or maybe two notches. But it was the second ramification that was even more important. On various occasions, including the Japan-US meeting of foreign ministers, the United States had issued warnings to China and called on it to exercise "restraint." China had clearly chosen to ignore these warnings.

The same day as the February 5 radar lock-on, US Department of State Spokeswoman Victoria Nuland criticized China in a statement she made during a regular press conference. "Actions such as this escalate tensions and increase the risk of an incident or a miscalculation. They could undermine peace, stability, and economic growth in this vital region." She followed this up by calling on both Japan and China to exercise greater restraint. "We are concerned that there is increased tension between Japan and China."

It later came out that the new secretary of state, John Kerry, had had a direct telephone conference with Yang Jiechi, the top man in the Chinese foreign policy establishment. After the telephone conference, in a sign of consideration for China, the State Department made a point of refusing to comment on whether they had discussed the radar lock-on. On the other hand, Secretary of Defense Leon Panetta gave a speech in Washington, DC, the next day, February 6, in which he strongly implied that the United States was very concerned about what had happened. "It's the kind of situation where there are territorial claims that could ultimately get out of hand and one country or the other could react in a way that could make things worse."

The first time China sent jet fighters to the Senkaku Islands vicinity, the PLA General Staff Department issued this message of encouragement. "All military forces and the People's Armed Police must be ready to fight and must have their eyes fixed on winning in battle. They must rise to their duty to prepare for military conflict and must reinforce their training for combat readiness." According to an article that appeared in the January 14 edition of the *People's Liberation Army Daily*, the official newspaper of the Chinese military, the General Staff Department instructed the PLA that its duty for 2013 was to "prepare for war."

According to the *PLA Daily*, this training objective was formulated in response to an "important order" that had been issued by Xi Jinping as chairman of the Central Military Commission. Whether or not such an order was issued by Xi Jinping, what is notable is that the article had spotlighted an order to prepare for war issued by the General Staff Department. There is little doubt the Chinese leadership's intent in running this story was to provoke Japan with the threat of war and to perhaps split the Japan-US alliance by causing the United States to vacillate.

Commenting on these developments that were unfolding on the Chinese side, Oriki Ryoichi, former chief of staff, Joint Staff, makes no attempt to conceal his concern. "It is my understanding that the situation has gotten more serious over the last two or three years."

At one time during the April 12-18, 1978, period, a total of 357 Chinese fishing boats manned by armed "fishermen" carrying automatic weapons had sailed up to the Senkaku Islands where they ignored Japan Coast Guard warnings and repeatedly violated Japan's territorial waters. This was when Fukuda Takeo was prime minister. Japan Coast Guard Director-General Takashi Kitamura comments, "The boats arrived suddenly. But more importantly, the reason for the action was unknown and could not be determined."

Four months after this, the Fukuda Cabinet dismissed calls for greater caution and signed the Japan-China Treaty of Peace and Friendship as scheduled. Two months after the signing, Deng Xiaoping visited Japan as vice premier. Speaking before the Japan National Press Club on October 25, 1978, Deng Xiaoping addressed the question of the Senkaku Islands before an audience of Japanese and foreign journalists.

> Diaoyutai is the name by which we call the Senkaku Islands. The difference starts with the names that we give these islands. It is true there are differences on this matter between our countries. When diplomatic relations were normalized, the two sides promised not to touch on this issue. In signing the Treaty of Peace and Friendship, again the two sides agreed not to touch on this issue. The wisdom of China is unable to find any other method to handle this issue but this. This is because if this problem is brought up, we would no longer be able to speak clearly. It is true that some people want to use this problem to throw cold water on our bilateral relations. For this reason, I think it is best to avoid this problem in our bilateral negotiations. It does not matter if we shelve problems like this for a while. It does not matter if it is shelved for ten years. The people of our generation do not have the necessary wisdom. We cannot find a solution to this problem, but future generations will have greater wisdom than we do. When the time comes, they will be able to find a solution that everyone can accept.

The Japanese government responded to Deng Xiaoping's "It does not matter if the problem is shelved for ten years," with tacit agreement. As has been noted, this statement provides the grounds for what the Chinese side has claimed is the "status quo" in the Senkaku Islands.

Kitamura speculates on what might account for the armed fishermen swarming into the waters around the Senkaku Islands. Around this time, some members of the ruling LDP were discussing building a temporary heliport on the Senkaku Islands to reinforcing Japan's effective control. Kitamura suggests this might have triggered the fleet of fishing boats but avoids making a definite statement. "I have to admit I cannot say for sure whether this was the reason or not."

The idea of building a heliport on the islands lingered on for a while—long enough to become instrumental in exposing the serious fissures that existed within Prime Minister Ohira Masayoshi's administration in May 1979. Transport Minister Moriyama Kinji, Okinawa Development Agency

Director-General Mihara Asao, and others advocated building a heliport in order to strengthen Japan's claim to effective control of the Senkaku Islands. However, this met with very strong opposition from China, which argued that this contravened Deng Xiaoping's formula for shelving the problem. In the course of the Diet debate that ensued, Foreign Minister Sonoda Sunao stated, "In consideration of our national interest, it would be best to leave the situation as it is." He also directly commented on the temporary heliport to express his displeasure. "We were not notified in advance." He concluded with a strong statement condemning the Okinawa Development Agency for the arbitrary steps it had taken without consultation. "We should refrain from acts that serve no purpose other than to broadcast our effective control."

Years later, Prime Minister Kan Naoto submitted a written response on this very point to House of Representatives Speaker Yokomichi Takahiro. According to this October 26, 2010, response, Foreign Minister Sonoda had issued a protest to Deng Xiaoping regarding the April 1978 armed fishermen incident and had requested that measures be taken to "ensure that such incidents never again occur." Sonoda effectively succeeded in obtaining a pledge when Deng responded, "The recent incident was completely accidental. The government of China will never cause such an incident."

In light of these developments, Sonoda moved to oppose the heliport construction project. Heading Japan's foreign policy establishment, Sonoda had concluded that the priority should be on Japan-China relations. As a result of the pressure from Sonoda, the Okinawa Development Agency withdrew the academic study mission that it had dispatched to the Senkaku Islands. Plans to construct a full-fledged heliport, fishing port, and lighthouses on the Senkaku Islands, which were being discussed in the LDP General Council, were either cancelled or postponed in the interest of Japan-China relations. Some years later, China suddenly and unilaterally enacted its Law on the Territorial Sea and the Contiguous Zone in 1992, a law declaring the Senkaku Islands Chinese territory. This is basically where the situation stands today.

It is interesting to note that Foreign Minister Sonoda Sunao was the father of Sonoda Hiroyuki, secretary general of the Sunrise Party of Japan and close confidante of Tokyo Governor Ishihara in the events that ended with the nationalization of the Senkaku Islands in 2012.

On the fleet of armed Chinese fishing boats that sailed to the Senkaku Islands in 1978, Kitamura offers this explanation based on materials that remain in the possession of the Japan Coast Guard. "It is not known whether the armed fishermen included PLA troops. In any case, the ships disappeared after a week. They did not land on the islands." Whatever China's intent might have been, Oriki, commenting from the perspective of the top uniformed SDF officer and the perspective he gained in various desktop exercises and simulations related to possible contingencies in the Senkaku Islands, "While saying that the incident was 'accidental,' China makes full use of such 'accidents.'"

Former Defense Minister Morimoto, whom Oriki worked under, describes the worst-case scenario in the following terms. "I don't even want to think about it, but suppose Chinese aircraft sneak through the cracks in Japan's political and defense systems and drop personnel on the Senkaku Islands. Once on the islands, they hoist the Chinese flag. Then what? This scenario is not necessarily unthinkable."

During his time as defense minister, Morimoto had put together a game plan for Japanese victory. In it, Japan would patiently and resolutely endure repeated Chinese violations of Japan's airspace and territorial waters, and would finally succeed in building a consensus in the international community that China is being extremely unreasonable. Ultimately, as Morimoto sees it, Japan could use this wave of international opinion to pressure China.

"The United States and Asia will intervene when and only when the international consensus says that China's actions are unacceptable. Bearing this in mind, it is imperative Japan not respond but patiently endure. The question that remains is how to use that consensus to achieve a solution."

From this perspective, Morimoto warns against over-reacting to each and every Chinese action and argues that Japanese over-reaction can easily lead the international community to conclude that it is Japan—not China—that is picking the fight. Morimoto expresses the fear that grips him when he imagines that outcome. "In that situation, it would not matter how loudly the government argued that the Senkaku Islands are covered by the Japan-US Security Treaty. Congress, which has the power to declare or not declare war, simply would not accept this position."

The first member of the Obama Cabinet to visit Japan after the nationalization of the Senkaku Islands was Secretary of Defense Leon Panetta. On September 17, 2012, Panetta and Morimoto engaged in the first Japan-US meeting of defense ministers. In the press conference that followed, Panetta said, "Obviously, we stand by our treaty obligations. But the United States, as a matter of policy, does not take a position with regard to competing sovereignty claims. It is extremely important both sides use diplomatic means to resolve these issues constructively and peacefully. These approaches have to be based on clear principles, principles that relate to international rules and regulations. It is in everybody's interest Japan and China find a way to avoid further escalation."

Panetta arrived in Beijing that evening and met with Defense Minister Liang Guanglie the following day, September 18. The next day, September 19, Panetta met with Vice Premier Xi Jinping, who by this time had already been identified as China's next supreme leader. In his exchange with Panetta, Xi Jinping referred to Japan's nationalization of the Senkaku Islands. "Certain political forces in Japan are unrepentant and have orchestrated a farce." He appeared to be spitting out the words with extreme displeasure. Turning next to the United States, Xi Jinping stated, "The United States should exercise caution in both word and deed and should not intervene in sovereignty disputes. We do not want the United States to take any action that will intensify the conflict or complicate the situation." These words were designed to check Panetta, who had just stated publicly in Tokyo that the Senkaku Islands were covered by the Japan-US Security Treaty.

Panetta responded with a general statement of US principles. "We do not take sides in territorial disputes." But Panetta did not stop there. For the first time, Panetta directly conveyed to the Chinese leadership the US position that "the Japan-US Security Treaty applies to the Senkaku Islands." The message demanded China exercise greater restraint.

Initially, the United States did not include that Panetta had looked Xi Jinping in the eye and told him "the Japan-US Security Treaty applies to the Senkaku Islands" as part of the official record. But as the situation changed, the US Department of Defense leaked this information through NHK, Japan's public broadcasting corporation. What changed was the Japanese public's reaction to the anti-Japanese demonstrations that raged in Beijing and other Chinese cities following the nationalization of the Senkaku Islands. Japan reacted not only with a hardening of its attitude toward China but also a growing sense of doubt and suspicion toward the United States. Disturbed by this turn of events, the US put this information on the Xi-Panetta meeting out to relieve Japan's growing malaise.

There is another theory as to why the United States did not initially publicize Panetta's statement that the Japan-US Security Treaty applies to the Senkaku Islands—that this was in response to a strong Chinese request that it be left out. Be that as it may, the fact remains that the statement that the United States will stand with Japan in defense of the Senkaku Islands was eventually put in the public record, albeit informally. But what did the US seek to gain in return? Most probably, the US had two reasons for leaking this information. The first was to preserve Japanese trust in the United States. The second was to signal restraint and ensure that Japan would not go beyond nationalization (such as sending SDF personnel to the Senkaku Islands).

AFP and other news organizations reported on comments Panetta made onboard the plane to Japan. Speaking to the press pool accompanying him, Panetta expressed his fears of what could happen should the dispute over the Senkaku Islands continue to escalate. "At some point, one side may make a mistake in judgment that leads to the use of force. This would immediately raise the possibility of conflict," Panetta had warned.

Immediately before the Senkaku Islands were nationalized on September 11, Secretary of State Clinton was in Vladivostok on behalf of President Barack Obama and underscored the US position: "The United States will do everything in its power to prevent the territorial problem from becoming more serious." It is almost certain that the record of the Xi-Panetta meeting was released as part of the same delicate balancing act that the United States was pursuing in its mediation diplomacy.

This is borne out by the developments that followed Panetta's visit to Japan and China. On September 20, Kurt Campbell, assistant secretary of state for East Asian and Pacific affairs, testified before the East Asia and Pacific Subcommittee of the Senate Foreign Relations Committee. "Deterioration in Japan-China relations is not in our national interest and could clearly undermine peace and stability in the Asia-Pacific region."

The unspoken American position on the Japan-China dispute over the Senkaku Islands and its effect on the United States was perhaps best expressed in an editorial in the January 25, 2013, *Washington Post*. "It's hard to believe that the United States could be dragged into a military conflict . . . over a group of tiny, uninhabited islands claimed by both Japan and China." While staring this specter in the face, the United States was struggling to figure out how the Japan-US Security Treaty could be used in reining in the military threat posed by a nuclear-armed China.

Morimoto lays out what he believes is absolutely essential for achieving this objective. As the first requirement, he identifies the high-level "battle of international opinion" that must be fought with China. Second, he emphasizes the critical importance of "well restrained responses."

As a scholar and lifelong student of American affairs, Morimoto is known for his extensive network of friends and acquaintances in the

White House, the Pentagon, and the State Department. Having discussed the Senkaku issue with Panetta when Panetta was at the top of the Pentagon's hierarchy, Morimoto says, "The United States looks on the Japan-China confrontation over the Senkaku Islands with a mixture of concern and discomfort. 'Please don't agitate the Chinese any further with no exit strategy in sight!' This is what the Americans must be thinking," Morimoto then goes on to speculate on the national psychology that prevails in the United States on this subject: "The US does not want a prolonged stand-off between China and Japan. The American nightmare is that the US gets automatically sucked into a war with China based on its obligations under the Japan-US Security Treaty. They very much want to avoid this."

It is true that Campbell, who served as assistant secretary of state for Asian affairs during Obama's first term and was caught up in trying to quell the Senkaku problem, repeats the official line "We support Japan as our ally." Yet he also seems to echo Morimoto as he explains the psychological position that prevails in the US government. "This is the advice I was giving Japan at that time. 'Please be very careful because you may be pulling the trigger on a series of events that will continue for a long time.' This was my advice. But unfortunately, that is what happened."

Campbell comments on the emergence of China and the new situation that it represents. "The key is to avoid reading too much into it." Campbell's words indirectly signal the US bottom line, which can be rephrased as follows. Japan and China are both major Asian powers. The worst scenario for the United States is for the two powers to look upon each other with unmitigated suspicion and for tensions to continue to build as a result of spiraling over-reactions.

Old Man Run Amok

"I am Ishihara and I am the Rip Van Winkle that has returned to the Diet as an 'old man run amok.' The questions that I pose are meant to serve as my last will and testament."

In early 2013, Ishihara Shintaro returned to the Diet for the first time in 18 years and was claiming center stage in the debate as the co-representative of the Japan Restoration Party. Standing before the House of Representatives Budget Committee on February 12, Ishihara prefaced his questions in a challenging tone. Prime Minister Abe looked on solemnly as he prepared for the exchange.

Ishihara was describing himself as an "old man run amok" in a self-deprecating manner. The phrase itself had its origins in the lament that Tanaka

Makiko, then minister of education, culture, sports, science and technology, had voiced in a post-Cabinet meeting press conference on October 26, 2012, just after Ishihara announced his decision to resign as governor of Tokyo and launch a new political party. "An old man run amok is coming, and we're in for a lot of trouble," she had said sarcastically. Her father was none other than Prime Minister Tanaka Kakuei, the man who had flown to Beijing in September 1972 to ink the treaty normalizing diplomatic relations between Japan and China. And it was during this visit that Prime Minister Tanaka had brought up the question of the Senkaku Islands in his talks with Chinese Premier Zhou Enlai in an effort to ascertain Chinese thinking on this thorny issue.

The written response submitted by Prime Minister Kan Naoto to the Speaker of the House of Representatives, as discussed above, refers to this meeting between Tanaka and Zhou Enlai and says that, when the two met in the Great Hall of the People on September 27, 1972, for their third day of talks, Zhou Enlai broached the subject of the threat posed by the Soviet Union, to which Tanaka responded saying, "Given our industrial power and the level of our technology, Japan can produce nuclear weapons but won't. Moreover, we will not possess any nuclear weapons." It was at this point that Tanaka had posed the fateful question. "What do you think about the Senkaku Islands? On our side, we have people who say all kinds of things."

After politely stopping his guest, Zhou Enlai offered this comment and sealed off further discussion on this subject. "I do not want to talk about the Senkaku Islands now. It would not be good to discuss this matter now. This became an issue because oil was discovered. If oil had not been found, neither Taiwan nor the United States would care about this."

Chuo University Professor Hattori Ryuji addresses this question in his 2011 book *Nicchu kokko seijoka: Tanaka Kakuei, Ohira Masayoshi, kanryo tachi no chosen* ([Normalization of Japan-China diplomatic relations: the challenges that faced Tanaka Kakuei, Ohira Masayoshi, and the bureaucrats], Chuokoron-Shinsha). According to Hattori, Tanaka intentionally raised this question notwithstanding the fact that the Senkaku Islands were under Japan's effective control. This, Hattori theorizes, was a ploy designed to rebuff Japan's conservatives who viewed the normalization of ties with China with considerable skepticism.

The thought that Zhou Enlai expressed on this occasion would later be affirmed by Deng Xiaoping to create the "leave this problem to future generations" formula. Ultimately, this would lead to the tacit agreement between the two countries that nothing would be done to change the status quo. It was Ishihara who stood up to break this seal of history, which he did by announcing his plan to have the Tokyo Metropolitan Government purchase the Senkaku Islands. And it was Tanaka Makiko, the daughter on whom Prime Minister Tanaka had doted, who ridiculed this and other Ishihara actions by labeling him "an old man run amok." Perhaps Ishihara had sensed the hand of karma at work when he returned to the Diet after an absence of 18 years, and perhaps this is why he chose to borrow this phrase and refer to himself as "an old man run amok."

"The Constitution is a major causal factor in the turmoil and decadence that beset this nation. The Constitution was drawn up unilaterally by the victors after the Second World War as a means of ruling the vanquished."

After outlining his unique interpretation of history, Ishihara moved on to address the one issue that excited him the most during his years as governor of Tokyo—the effective control of the Senkaku Islands. "What the government is now doing in the Senkaku Islands cannot be called effective control! A lighthouse should be erected on the highest promontory of Uotsurijima." Ishihara heaped scorn on Prime Minister Noda and his DPJ administration's inaction. When Abe took the podium to respond, his words sounded like a love call that advertised to the world the good relations that linked these two ideological bedfellows. "It is because I place such importance on environmental issues that I have appointed Ishihara Nobuteru (Shintaro's eldest son) to be my minister of the environment."

"This is a sensitive issue, so I don't expect a straightforward response. But I hope my questions will prove effective in raising awareness."

The question and answer session continued for an hour and forty minutes, most of it used by Ishihara to speechify. At the end of the session, Ishihara expressed support for Abe and left the Diet wearing a triumphant expression. He appeared to be satisfied with his own performance on the center stage of national politics after an interlude of so many years.

Sankei Shimbun had carried an interview with Abe on May 12, 2012, when the plans to nationalize the Senkaku Islands were not yet public knowledge. After stating that, "I absolutely support Ishihara," Abe went on to comment on Japan-US relations: "Constant and uninterrupted effort is essential for maintaining the alliance. It's like a marriage . . . It's a relationship based on trust. If trust is lost, the Japan-US alliance will be no better than a piece of scrap paper. The truth is that no soldier will risk his life for an untrustworthy friend."

Morimoto looked askance at Abe, who was prone to such pronouncements. With his deep knowledge of the cold and cruel world of national security, Morimoto made no effort to hide the anxiety he felt as he considered the Japan-China confrontation over the Senkaku Islands and the disturbing chill that was beginning to be felt between Japan and the United States. "The idea that Japan and China would come to blows was a joke as recently as three or five years ago. Today, nobody is laughing any more," Morimoto rues.

"Maybe there was something wrong with us when we imagined the possibility of war with China to be a joke and nothing more." Morimoto sounds embarrassed as he reminisces how Japan lived through the postwar years. At the same time, he reaffirms his "resolution" to face up to the nation's security issues. He then concludes with a warning directed to all Japanese leaders in the aftermath of the nationalization of the Senkaku Islands. "International affairs are without mercy. Hope has no place in international politics. Hopes and prayers will change nothing."

Postscript

"This ensures that China will see the nationalization of the Senkaku Islands as having been a Japanese national conspiracy. Brace yourself. This is going to be a long battle," muttered Richard Armitage, the former deputy secretary of state, on October 25, 2012. Just two days earlier, Armitage had been in Beijing at the unspoken behest of President Barack Obama. During his stay in Beijing, he had engaged in heated exchanges on the Senkaku Islands with Vice Premier Li Keqiang and others. Now he was back in his Tokyo hotel watching the news.

Around the same time, the Chinese side was busy circulating its interpretation of how Noda Yoshihiko and his DPJ had made the decision to nationalize the Senkaku Islands. "It was a national conspiracy, with Noda and [Tokyo Governor] Ishihara colluding to perpetrate this conspiracy," went the Chinese story. The day after Armitage returned to Japan from China—October 25—Ishihara Shintaro called a press conference to announce that he was resigning as governor and was launching a new political party, the Sunrise Party. What Armitage's gut told him was that China's immediate knee-jerk reaction would be to tie Ishihara's announcement to the Senkaku Islands. Hence his dark prediction.

About a month later, I was in Washington, DC, to meet and exchange views with senior Obama administration officials working on Asia policy. During the trip, I also met with a number of old friends, some of whom had already left their government posts and others who were still on the US government frontlines. All of them without exception voiced the same very candid question. "Why did Japan have to act so hurriedly to nationalize the Senkaku Islands? What was so special about this timing?" Not one of these former and current US policymakers believed the Chinese national-conspiracy story. However, all of them doubted the wisdom of having nationalized the Senkaku Islands—a move that was certain to violently agitate the emerging superpower that was China. It was clear to me that all of them, without exception, had come to harbor a certain dissatisfaction with and distrust of Japan.

Japan hardly needed any more headaches and negative developments. The Japanese economy had come to a standstill, and the world was beginning to dismiss Japan for its self-marginalizing. On the domestic front, an air of stunned hopelessness hung over the nation in the wake of the Great East Japan Earthquake. The situation had only been made worse by the decision to nationalize the Senkaku Islands, a decision that was sure to seriously impact Japan's national security future. China was feeding the rumor mills with its conspiracy theory and waves of suspicion were washing over the United States. If left unaddressed, these rumors and suspicions could eventually mean trouble for future Japanese generations.

I came away from my many conversations and discussions in Washington wondering what had happened—what had gone wrong, if wrong it was. But what was initially a simple query grew to become an overarching obsession by the end of 2012. During New Year's 2013, the thought came to me: "Someone has to leave some kind of record for the future—a record that can withstand critical examination by future historians." The first thing I did was to pick up the phone and call everyone that came to mind. I was looking for anyone who would listen to what I had to say about the gnawing question that I had stumbled across. Before I knew it, I had launched into writing this book. The New Year was not yet two weeks old.

The thought of writing this book came to me just as my previous book, *Beichu hyakunen senso: Shin reisen kozo to nihon no meiun* [The US-China hundred year war: Structure of the new cold war and Japan's fate], was going to be released. I was also in the midst of translating *Obama and China's Rise: An Insider's Account of America's Asian Strategy*, the memoirs of Jeffrey Bader, who had been the Obama administration's senior director for Asian affairs on the National Security Council. Yet busy as I was, I suspect the fact that I began working on this book in tandem with these other projects helped me approach Japan-China relations, US-China relations, and the structure of the Japan-US-China triangle from a more comprehensive and multi-tiered perspective.

I would like to take this opportunity to express my special thanks to Nikkei Inc. CEO Kita Tsuneo and to Okada Naotoshi, Managing Director and Editor-in-chief of *Nihon Keizai Shimbun* (*Nikkei*) at Nikkei's Tokyo Headquarters, both of whom graciously viewed my writing activities as an exercise in honing my skills as a journalist. I would also like to thank Chief Editor Matsumoto Motohiro and Copy Editing Assistant Director Fujiwara Toyoaki at the electronic edition of *Nikkei* (titles as of this writing), who approved and supported the serial publication of this book in their paper.

I was fortunate enough to be able to interview two central actors in this narrative—Noda Yoshihiko and Nagashima Akihisa—on multiple occasions and appreciate that they openly and candidly shared their thoughts with me. I can find no other word than "gratitude" to express my indebtedness to them for having understood the disturbing question that stood behind the writing of this book. I am likewise indebted to two former foreign ministers, Maehara Seiji and Gemba Koichiro, to former Chief Cabinet Secretary Sengoku Yoshito, and to the many other DPJ executive officers who shared their views, insights, and information. Finally, I would also like to express my deepest thanks to the many other individuals too numerous to name without whose support and assistance the writing of this book would not have been possible.

In June 2013, President Obama welcomed China's new supreme leader, Xi Jinping, to their first summit meeting. The venue for the meeting was a posh estate in California. According to both Japanese and US government sources, during the meeting, President Xi repeated China's usual statements and claims regarding the Senkaku Islands and solicited President Obama's understanding. In response, President Obama acknowledged that the Senkaku Islands were under the administration of Japan and encouraged President Xi to "talk to Japan."

At just about the same time, Qi Jianguo, deputy chief of the People's Liberation Army, spoke at an international conference in Singapore where he addressed the Senkaku issue and expounded upon the shelving-of-the-problem argument. On the Japanese side, a non-partisan mission to China headed by former Chief Cabinet Secretary Nonaka Hiromu publicly stated that an agreement had been reached on shelving the problem in the 1972 meeting between Prime Minister Tanaka Kakuei and Premier Zhou Enlai.

As predicted by Richard Armitage, the war of nerves between Japan and China over the nationalization of the Senkaku Islands has only just begun and will almost certainly see skirmish after skirmish for many years to come. It is imperative Japan understand the decision-making process that culminated in the nationalization of the Senkaku Islands, which it claims as an inherent territory of Japan. Nothing would make me happier than to have this book serve that purpose in some small way.

Early summer of 2013
Sunohara Tsuyoshi

REFLECTIONS
Was Nationalizing the Senkaku Islands the Right Choice?

Nagashima Akihisa, Special Advisor to Prime Minister Noda, and Sunohara Tsuyoshi

China Rising

Sunohara: Looking back from our vantage point of May 2015, how do you view the entire process of nationalizing the Senkaku Islands?

As you know, tensions in the South China Sea are extremely high because of what China has been doing. This is bringing the confrontation between the United States and China to the forefront. At the same time, the Diet is beginning to debate the Abe administration's national security legislation package aimed at paving the way for Japan to exercise its right of collective self-defense. This also ties in to what is called China's rise. In my opinion, the proposed legislation actually reflects an appropriate and correct political judgment based on a strategy for beefing up Japan's defense ahead of China's rise.

But with all of these developments in mind, do you believe it was best that the Senkaku Islands were nationalized at that time? Of course, in asking this, I am also asking you to speculate on what the situation would be now if the islands had not been nationalized then.

Nagashima: The answer to that question is obvious and I have written about it in my book, *"Katsubei" to iu ryugi: Gaiko, anzenhosho no riarizumu* (A style known as utilizing America: Foreign affairs and national security realism). It all begins and ends with Mutsu Munemitsu's "I want to believe that there was no other way available." (from his *Kenkenroku*) I think that was very close to the last possible chance we had to nationalize the islands. The point is that, beginning in 2008, Chinese ships had started to violate our territorial waters. Various things were happening in the Chinese leadership in 2007, 2008, and 2009. That is about when China reversed its policy of keeping a low profile. This also coincides with the proposal made by a top Chinese navy officer to US Pacific Command chief Timothy Keating: "Let's divide the Pacific. You take the east and we'll take the west."

Sunohara: Yes, that is right. (wry smile)

Nagashima: Another concurrent development was the shock of the Lehman Brothers collapse, which sent the Western economies into a tailspin. At that time, China's fiscal position was extremely sound and strong.

Sunohara: I have heard that the Chinese see the United States as a "nation of finance," and then the US stumbled in the finance field. Some have said that this is when China began to think, "The American age has come to an end."

Nagashima: Yes, China came through with a massive four trillion yuan (approximately 56 trillion yen) fiscal stimulus package. China's fiscal stimulus buttressed the world economy at a very difficult juncture. It was around this time that China began to feel that a strategic opportunity was dawning. Another factor is that China had used the preceding 25 years to build up immense military power.

With that as a point of demarcation, China began its naval expansion. Two years before the Senkaku Islands were nationalized, we had that collision incident with the Chinese fishing boat, which is why I felt that Japan could not retreat. For the government, for the people, and also from a strategic perspective, Japan had to take a stand. Actually, my feeling was that Japan would not be able to control the situation if we just pretended not to see anything.

Sunohara: I completely agree. Professor Joseph Nye of Harvard University, a long-time acquaintance, often says, "In hindsight, you can say anything you want about the past." But for this particular case, I really agree that the situation today could have been very tough if the decision to nationalize had not been made at that time.

On the other hand, Prime Minister Noda's decision to nationalize the islands was not really triggered by some strategic political judgment. The trigger was much more artificial. The whole thing started with Tokyo Governor Ishihara Shintaro's announcement that Tokyo would purchase the islands. This is the most problematic point in the entire process.

If we ask whether nationalization was unavoidable from the national defense perspective and whether the Noda administration had arrived at its decision based on various strategic considerations, the answer would have to be, "Yes, but that is not all." The motivation that was always there in the background was the idea of blocking Ishihara. Writing this book, I always felt uncomfortable and conflicted about this motive and its ramifications. (laugh)

Nagashima: I understand what you are saying. (wry smile) However, there are two things I want to say on that. The first is the complexity and ambiguity of history. I am not going to deny that this was not done autonomously and on our own initiative. After all, we were reacting to Ishihara. But we were also thinking, "So, the time has finally come." In other words, we were not completely passive in this.

Our thinking was that China is going to do something sooner or later. What should Japan do when the time of reckoning comes? It is true that we were running all sorts of simulations ever since that Chinese fishing boat rammed a Coast Guard patrol ship. The government would have definitely run these simulations even if Ishihara had never made his announcement on buying the Senkaku Islands. Then, there was that announcement. Our response was, "This is a good chance. We cannot ignore this and sit idly by." That's when we took the first step forward.

Sunohara: Yes, as I wrote in the book, this issue had been considered by a succession of administrations before the Noda Cabinet.

Nagashima: You are right. Remember, there were plans to purchase the islands going back to Prime Minister Koizumi's time.

Sunohara: I have looked into that history. Also, there was that incident when Abe was chief cabinet secretary. He "lowballed" the owner with a very cheap offer and was rebuffed. (laugh) Ishihara said the same thing. So as you have pointed out, this was an accident of history. Noda was the prime minister, you were his advisor, and Ishihara was still going strong as governor.

It seems to me that, at the time, Ishihara still hoped to make his oldest son, Nobuteru, who was already a Diet member, prime minister one day. With that in mind, he probably wanted to set off some fireworks. He was looking around and found his opportunity in the Senkaku Islands. This is all conjecture, of course.

So there was a perfect confluence of internal and external conditions leading to the nationalization of the Senkaku Islands. And this confluence of conditions reverberated domestically and internationally in a very complex manner. That is how I see it.

Nagashima: That's why I called it a quirk of history. The Chinese side was probably thinking, "Why is Japan doing this?" Even while they were trying to figure this out, the Japanese initiative on purchasing the islands kept moving forward until China was left with no choice but to react in a very strong manner. I think that is part of the explanation. The wheels of history seemed to be moving inexorably in that direction.

Sunohara: The main actors themselves were probably acting without knowing exactly where they were headed. I can just imagine the confusion of those who were watching from the sidelines or from afar. It's only natural that they couldn't figure things out. I would count the United States among them. Even Kurt Campbell, the assistant secretary of state who stood on the Japan policy front lines, wasn't quite sure what was happening.

Imagine how confusing the situation looked to China. It's against this backdrop that wild conspiracy theories like the Noda-Ishihara conspiracy idea gained currency. (laugh) What really surprised me was that there were some indications that people in Washington also initially credited this story. Now this is the real kicker! (laugh) Your presence, Nagashima, was being cited as evidence of this conspiracy. From the Chinese perspective, you were both an aide to Prime Minister Noda and an Ishihara protégé. (laugh)

Nagashima: So I'm the source of all evil. And I was the one that brought down Japan-China relations. (wry smile)

Sunohara: I quoted you in the book as vigorously denying this allegation, but I am going to ask you again for the record. Are you saying there was no conspiracy? (laugh)

Nagashima: Absolutely! There was no conspiracy. The cross-currents of history put me there. All sorts of factors were at play, and totally by chance, my background got caught up in the mix. That's all there is to it. I neither plotted a conspiracy nor was I used by people plotting a conspiracy. (laugh)

Sunohara: You mention "by chance." By chance, Noda was the son of a Self-Defense Forces (SDF) officer. In a sense, this prime minister turned out to be very gutsy. Then you were there standing by his side, Nagashima, with your detailed knowledge of the Japan-US Security Treaty. A question naturally arises at this point. What would have happened if Kan Naoto had remained prime minister? What would have happened if Hatoyama Yukio were still prime minister? Or let me take this question further back in history. What would have happened under earlier Liberal Democratic Party

(LDP) administrations such as under Fukuda Yasuo or Aso Taro or the first time Abe Shinzo was prime minister?

Nagashima: It's true the human factor plays an important role, especially at these critical junctures in history. So was that a good thing, or was it a bad thing? We will just have to wait for history to render its judgment. You have to remember that it was already five years since the collision.

As I look back, and as I consider what you said at the start concerning the current situation in the South China Sea, I feel that these events served as a wake-up call for the United States. The Americans must have been asking themselves, "What's going on? Why are the Japanese reacting by nationalizing the islands when they have always refrained from reacting to China's outbursts? What does this all mean? What's happening in East Asia?" I am convinced this served to focus America's attention on this part of the world.

It is true that even before this, Secretary of State Hillary Clinton had made some pointed remarks at an ASEAN Regional Forum (ARF) to check China. I'm sure the United States was already struggling with the question of how to deal with China. The US always had its own strategic calculations and objectives and was urging both Japan and China to exercise self-restraint. This is because the US feared being sucked into a conflict between Japan and China. For the first time in the history of the alliance, the US was seriously thinking about the possibility of being pulled into a conflict involving Japan. I have to admit that I felt a strange sense of relief in this turn of events because I was sick and tired of all the arguments about the reverse situation where Japan is pulled into an armed conflict involving the United States. (laugh)

The End of the Japan-US Alliance?

Sunohara: I travelled in the US during the long holidays in May. The United States has definitely changed compared to last year.

Nagashima: Yes, things have changed.

Sunohara: On China, the attitude used to be that the US would pat China on the head or would continue its policy of supportive intervention and China would eventually behave better. Some 60 or 70 percent subscribed to this optimistic projection. But on this trip, the majority seemed distrustful of China.

So in a way, the Senkaku problem was a wake-up call for the US and caused the Americans to turn their eyes to what was really happening in China and the truth about the Chinese dragon's fangs. As I mentioned earlier, there were clear indications during the early days that some people in the US believed the Chinese conspiracy theory.

Nagashima: I think that's right. Congress has changed significantly. The other day, I was talking to some senior staff members at a meeting in Washington. They were saying the "red team" (China appeasers) has been disbanded and that everyone has now moved over to the "blue team" (China skeptics).

Sunohara: What you said about the reverse risk of being sucked into a conflict by an ally is very interesting.

What if America gets sucked into a war with China over a few uninhabited rocks in the middle of the ocean because of something stupid that Japan does? That is the American perspective. Jeffrey Bader, a friend of mine and a former aide to President Obama (senior director for Asian affairs on the National Security Council), has written about this very thing in his personal memoirs.

But the majority of Japanese would respond, "Get real! It runs the other way." The people around Abe probably think the same way.

Going back further, Tom Schieffer, the US ambassador to Japan during the Bush administration, very clearly said this about the Japan-US alliance. Suppose North Korea fired ballistic missiles at US bases in Guam or Hawaii, and suppose Japan knew that the missiles were on their way to their targets. If the SDF Aegis warships did not shoot the missiles down because official policy said Japan cannot exercise the right of collective self-defense, that would be the end of the alliance.

I had dinner with Schieffer the other day for the first time in a long while. This topic came up again in our conversation, and I posed the following hypothetical question. Suppose People's Liberation Army (PLA) soldiers disguised as fishermen landed on the Senkaku Islands and raised the Chinese flag, even though Japan had done nothing to provoke this. Further suppose the Japan Coast Guard came under attack when it approached the island to remove the PLA soldiers. If the United States did not stand up pursuant to the provisions of the Japan-US Security Treaty, that too would spell the end of the alliance.

But the real question was: What would happen after that? Japan would probably conclude that we cannot rely on the US and voices would be raised in Japan for serious rearmament and developing our own nuclear weapons. Once that starts, no one would be able to stop the process. So the basic conclusion was that our present challenge is for both Japan and the US to do everything possible to avoid that outcome. That was the discussion we had.

The Diet—in what is being called the "national security legislation Diet"—is currently deliberating the exercise of the right of collective self-defense. The problem is that the Diet is going back to the old hypothetical argument that was originally posed by Ambassador Schieffer. What I mean is that the Diet is indulging in self-centered, myopic, one-sided, and shallow discussions that ask, "Does the exercise of collective self-defense mean we are going to end up defending America?" or "Are we going to be co-opted into fighting for America's global strategy?"

What I find so unsatisfying about the Diet debate is that the question "Will the United States really live up to the provisions of Article V of the Japan-US Security Treaty" was discussed exhaustively when the nationalization of the Senkaku Islands was being debated. This was placed under the microscope and examined closely. But where did all that discussion go now that we are talking about this in reverse? (wry smile)

The DPJ is now in the opposition, and I am not saying they are the only ones, but what a wasted opportunity this is becoming. This is a great chance for Japan to shed its old skin and develop a more mature understanding of national security and international politics. But we have utterly failed to take advantage of this golden opportunity.

Some liberals continue to exhibit a strong emotional reaction based on their idealism. Thus they declare, "We don't want war," or they sound the alarm: "The SDF will be sent to fight on the other side of the world." Perhaps they don't understand that in the twenty-first century, we no longer live in an environment where Japan is constantly and unilaterally exposed to the risk of being pulled in by America to be used by America.

I know Prime Minister Abe's LDP administration cannot reveal the truth about everything in Diet debate or where TV cameras are rolling. But I cannot help but feel they are not doing a good enough job in responding to the questions put to them in the Diet. For example, why not say, "Please try to remember the Senkaku debate." If we want the United States to come to our defense in accordance with the provisions of Article V of the Japan-US Security Treaty in an emergency, we have to be prepared to help the United States in, say, a missile attack from North Korea.

There are limits to what Japan can do. Of course we should cherish and preserve the Constitution's core values such as renunciation of war and renunciation of war as a means of settling international disputes. At the same time, Japan must adjust to the international environment of the twenty-first century and demonstrate that, to the extent possible, we are doing what we can for the United States. Failing this, the United States may well abandon Japan at some point in the future.

I am not siding with the anti-Americanism advocates that you see on the streets, nor am I suggesting that Americans are advocating the foolish position that America should abandon Japan. What I am saying is that it is about time the Japanese people woke up and looked directly into the face of the essential features that characterize international relations and international politics.

People in the foreign policy field like to say, "There are no permanent enemies, and no permanent friends, only permanent interests." It is time for Japan to appreciate these words and take them to heart. Reciprocity and the spirit of give-and-take are an important foundation in international relations. This is the reality that exists in international politics.

Nagashima: I totally agree.

Sunohara: This is an old story from back when Japan still had a Socialist Party, but let me tell it anyway. Various emergency situations were being debated on a TV program, and someone from the LDP asked a Socialist member of the Diet, "What should Japan do in such-and-such contingency?" The Socialist was caught off guard and hemmed and hawed until he suddenly blurted out, "But we have the Japan-US Security Treaty!" (laugh) I guess there might be some black humor in this exchange, but I was totally astonished and disgusted by this response. The response was not meant to be funny, nor does it contain a dark joke that we can laugh about. My guess is that the Socialist member of the panel simply blurted out what he was always thinking in his heart. My point is that this type of thinking remains entrenched in the minds of a majority of the Japanese people to this day.

I don't intend to be an uncritical Abe supporter, but it is about time this deception and fiction was exorcised from Japanese politics and foreign relations. If it is not exorcised, we should be forewarned that we have already entered an age when Japan cannot effectively defend the nation and protect the rights, property, safety, and peace of the Japanese people as required under the Constitution.

Peacetime Costs and Contingency Risks

Nagashima: Given that the Japan-US Security Treaty is, as someone once said, no more than a piece of paper, both sides must work to give concrete shape to its provisions. In the context of what you were saying, I believe it is critically important to reaffirm the meaning of Articles V and VI of the Japan-US Security Treaty.

Article V states that the United States assumes joint responsibility for defending Japan against external threats. In a normal mutual security agreement, in exchange for this guarantee, Japan would be required to take on the same responsibility for defending the United States in the event of a crisis. But Japan has been saying, "Sorry, but we can't do that because of our constitutional constraints."

The Abe administration is now working to enact laws that will enable collective self-defense. But what we are getting is something that is just a hair better than the right of individual self-defense. In other words, what Japan is aiming at is "faux collective self-defense." (wry smile) It simply is not that easy to get to where Japan can exercise its military might for the United States. What this means is that the United States has accepted the contingency risks. That's where Article VI (provision of bases and facilities) comes in, and Japan accepts this responsibility. This is the basic structure of the Japan-US Security Treaty. The structure is fundamentally warped and unbalanced, but this is how a semblance of balance is achieved. Japan pays to cover the peacetime costs in exchange for the United States taking the contingency risks.

The issue with peacetime costs is that Okinawa has been made to bear an inordinate portion of the total. Regarding the relocation of Futenma Air Base, Hatoyama famously said, "At least relocate to a site outside Okinawa, and relocate to another country if at all possible." Ever since, the discussion of how peacetime costs are allocated has become very heated. But as I said a moment ago, the peacetime costs borne by Japan are meant to balance out the contingency risks borne by the United States. From the American perspective, they are going to say, "Why doesn't Japan bear any of the contingency costs?" Dissatisfaction exists on both sides, and this is the source of instability in the alliance.

Past administrations have struggled with the question of how to achieve a balance. Japan has endeavored to balance the situation by accepting part of the contingency risks. Going back in history, you see Kishi Nobusuke and the revision of the Japan-US Security Treaty in 1960. Then there is

Nakasone Yasuhiro, who came through with the commitment to block-ade four straits and to defend the sea-lanes. More recently, we have Noda Yoshihiko and Abe Shinzo. There is a definite continuity between what Noda and Abe have endeavored to do. Negotiations are going forward on two fronts: On the one hand, Japan will accept a greater share of the con-tingency risks. And on the other hand, an effort will be made to reduce the peacetime costs in Okinawa and elsewhere (e.g., burdens related to military bases and expenses related to US forces in Japan).

The problem is with liberals who say they want to lower the peacetime costs but are unwilling to shoulder any contingency risks. (wry smile) From the American perspective, the response is, "Don't be silly." Eventually, they will say, "Who do you think we are? Don't play us for a fool."

Sunohara: You used the word "silly," and I apologize to you in advance for saying this, but the person who stands at the very front of the "silly" line is Hatoyama Yukio, who came to office as the DPJ's first prime minister. If I had to name a second person responsible for the imbalance, that would be Koizumi Junichiro.

You mentioned the continuity between Noda and Abe. By the same token, I see a continuity between Koizumi and Hatoyama. Of course, the two were separated by a number of intervening administrations—the first Abe administration, the Aso administration, and the Fukuda administra-tion. But Koizumi and Hatoyama are on a continuum in the sense that both were only interested in reducing peacetime costs. Neither of them made any reference whatsoever to bearing the contingency risks.

Nagashima: I see.

Sunohara: We don't normally think of Prime Minister Koizumi this way because he was the one who sent the SDF to Iraq. That's the image that we have of him. But that was in large part influenced by the emphasis on his personal relationship with President George W. Bush.

I was posted in Washington at that time and was observing the Koizumi administration from the American vantage point. Quite frankly, it would be hard for me to say Koizumi shared the kind of ideology or philoso-phy that we see today in Abe. By this I mean Koizumi was not particularly committed to further developing the Japan-US security arrangements or upgrading the alliance.

Nagashima: I completely agree with you. Abe today has Yachi (Shotaro) at his side, which places him on a firm footing in the area of strategic thinking. And he established the Japanese National Security Council (NSC). From the American perspective, they are now dealing with a very stable administration. So relations with the US are naturally going to improve. From where I stand, this is a very natural development. It's not that Abe is being obsequious or that he is yes-manning the United States. That's not it at all. He is appreciated because he does what has to be done.

The same applies to Noda in his relationship with President Obama. The relationship went well because Noda did what had to be done. He moved forward on the Trans-Pacific Partnership, acted on easing the three principles governing weapons exports, and purchased the US F-35 fighters. Obama may have looked down at him at the start, but Noda came through on these critical decisions.

At first, Obama asked, "What number DPJ administration are you?" (wry smile) That was at the first summit meeting that Noda attended in New York immediately after he assumed the office of prime minister. Obama turned to him and said, "Starting with the LDP's Aso Taro, you are the fifth Japanese Prime Minister that I am sitting across from." It's very likely that he looked down on Noda in the beginning. But that attitude changed.

Sunohara: I don't know whether President Obama initially held Noda in contempt or not, (wry smile) but there was definitely a sense of "once bitten twice shy" on the American side, particularly with regard to the DPJ. They were very suspicious and worried it was going to be a repeat of the Hatoyama Cabinet pattern. It was very clear from my conversations with Obama administration people that America's assessment of the Noda administration underwent a significant change midway through. (laugh)

Nagashima: To be precise, the repair and restoration of our relations with the United States began during the latter portion of Prime Minister Kan Naoto's term. But the improvement was not particularly conspicuous. So let's give the credit to the Noda administration that I was part of. (laugh)

Sunohara: I didn't sense anything like that in Koizumi.

Nagashima: You are right. The US economy was doing well during that period, and with the shock of 9/11, the Koizumi administration reflexively announced its support for the war on terror. On the surface, the Koizumi years appear to have been a success story.

Sunohara: In that sense, I think that Abe has thrown everything into this. On the other hand, Yasukuni Shrine means something different for Abe than it does for Koizumi.

For Abe Shinzo to really rise above Kishi Nobusuke [his grandfather] as a politician, he has to approach the Japan-US Security Treaty head-on and repaint the whole thing so that Japan can really stand on an equal footing with the United States. Just looking at the Japan-US Security Treaty, this is what I believe Abe has to do.

In an election where the people are being asked to make a choice, the key issue should not be the consumption tax rate. The recent election should have been fought over national security. But Abe didn't do that. If he had, he would have lost the election.

Nagashima: For sure. (laugh)

Sunohara: The election was fought over the question of postponing the consumption tax rate hike. How can you lose in an election like that? Voters are obviously going to applaud postponing a rate hike that will hit them in the pocketbook. Imagine what would happen if he had said, "This election seeks a vote of confidence on our national security legislation." That kind of honest approach to politics and elections would definitely spell defeat for the ruling party.

Nagashima: Noda is a good example of how that can happen. (wry smile)

Sunohara: That's right, just like Noda. (laugh) But Prime Minister Abe and Chief Cabinet Secretary Suga Yoshihide are veteran politicians. With all their political dexterity and all the tricks that they have up their sleeves, they would never make that mistake. But there is also a negative to the path that they chose. We are now (early summer of 2015) seeing this negative play out. Whereas the current session of the Diet is dedicated to debating and enacting the package of national security legislation, we are seeing a parade of old fictions resurrected. It is as if we were sleep-walking through a flashback to the old days—a sort of deja deja vu.

For example, the defense minister has explained in the Diet debate that "The SDF will not be exposed to any higher level of risk." This is deception, pure and simple. As you just said, under the proposed laws, Japan will be taking on some contingency risks. This means that, as professional soldiers in the broad sense, SDF personnel will be exposed to heightened risk.

But that's not where the real problem lies. The critical question is whether the Japanese people are aware of this heightened risk, and whether the SDF personnel going to their posts sense that the people are aware of the risk they are exposing them to. The critical question is whether politics ensures that the people share this awareness. You know what I mean?

Nagashima: I am planning to ask Prime Minister Abe straight-out if his real purpose isn't to restructure the Japan-US alliance. The salient feature of the Japan-US alliance structure is the balance, or imbalance, if you will, between peacetime costs and contingency risks. Ever since Abe's grandfather (Kishi Nobusuke) was prime minister, Japan has been trying to rebalance this. I want to believe he is continuing on this path. And if he is, I want to know why he does not directly address the contingency risks. It is only because we are accepting some contingency risks that we can talk to the United States about reducing the peacetime cost burden. I want to drive that point home.

Sunohara: It's interesting to follow how the media reports the debate and how the debate evolves. The liberal media first came out with the warning, "SDF personnel will be at greater risk." They were back to the "peace at any price" thinking that was rampant during the Cold War era. Next, the government tried to quell the fears by denying the heightened risk. It was only quite a bit later that the government began to give the debate a more positive spin by saying the legislation will allow us to reduce the people's exposure to more substantial risks. Why can't the government convey this message to the people in a more straightforward way?

For example, why doesn't the government say this is part of an effort to form a tight scrum with the United States to create a robust system for protecting Japan in the face of unreasonable demands and threats from the Chinese government and people? Seen that way, this approach enables the Japanese nation and people to eliminate an enormous risk at a very low price. Having settled that, the government could then explain that this is why we are exposing the SDF to heightened risk. In any case, isn't that ultimately the SDF's mission?

Nagashima: It goes without saying that no one in the SDF wants to die in vain. But I am certain they are prepared to accept the heightened risk and to stake their lives willingly if it is for the future of the nation and in the national interest.

Sunohara: All the SDF officers I meet say the same thing.

Nagashima: In that sense, I feel that the LDP and Komeito Diet members, the opposition Diet members, and the government bureaucrats are all undermining the honor of the SDF. The SDF personnel themselves are at peace with their mission and recognize that, yes, the risks are going to be greater. It is the politicians who are flinching and engaging in deception.

The national security legislation will expand the scope of SDF activities. But the government keeps on saying there will be no heightened risk. So I put this question to them: How is that possible? When the scope of activity expands, it's only natural the risk level should rise. And what is the government's answer? "We are taking all available precautions." (wry smile)

Sunohara: And then they say the field commander can decide to withdraw or evacuate his forces any time.

Nagashima: The risk level goes up. That is the plain truth. But it has to be explained that there are so many critical advantages to be gained.

Sunohara: It should be clearly explained to the public that in terms of straightforward cost-benefit accounting, there is a huge difference between being able to exercise the right of collective self-defense and remaining in our current hamstrung condition.

Nagashima: That is what it will take to convince the public and to reassure the SDF. The situation has to be presented in these terms. But what the government is trying to do is to slip by with all the talk about precautions and safety measures.

Sunohara: That has got to be clearly explained. I hope you will hit them head-on with your questions.

Nagashima: I will.

Sunohara: I am sure everyone in the SDF feels the same way.

Nagashima: You are right. How is it acceptable to say we will only go where it is safe and will suspend our activities if it gets dangerous? How are you going to suspend logistical support activities in the middle of a battle? How can you just walk away from a life-and-death war? (wry smile)

Sunohara: You can't say "Hey, there are people dying here. We're going home." As soon as you say that, I can just hear the response. "You must be kidding!" That would be the natural response.

Nagashima: "Why did you come here in the first place," they would protest.

Sunohara: It's all extremely deceitful the way this is being presented. I don't deny that Japan has a long legacy and a difficult history, and it is very difficult to change all of this overnight. But the question that is bothering me is what will happen if the legislative package currently before the Diet gets passed with smoke and mirrors. Deception is not the right way to do this. Deception is not going to foster a higher level of understanding and sophistication.

Nagashima: That's right.

The Meaning of National Autonomy

Sunohara: I wonder if we could move on a little and talk about "the world according to Ishihara Shintaro." (laugh) The question is: What is "national autonomy"?

Going back to the Senkaku Islands, this has a lot in common with the problem of Japanese citizens abducted by North Korea. Conservatives have been persistently arguing and asking: What kind of a sovereign nation is it that can't defend its own territory, protect its own people, and regain what has been taken from it? The situation gets very murky if you add conservative ideology to this mix, and even murkier if you add anti-Chinese sentiments such as have existed since ancient times or add anti-Western ideologies or add the xenophobic sentiments encapsulated in the pre-Meiji slogan of, to borrow an old expression, expelling the barbarians.

Postwar Japan has made a conscious effort not to think about this question, but we can't go on like this any longer. We live in a world where the Cold War stand-off between East and West has become the stuff of history books. We live in a world of rapid globalization and a world of polarity. To live in this world, Japan must stand on its own feet, think with its own head, and act on its own will. In the process, Japan will naturally have to reflect on the meaning of territory, sovereignty, and national autonomy. Politics will have to make an effort to foster a public consensus on these issues.

Otherwise, Japan will never be able to graduate from being what Ishihara and those around him call an "emasculated nation" with "hand-me-down democracy." I really want politics to get on with this task. But right now, no one shows any sign of doing that. (wry smile)

Nagashima: I suspect they will try to get away without ever touching on those issues. After all, the bureaucrats are writing their lines. Abe might go there if he had a free hand in replying to the questions put to him, but he doesn't. And the bureaucrats who write and vet his answers are only thinking about putting in the hours so their important bills can be enacted without amendment and without incident.

Sunohara: Yes, but that is not the style of politics we need. Politicians have to speak in their own words.

We hear a lot of criticism of America of the conspiracy-theory variety—that it is a hegemon or that it is doing all kinds of things behind the scenes. But many of my American friends and acquaintances are personally shouldering the heavy weight of supporting the United States as a nation. For example, in the middle of a normal conversation, someone might say, "My son is now in Iraq," or "My son-in-law was killed in Bosnia, and I'm trying to be a father to my grandchild." You hear this kind of thing all the time.

Nagashima: The same with the professor who mentored me when I was studying in the States. His third son is a Marine and has done four tours of duty in Iraq.

Sunohara: All of the American people, whether consciously or not, are carrying a heavy burden. On a national and personal level, they are all shouldering certain risks. To a significant degree, that is why America can remain America.

Nagashima: That is right.

Sunohara: If Japan says we won't take that kind of risk, then we have no choice but to continue living under the protection of the United States for the rest of the twenty-first century—no alternative but to live under the asymmetrical alliance, leaving Okinawa's Futenma Air Base where it is, spending more and more money to support US forces in Japan, and constantly begging them to please protect us. The question we should be asking now is: Is that really what we want? Is that really what is best for Japan?

Nagashima: That's certainly what Japan looked like in the 1970s. The argument about the division of roles and responsibilities goes straight to the core and culminates in saying Japan should pay for the protection it is receiving. It was Nakasone who changed this.

Sunohara: I guess this brings you to the argument typical of the Ron-Yasu generation, (laugh) and you can say that the nationalization of the Senkaku Islands was one example of a step that postwar Japan simply could not avoid taking.

Nagashima: Actually, it was And it would make me very happy if you would view this entire episode as part of an effort to get out of the rut that postwar Japan was in.

Sunohara: I wrote about this in the book and identified you as a member of the Ron-Yasu generation. For Noda, I wrote about Rikidozan and Walt Disney. Finally, I associated Ishihara Shintaro with the "Take that, America!" generation. Noda said, "Our postwar generation watched Disney and we were awed and attracted to America." Noda told me this enabled him to act as an interpreter between the Ishihara generation and the Nagashima generation. I suppose what he meant was that he could be a bridge between the wartime and postwar generation and our Cold War generation. (laugh)

Nagashima: My generation is also able to bridge the generations.

Sunohara: I want to ask about when you were negotiating behind the scenes with Ishihara. Did you sense the kind of things we have been talking about?

Nagashima: You mean about the structure of the Japan-US alliance? There's that "US forces as guard dog" theory that Shiina Etsusaburo argued. But that was unacceptable to Ishihara because he believed in autonomy. He evidenced a very strong sense that the current over-dependence was unacceptable.

Sunohara: That certainly sounds like him.

Nagashima: Max Weber described politics as a strong and slow boring of hard boards. But strong and slow boring, as Weber described it, to ultimately change the basic structure of the alliance is not the Ishihara style. He has always shown a preference for the unconventional. He wants to get things done by surprising and awakening the public by saying something shocking. This has been his *modus operandi* for generating movement and change. In the final analysis, he is perhaps more of a writer than a politician.

Sunohara: That's always been true. Still, I am reminded of the Narita Express. That entire project was basically conceived and done top-down when Ishihara was minister of transport.

Nagashima: How so?

Sunohara: In those days, I was assigned to micro-economic issues and was covering the Ministry of Transport (now the Ministry of Land, Infrastructure, Transport and Tourism) and the Japan Railways Group. I did a lot of investigative reporting in that area. On several occasions I interviewed Ishihara when he was the minister in charge of the project. What I was thinking at the time was that the Narita Express project would have never gotten off the ground if it had been left in the hands of the LDP transportation lobby in the Diet or the old conservatives at the Japan National Railways. They would still be talking about the Narita Express to this day. Getting this project done really proved Ishihara's worth as a politician. (laugh)

Nagashima: I see.

Sunohara: But the Senkaku Islands and the entire national security field are a little different.

Nagashima: But as governor of Tokyo, what he really wanted to do was to get joint military-civilian use of Yokota Air Base. The base was emblematic of the one-sided relationship that we call the Japan-US alliance. Moreover, he viewed it as a vestige of the postwar occupation of Japan. For him, maintaining an air base of that size so close to an urban environment was unforgivable. In a way, this worldview can be linked to Hatoyama Yukio's thinking. Shortly after Hatoyama became prime minister, he said that he found it extremely strange and abnormal that 60 years after the end of the war, part of the nation remained occupied by foreign military forces that acted as if they owned the place.

Sunohara: In a sense, this sentiment binds a lot of people, including Abe Shinzo and Hatoyama Yukio. I hope I am not being rude in saying that other adherents of this sentiment include Noda Yoshihiko, Ishihara Shintaro, and yourself, Nagashima Akihisa. All of you are bound together by a basic awareness and aspiration for autonomy.

I always ask my American friends to please not misread what's going on in these people's minds. Hatoyama is not crazy, nor is Ishihara an outlier. All Japanese harbor this feeling somewhere in their psyche.

Nagashima: To borrow a phrase from Fukuzawa Yukichi, who founded my alma mater, Keio University, it's all about self-reliance and self-respect. The only real difference between Ishihara and these other people is in how they express it and how they hope to achieve it. It is a question of style.

Sunohara: One approach features minor adjustments, tweaks, and patience. The other approach is rough and tumble and aims to achieve the objective in a single leap. And then there are people who cannot see any further than the tips of their own noses and just muddle through.

Nagashima: Do you remember the "bottle cap" analogy that used to be used to describe the Japan-US alliance? The argument was that Japan should not be allowed to re-militarize and that therefore it was necessary to maintain a US presence in Japan as a "bottle cap" designed to prevent Japanese remilitarization. When I was a student in Washington, I spent a lot of time researching documents and materials and came across the reverse argument. This was the "incubator" analogy and was being pushed by China to argue that US cooperation would nurture Japan's standing in national security matters. The idea was that Japan would eventually grow big and strong, at which point it would break its ties with the United States and opt for autonomy and self-reliance. This is the heart of Chinese suspicions and fears.

Sunohara: But what does Japan have to gain today from turning its sword to China? China does not have resources that Japan would covet. They say China's population is 1.3 billion, but China will soon begin to feel the effects of a rapid aging of society. This will affect its labor force as well as its status as a consumer market. In that sense, maybe the optimal path for Japan would be to sign a "non-aggression pact" with China. (laugh)

Nagashima: Terrible idea. That would simply mean a repeat of the fate that befell the prewar Japan-Soviet Neutrality Pact.

Sunohara: What I mean by signing a Japan-China non-aggression pact is to emphatically state that there is absolutely no strategic value to invading China. And the point of this would be to break away from the history that remains so central to Chinese thinking today. Japan has to be smarter in how it acts in the future. In a certain sense, it needs more wile in its actions.

Nagashima: That's right.

Sunohara: In that sense, there was absolutely no wile on the Japanese side when it was nationalizing the Senkaku Islands. More than anything, the government was feeling cornered and felt its hand was being forced. This is what I would say if I were to criticize the nationalization process. Couldn't we have had a more broadly based "Team Japan" approach?

Nagashima: At the time, we did discuss the matter very extensively in our sort-of NSC.

Sunohara: I guess you are right. On the other hand, you were working with a very small group of people. You had Prime Minister Noda and Foreign Minister Gemba at the center. And then there were Deputy Chief Cabinet Secretary Nagahama and Special Advisor Nagashima in close-to-core positions. Added to this core group were Assistant Chief Cabinet Secretary Kawai from the Foreign Ministry and Vice-Minister of Foreign Affairs Sasae. Wouldn't you say this was a very limited circle of people? Given the status of the Japanese government at the time, maybe it was not possible to field a larger and more imposing team of people. That is one area I hope Abe will do better in.

Nagashima: That is exactly why Japan established its NSC. The idea is to handle these issues with the participation of the whole government.

What if Tokyo had Purchased the Senkaku Islands?

Sunohara: What would have happened if Tokyo had bought the Senkakus? If the government had backed out of purchasing them, would Governor Ishihara have gone through with his proposed acquisition? And what would have happened then? Would you care to speculate on this?

Nagashima: I don't know the answer to that. At the very end, I visited Ishihara at his home in Denenchofu to tell him that the government was going to purchase the Senkaku Islands.

Sunohara: I wrote about that in the book. "Is that right? Make sure you spend that 1.5 billion yen wisely," he said to you.

Nagashima: It was his normal mixture of scorn and irony. "You people are really stupid. You've allowed yourselves to be fooled by the Foreign Ministry." He was being his usual self. There was no trace of disappointment in his voice. I remember how I was caught off guard by his cool reaction. But maybe I did sense a bit of resentment when he said Kurihara had tricked him and that he had been betrayed.

Sunohara: But Sonoda was there that day, and as soon as the subject of the Senkaku Islands had come to an end, the two of them started talking about some other secret matter. They suddenly noticed you were still there and Ishihara said, "Why are you still sitting there? You're dismissed!" (laugh) If you would allow me to engage in some speculation, maybe Ishihara was the consummate plotter and it was his intent from the very beginning to have the government purchase the islands. If you think of it that way, it suddenly becomes very easy to explain his cool and nonchalant attitude upon hearing that the government was going to buy the islands. (laugh)

Nagashima: That would put you right back in line for the conspiracy theories that we talked about earlier. (laugh) I really can't say what the truth was. And all the donations that poured in to buy the Senkakus are still in a state of limbo. They can't return them to the donors because there were just too many anonymous donations.

Sunohara: That's true. Going back to an earlier topic, just for the sake of discussion, let's say the government had given up on purchasing the islands. Do you think the Tokyo Metropolitan Government would have followed through with the deal? Or once the purchase had been done, perhaps the Tokyo Metropolitan Government would have approached the government to say, "Can you take these islands off our hands?"

Nagashima: As far as Ishihara was concerned, he needed things to "look right."

Sunohara: So maybe he would have built a lighthouse before selling the islands to the government.

Nagashima: Maybe.

Sunohara: What about China? How would China have reacted if the Tokyo Metropolitan Government had held title to the islands, even if only for a brief time?

Nagashima: I don't know the answer to that one, either. A fair number of people subscribe to the view that things would not have been so bad if Tokyo had ended up owning the islands. The idea is that we would not have seen Chinese naval vessels and all that if the Tokyo Metropolitan Government were the owner. In other words, these people say China acted the way it did because it was the national government that made the purchase. That's why people come up to me and say, "How could you have been so stupid? You should have let Tokyo buy the islands." (wry smile)

But I can't say for sure. Suppose Ishihara had bought the islands and proceeded to make the changes he wanted. I don't think the Chinese side would have sat by quietly and watched. It's quite possible they would have exploded. Even if the Tokyo Metropolitan Government had purchased the islands, the national government would still have to take ultimate responsibility. So what's the difference? The better option would have been for the government to make the purchase from the start. That's what it all comes down to.

Sunohara: Let me present another hypothetical. What if the government had approached the Chinese side secretly with this suggestion: "As a nation under the rule of law, the government cannot stop the Tokyo Metropolitan Government from purchasing the islands. But we can prevent new construction on the islands. Can we strike a deal with you on these terms?" Would it have been possible to reach an agreement with this type of solution?

Nagashima: That's an interesting question.

Sunohara: There is a reason I ask. A while ago, Nikai Toshihiro, chairman of the LDP General Council, travelled to Beijing and met with President Xi Jinping. What really caught my attention was something that Xi Jinping said then. The common interpretation is that Xi Jinping was referring to the so-called history problem—the issue of visiting Yasukuni Shrine and all—and that he meant to check Abe, but what Xi Jinping said was, "The Japanese people are innocent," and "Certain militarists and Class-A war criminals caused Japan to take the wrong road." This is the standard line that has been repeated since Zhou Enlai and Mao Zedong, and this is the line that forms the foundation of Japan-China relations. Therefore, China's reasoning is that it cannot overlook the visit of Japanese political leaders to Yasukuni where these Class-A war criminals are enshrined.

For Japanese political leaders representing the whole of the people, the prime minister, for example, to violate China's long-standing views and visit Yasukuni tramples on the principle left to posterity by Zhou Enlai and Mao Zedong and insults the legitimacy of Chinese Communist Party rule.

Within this perspective, it can be said that China views Ishihara as something like a descendant of those certain militarists who led Japan astray. (wry smile) While the national government ultimately purchased the islands, what would have been the impact on China if the Tokyo Metropolitan Government had become the owner? Paradoxically, the impact on China would have been completely different. But purchase by the national government negated the position that had been repeated by Xi Jinping, Zhou Enlai, and Mao Zedong that the Japanese people and the Japanese government are innocent.

Nagashima: You mean that nationalization negated the "dualism" that is fundamental to the Chinese position. Perhaps nationalization did touch something that was deep and fundamental in the Chinese psyche.

Sunohara: That certainly may be there. I discussed this point extensively with Professor Kawashima Shin of the University of Tokyo and other experts. They pointed out that the Chinese side reacted very strongly to the term "nationalization."

Nagashima: But we explained that point again and again. *Asahi Shimbun* used the term "nationalization," but we said that what we were doing was not "nationalization" per se but was nothing more than the transfer of title to a piece of real estate. We also explained that no structures would be erected and the status quo would be maintained.

Sunohara: In other words, "We will not do anything like what South Korea has done on Takeshima." (wry smile)

Nagashima: We explained that this would be the closest thing possible to maintaining the status quo. It seemed to us at the time that the Chinese side somewhat understood what we were saying. At least that's what we thought.

Sunohara: Let's back up a bit. It is clear that China needed to uphold the legitimacy of the Communist Party's one-party rule that has continued since Zhou Enlai and Mao Zedong and which has now been passed down to Xi Jinping. The reins are being tightened with the anti-corruption campaign and other programs, but ultimately it is a matter of safeguarding the party's legitimacy. Coming at such a sensitive time, the nationalization of the Senkaku Islands must surely have rubbed the Chinese leadership the wrong way. Could it be that this is the candid truth of what the Chinese side was thinking?

Nagashima: Omae Kenichi has suggested something similar. A moment ago, you asked whether it would have been possible to reach a secret agreement with China whereby the Tokyo Metropolitan Government would buy the islands but would be prohibited from building any form of structure. Two points come to mind. First, the situation was too tense to allow anything like that. The power struggle going on inside Zhongnanhai was incredibly intense. I would guess that it would have been impossible to hammer out a secret agreement. The second point concerns Ishihara. If the Tokyo Metropolitan Government had acquired the islands, would the national government really have been able to keep him from doing anything more? Considering the momentum that he had at the time and the public support he had garnered, it's difficult to say what might have happened.

Sunohara: It is true that the Tokyo Metropolitan Government had chartered a large ship in the 1,000-ton range to survey the area around the Senkaku Islands. That came as a real shock to Noda. That incident served to magnify his concern and resentment. "This, after all we have done?"

Nagashima: Prime Minister Noda asked me at a relatively early stage, "What do you think about nationalization?" It was in May that he asked me this. My answer was, "The national government should take responsibility and purchase the islands." The prime minister responded, "Yes, that's the way it should be." But this did not mean that he was green-lighting nationalization. Shortly after this, we embarked on an examination process to review the possibilities and ramifications of purchasing the islands. I doubt the prime minister had arrived at a final decision before his August 19 meeting with Governor Ishihara at the Kantei.

Sunohara: It did appear as though alternative paths had been prepared for moving forward in any of several directions. However, the point seems to have been that this had to include a path to nationalization. That is why I wrote in the book that the Noda administration had not yet reached a final-final decision when the first newspaper reports appeared.

Nagashima: That's right. No final decision had been made on nationalization. We had just started studying the issue with nationalization as one of the options. And then the first article ran on July 7, the anniversary of the Marco Polo Bridge Incident, of all days.

(At the Diet Members' No. 1 Office Building, May 29, 2015)
The Japanese-language book was published in July 2013 by Shinchosha.

About the author

SUNOHARA Tsuyoshi was born in Tokyo in 1961. He started working for the *Nihon Keizai (Nikkei) Shimbun* in 1983 after graduation from Sophia University (Faculty of Economics, Business Administration program). At *Nikkei*, he worked on the business desk, the Washington bureau, the political bureau, and the international bureau. He has served as a Fellow in the Columbia University School of Journalism's Advanced Global Reporting program, a Visiting Scholar at the Center for Strategic and International Studies (CSIS), and Visiting Researcher at the Henry L. Stimson Center, among other distinctions. Back at the *Nikkei*, he was appointed Global Business Managing Executive Officer in 2016 and Senior Managing Executive Officer in 2019, serving concurrently as Professor by Special Appointment at Sophia University. He has served as Chief Operating Officer for the Mt. Fuji Dialogue to promote intellectual exchange between Japan and the United States since 2014. Among his many publications from Shinchosha are: *Zainichi beigun shireibu* (United States Forces command headquarters in Japan, 2008); *Beichu hyakunen senso: Shin reisen kozo to Nihon no meiun* (The Sino-US hundred years' war: Japan's fate in the new cold war structure, 2012); *Kaku ga nakunaranai nanatsu no riyu* (Seven reasons the world does not go nuclear free, 2010); *Zero no idenshi: Nijuisseiki no "Hinomaru sentoki" to Nihon no Kokubo* (The Zero gene: Japan's quest for a domestic-built fighter plane and national defense policy, 2012).

（英文版）暗闘 尖閣国有化
Fencing in the Dark: Japan, China, and the Senkakus

2020年2月27日　第1刷発行

著　者	春原　剛
英　訳	公益財団法人日本国際問題研究所
発行所	一般財団法人出版文化産業振興財団
	〒101-0051 東京都千代田区神田神保町2-2-30
	電話　03-5211-7283
ホームページ	https://www.jpic.or.jp/
印刷・製本所	大日本印刷株式会社